The Wannabe Fascists

The publisher and the University of California Press Foundation gratefully acknowledge the generous support of the Anne G. Lipow Endowment Fund in Social Justice and Human Rights.

The Wannabe Fascists

A GUIDE TO UNDERSTANDING THE
GREATEST THREAT TO DEMOCRACY

Federico Finchelstein

UNIVERSITY OF CALIFORNIA PRESS

University of California Press

Oakland, California

© 2024 by Federico Finchelstein

Library of Congress Cataloging-in-Publication Data

Names: Finchelstein, Federico, 1975– author.
Title: The wannabe fascists : a guide to understanding the greatest threat to democracy / Federico Finchelstein.
Description: Oakland, California : University of California Press, [2024] | Includes bibliographical references and index.
Identifiers: LCCN 2023044864 (print) | LCCN 2023044865 (ebook) | ISBN 9780520392496 (hardback) | ISBN 9780520392502 (ebook)
Subjects: LCSH: Fascism—21st century.
Classification: LCC JC481.F525 2024 (print) | LCC JC481 (ebook) | DDC 320.53/3—dc23/eng/20231221
LC record available at https://lccn.loc.gov/2023044864
LC ebook record available at https://lccn.loc.gov/2023044865

Manufactured in the United States of America

33 32 31 30 29 28 27 26 25 24
10 9 8 7 6 5 4 3 2 1

To Lauri, Lulu, and Gabi

Contents

Introduction: How Populism Is Turning into Wannabe Fascism *1*

1. Violence and the Militarization of Politics *22*
2. Fascist Lies and Propaganda *56*
3. The Politics of Xenophobia *94*
4. Dictatorship *141*

    Epilogue *179*

    Acknowledgments *187*
    Notes *189*
    Index *243*

Introduction

How Populism Is Turning into Wannabe Fascism

A few days after Donald J. Trump lost his reelection bid in November 2020, I wrote an op-ed in the *Washington Post*, warning of the possibility of a coup attempt if the defeated president continued to deny the election results.[1] I argued that Trump was edging away from being a typical right-wing populist and moving toward becoming a fascist—a dire threat to our democracy. While some considered this to be an alarmist take, the storming of the Capitol on January 6, 2021, proved otherwise. My op-ed wasn't the first time I had published a warning. Before Jair Bolsonaro was elected president of Brazil in 2018, I outlined the parallels between Bolsonaro's tactics and those of the Nazis in an article for *Foreign Policy*. These pieces, among others, point to my primary concern as both a historian and a citizen: global populism is turning into fascism and this trend represents a major threat to the future of democracy.[2]

The subject of this book is personal to me. I was born in Argentina one year before a gruesome dictatorship took shape.[3] Like many other Argentines, I am still trying to come to terms with the fascist crimes against humanity committed in the country of my childhood—the disappearances, the concentration camps, the citizens tortured, drugged, and thrown into the Atlantic from military planes. Official estimates range from ten thousand to fifteen thousand murder victims. Human rights groups estimate that thirty thousand disappeared. There was also the theft of babies born to illegally detained mothers. One of the reasons I became a historian was because I wanted to understand how the so-called Dirty War and its fascist ideology became a reality in a modern nation with a strong, progressive civil society. I migrated to the Unites States in 2001 and even here the presence of fascism continues to shape my focus as a writer and citizen. As in Argentina and other parts of the world, "the long shadow of fascism" is a clear and present danger in the United States, but it appears under the guise of a new breed of politician whom I call the *wannabe fascist*. Like the fascists and dictators of my youth, this new political archetype aspires to destroy democratic institutions, yet has, so far, failed to succeed. I see this book as contributing to the historical and present understanding of this peril to democracy. Trump may no longer be president, but he and his followers are still flying alarmingly close to fascism. The more we know about past fascist attempts to deny the workings of democracy, the more alarming these wannabe fascists appear.

Wannabe fascism is an incomplete version of fascism, characteristic of those who seek to destroy democracy for short-term personal gain but are not fully committed to the fascist cause. In 1924, the first fascist dictator, Benito Mussolini, explained the difference between true fascists and fake ones: "I will distinguish between the fascists by will, by passion and by faith and, on the other hand, those fascists who are semi-wandering men, who have always raised their ears to feel the voice of public opinion."[4] For Mussolini, the former were the true fascists who did not stumble on the road to power, while the latter aspired to fascism but lacked resolve and ultimately wavered, proving to be weak and ineffectual.

While Mussolini might have been disappointed by the wannabe fascists, I see them as a dangerous threat to democracy, extremists who have not (yet) reached the levels of ideological fervor, violence, and lies achieved by historical fascists. Wannabe fascists do not openly advocate for fascism, but they gravitate toward fascist political styles and behaviors. The historical fascists, wannabe fascists, and many populists are traveling different but interconnected paths.

Trump's hesitation to go full fascist in 2021 put him in the category of wannabe fascist, a semi- or pseudofascist wannabe dictator who lacked the ideological commitment and extremism of Adolf Hitler and Mussolini. The same, of course, applies to a long list of mini-Trumps: Jair Bolsonaro, Nayib Bukele, Narendra Modi, Viktor Orbán, and others. They have blurred but not erased the separation of powers. They have not succeeded in unifying the state and civil society. They have not fully destroyed the legal system. In terms of violence and militarization, they have not matched the extremism of classic fascism. In terms of hatred, they have not unlocked its genocidal potential. They employ propaganda and lies but have not fully developed an Orwellian state machine. Somewhere along the road to creating totalitarian dictatorships, they faltered. Their fascism is aspirational.[5] Today's wannabe fascists are weaker and more incompetent than classical fascists, but this should not ease our minds.

Since they travel the same paths, and since they seek fascist politics as a vocation, we should not shy away from using the f-word to call out the violence, xenophobia, lies, and dictatorial behavior of the wannabe fascists. Leaders like Trump, Bolsonaro, Modi, and Orbán are helping to take contemporary far-right populism back to its fascist roots. Their style and behavior display key features of fascist rule: the glorification of violence and the militarization of politics; racism and discrimination; and propaganda techniques that were pioneered by Nazi propaganda chief Joseph Goebbels.

This book defines and is organized around the four key elements of fascism: political violence, propaganda and misinformation, xenophobia, and dictatorship. In order to underscore the risk of fascism in the present, I will explain how new challenges to democracy can be countered by learning some of the lessons from history. The antidemocratic radicalization of populist movements such as Trumpism echo the fascist era of the mid-twentieth century, when dictatorial regimes adopted xenophobia, violence, coups, and anti-science to seize and retain power. Paraphrasing the philosopher Walter Benjamin, my idea is to brush Trumpism and its global associates against the grain of previous histories. More precisely, I will consider them as representing a different chapter in the long history of antidemocratic politics. In other words, they represent different "documents of barbarism" to think about in the present.[6] Learning about the connected histories of fascism and populism, but also their contextual distinctions, reminds us why democracy matters and why wannabe fascists need to be stopped.

Additionally, this book will challenge two mutually exclusive assumptions of the prevailing wisdom, that either we are currently witnessing extreme cases of populism, or that fascism and not populism is the key to analyzing the present. While populism leads to democracy's deterioration, fascism destroys it. In this context, seeing something like Trumpism as a populism-only approach does not fully appreciate that democracy is in grave danger, while seeing it as a fascism-only approach often does not recognize that democracy can still be defended and saved from fascism. I don't believe these views are incompatible, and I will locate the source of the present danger of fascism in the histories of both fascism and populism and explain how it has led to the present outcome: the wannabe fascist leader.

The recent debates that scholars have undertaken around the use of the f-word with regard to Trump have, to my mind, only yielded more confusion. Many of them are centered on arcane epistemological issues, simplistic ideas about the lack of correlations, and ignorance about the historiography of fascism. Indeed, it is peculiar that although many of these scholars are not experts on fascism, they often stress an essentialist reading of what is and what is not fascism.[7] I also part ways with these scholars on important issues, such as the relevance of non-European and non-US sources; nearly all of these approaches fail to take a larger, global view of the question. Indeed, as a specialist in both Latin American history and European history who is also interested in primary and secondary sources from and about India, Egypt, China, Japan, and the Philippines, among others, I take a global perspective on fascism and populism. In this book, as in my work as a whole, I let these sources speak for themselves, giving the reader a clear view of the problems.

As a historian of fascism and populism, I am frequently asked whether the recent rise of right-wing populists really represents a threat to democracy around the world. Are we living on the edge of a new dark age of fascism? People ask me whether Trump and others, like the leaders of India, Brazil, Hungary, and El Salvador, are really populist demagogues, and what fascism actually is. Drawing on my three decades of research on the histories of fascism and populism in Latin America and Europe, I will answer these questions in this book and explain clearly the current state of world autocracy. My aim is to help establish a better understanding of this dangerous and frightening political turn for those may want to push back against these antidemocratic threats. It will examine the ideologies and actions of autocratic leaders both past and present and will offer lessons on how to quash them in the future.

What is fascism? In historical terms, fascism can be defined as a global ideology with separate national movements and regimes. A counter-revolutionary formation of the extreme right, it was ultranationalist and xenophobic. Fascists were essentially anti-egalitarian and despised liberalism and socialism.[8] The primary aim of fascism was to destroy democracy from within in order to create a modern dictatorship from above. Fascists proposed a totalitarian state in which plurality and civil society would be silenced and there would be few distinctions between the public and the private, or between the state and its citizens. Fascist regimes shut down the independent press and destroyed the rule of law.

Fascism defended a divine, messianic, and charismatic form of leadership that conceived of the leader as organically linked to the people and the nation. It considered popular sovereignty to be fully delegated to the dictator, who acted in the name of the community of the people and knew better than they what they truly wanted. Fascists replaced history and empirically based notions of truth with political myth. They had an extreme conception of the enemy, regarding it as an existential threat to the nation and to its people. Such an enemy had to be first persecuted and then deported or eliminated. Fascism aimed to create a new and epochal world order through an incremental continuum of extreme political violence and war. Global unity came through conquest and domination. A global ideology, fascism constantly reformulated itself in different national contexts and underwent constant national permutations.

Fascism was officially founded in Italy in 1919, but the antiliberal and anti-Marxist politics it represented appeared simultaneously across the world. From Japan to Brazil and Germany, and from Argentina to India, Nicaragua, and France, the antidemocratic, violent, and racist revolution of the right that fascism epitomized was adopted in other countries under different names: Nazism in Germany, *nacionalismo* in Argentina, *integralismo* in Brazil, and so on. Fascism was transnational even before Mussolini used the word *fascismo*, but when fascism became a regime in Italy in 1922, the term received worldwide attention and acquired different meanings in local contexts.

What is populism? Populism is an authoritarian form of democracy. It first came to power after 1945 as an original historical reformulation of fascism. Historically, it has subsequently thrived during political crises, when it has offered itself as the antidote to the politics of the day.[9]

While fascism involves fanatical right-wing ideological beliefs, populist leaders and followers are more pragmatic in their antidemocratic beliefs than fascist. Unlike with fascism, which is always a right-wing ideology, movement, and regime, populists can identify with the right and left of the ideological spectrum. Like the classic fascists, wannabe fascists are always right-wing populists.

Populist leaders claim to do the work of politics while keeping themselves free from politics. They increase the political participation of their own followers while excluding others, notably limiting the rights of political, sexual, ethnic, and religious minorities. Populism conceives of the people as One—a single entity consisting of leader, followers, and nation. This trinity is rooted in fascism but is confirmed by votes and elections, which populist leaders embrace. While populism stands against liberalism, it abides by the ballot box. Populism's homogenizing view of the people conceives of political opponents as the antipeople. Opponents become enemies—nemeses who, consciously or unconsciously, stand for the oligarchical elites and traitors to the nation. Populism defends an illuminated nationalist leader who speaks and decides for the people. It downplays the separation of powers, the independence and legitimacy of a free press, and the rule of law.

The relapse of populism into fascism or semi-fascism is not a new phenomenon. A few significant historical examples of this relapse have appeared in the past century, ranging from neofascist Peronism in the 1970s to the Golden Dawn in Greece and other European movements of the extreme right. Even if it does not renounce democratic electoral procedures, populism as a movement can become neofascism when it transitions from viewing its population as homogenous to basing its national identity on a particular ethnic community, while simultaneously sharpening its rhetoric about the nation's enemies from the general (elites, traitors, outsiders, etc.) to a specific racial or religious foe who is the target of political violence. As a regime, populism becomes a dictatorship (fascist, neofascist, or nonfascist) when it voids its association with its defining democratic features. To put it differently, when elections are finally banned or are no longer free, when the intimidation of the independent press leads to its suppression, when dissent is not only deemed illegitimate by those in power but is also prohibited and punished, when undermining the separation of powers morphs into unifying them under the leader, and when the populist logic of polarization is translated into actual political persecution, populism ceases to be populist. In these cases, the populist tendency to corrupt constitutional democracy leads to its violent elimination.

Populism and fascism are connected and yet separate forms of autocratic leadership. Fascists and populist leaders are autocrats in the sense that their politics aim to impose their undisputed authority. However, only fascists seek to become full-fledged dictators, wishing to fully impose their will with permanent power. By contrast, populist leaders challenge but do not destroy democracy.

After 1945, it was believed that fascism had been stamped out forever. It had not. Fascist thought and fascist movements retained some of their strength and appeal even though they no longer controlled states and they were significantly diminished in numbers and legitimacy. The fact that Trumpism rose to the center of world power must now give us pause. This book will examine the national and international implications of this new type of post-fascist politics that reformulated right-wing populism and fascism and materialized in America on the escalator of a golden Manhattan tower on June 16, 2015, when Trump launched his candidacy for the presidency. When Trump was elected president the following year, the United States became the epitome of what a twenty-first-century novel threat to democracy looks like, a newer version of fascism and semi-fascism mixed with previous populist traditions.

By reconnecting fascism and populism in unexpected ways, Trump represents a new type of global autocratic ruler: the "wannabe" fascist. This new type of populist politician is typically a legally elected leader who, unlike previous populists who were eager to distance themselves from fascism, turns to totalitarian lies, racism, and illegal means to destroy democracy from within. The wannabe fascist can be defined as a populist aspirant to fascism. Wannabe fascism remains a vocational form. It is not full-fledged fascism because it has not yet descended into dictatorship and has not fully relied on terror to monopolize violence and use it without restraint.[10]

To understand the wannabe fascist, we need to go back to the moment in history when populism was for the first time born out of fascism after World War II, initially with Juan Perón in Argentina and then with other Latin American leaders like Getúlio Vargas in Brazil, Rómulo Betancourt in Venezuela, and Víctor Paz Estenssoro in Bolivia. These populist leaders created a new form of political regime that combined democracy with illiberalism. Populists invoked the name of the people to stress a form of highly hierarchical leadership, to downplay political dialogue, and to solve a perceived crisis of representation, increasingly by attacking institutional checks and balances. They asserted a direct link between the people and the leader, relying on a form of leadership that might best be described as religious, namely, a political theology. Populists bolstered social and political polarization. In their view, fewer public spaces should be left for the expression of the views of political minorities. The political rights of these minorities are not eliminated, but their democratic legitimacy is undermined. Populists conceive of these minorities as enemies of the people and the nation. Populism, in short, is an authoritarian form of democracy.

Nonetheless, populists rejected key aspects of fascism, including extreme forms of repression and racism, and although they were intolerant of political diversity they recognized that, by 1945, a continuation of fascism would need to renounce some of its dictatorial dimensions, reforming its legacy in a democratic key.

Consider the case of Juan Perón and Peronism, the movement he created in Argentina. Perón was the strongman in a military junta dictatorship that ruled from 1943 to 1946. As a young officer he had participated in the pro-fascist coup of 1930 and was later deployed as a military observer in Nazi Germany and fascist Italy. Despite coming to power by force in 1943, Perón encouraged and participated in free democratic elections in 1946. Modern populism was first proposed as a third position aimed at overcoming the Cold War dilemma of choosing between communism and liberalism. Rather than adopting a preformatted version of neofascism, Peronism was the first movement that attempted to adapt the legacy of fascism to a novel democratic framework and became the first example of a modern populist regime.

After the global defeat of fascism at the end of World War II, fascism, coups, and military dictatorships had become toxic to most societies. So former fascists and militant dictators tried to regain power through democratic means. Politicians like Perón understood that elections provided a critical source of political legitimacy. Drawing on the charisma, celebrity, and political skills of his second wife, the actor Evita Perón, Colonel Juan Perón won the 1946 presidential election, becoming the first populist leader in history to be democratically elected head of state.

Populism borrowed elements of fascism. Like Mussolini and Hitler, leaders like Perón and Vargas transformed political arguments into all-or-nothing fights for a new moral order. They claimed to be the solution to an impending cataclysm. They denounced the ruling elites, thwarted independent journalism, and advanced a deep dislike for pluralism and political tolerance. But because Perón and Vargas remained popularly elected, they stand apart from the fascists with whom they are otherwise linked. Peronism and Varguism also renounced racism, the glorification of violence, the militarization of politics, and totalitarian propaganda.

Like Perón and Vargas, other Latin American populists in Ecuador, Venezuela, and Bolivia came to power by affirming the legitimacy of electoral results in the late 1940s and early 1950s. Holding power depended upon winning real elections and putting aside the fascist politics of xenophobia, with its endless lies and extreme repressive methods. Perón and his Latin American populist counterparts *were* popular. When they were ousted from power, it was often by coups, not elections—which their movements kept winning.

More recent populist leaders, like Silvio Berlusconi in Italy and Hugo Chávez in Venezuela, followed a similar pattern. Instead of making baseless accusations of electoral fraud, they staked their grandiose claims upon the democratic idea that elections represent the will of the people. Berlusconi lost elections in 1996 and 2006, while Chávez lost the 2007 Venezuelan constitutional referendum that attempted to abolish presidential term limits. Both accepted the results even though they lost by extremely slim margins. Populism affirms the authoritarian idea that one person can fully personify "the people" and the nation, but it must be confirmed via democratic procedures. Although populism has traditionally respected the ballot box, it hasn't always advanced democracy; indeed, it frequently manipulates it. But it still derives power from, and depends on, the integrity of the electoral system.

The wannabe fascists, on the other hand, follow the fascist playbook and lie their way out of electoral defeat. Italian fascists and German Nazis in the 1930s saw no value in the electoral system and only used it to claim legitimacy and leadership when it benefited them. They then worked to destroy democracy from within. Fascism denies the very nature of democracy, the legitimacy of democratic procedures, and their electoral outcomes. Its proponents claim that votes are only legitimate when they confirm by referendum the autocratic will of their leader.

So, there is a clear conceptual divide between historical populists who abide by the *truth* of the ballot box and fascists and wannabe fascists who *lie* about electoral results and subvert democracy. For traditional populists, electoral results matter.

But this distinction is beginning to fade. Donald Trump blazed a trail for other aspiring autocrats. By denying the 2020 election results and fomenting the Big Lie about voter fraud, Trump represents a turning point in populist politics, enabling and inspiring others to deny the electoral legitimacy of their opponents. Leaders like Bolsonaro in Brazil, Benjamin Netanyahu in Israel, and Keiko Fujimori in Peru have used falsehoods about legality and elections deception to create an alternative reality where they can rule, now or in the future, without the burdens and limitations of democratic procedures.

Trump is a major influencer of wannabe fascism, but he is not unique. Like the classic fascists and populists that preceded them, the wannabe fascists represent a global phenomenon that has been generally ignored by prevailing American- or European-centric views. Writing against these reductive, and paternalistic, traditional narratives, this book contributes to decentering them.

Global South experiences are not a mere by-product or mimetic reflection of the history of fascism and right-wing politics in the North. This book will show the dissemination of converging ideologies, practices, and discourses from North to South and South to North, while also paying attention to the peculiarities and differences of fascist, populist, and wannabe fascist leaders and ideologues in their own contexts.

Of the many explanations for Trump's attacks on democracy, the most erratic are those that invert his nationalism by claiming that he represents an anomaly situated outside of American traditions and history. Trump, it is claimed, cannot be a fascist, or fascistic, because there is no such thing as fascism in America. Trump therefore belongs to a special historical pathway that separates him from global fascism and post-fascism.[11]

According to these arguments, America is either too good for fascism or its right wingers are too inarticulate and unintelligent to engage in fascism, while its institutions are strong enough to withstand the crude Trumpian threat to democracy. Rather than being a by-product of global and American racist, populist, and fascist traditions, Trumpism is an empty-headed phenomenon that can be historically bracketed and summarily dismissed. This book will argue that the more we know about past fascist attempts to deny the workings of democracy, the more worried we should be about present post-fascist and populist forms.

As students, citizens, and readers, we need to shine a light on these connections between past and present because we are living in a time when human rights, secularism, and democracy are under attack. The aim of this book is to recognize the fascist danger of Trumpism and future Trumpists and their global populist allies. We need to know them better before it is too late.

The different chapters in this book address the following questions: why has current populism been morphing into fascism, and why and how is the answer to that question connected through transnational histories and collective national experiences?

Fascism is a global nationalist ideology with distinctive national movements, but it always comprises four essential features. Defining these four pillars allows us to clearly understand fascist history and its playbook. This introduction presents the current turning point in the histories of fascism and populism, while the four chapters address each of the pillars of fascism. Finally, the epilogue briefly addresses the impact of this new fascist turn by global autocrats and how history offers lessons to stop them.

This book explains how the ongoing recalibration of populism signifies a third autocratic wave of attacks against democracy after the first wave of fascism (1919–1945) and the second wave of populism in power (1945–2000s). The first wave of fascism was exemplified by leaders like Mussolini, Hitler, and Plínio Salgado in Brazil. The fascist model was extremely influential, inspiring leaders who ranged widely across the political spectrum in the interwar years, from Georges Valois in France to Ahmad Husayn in Egypt. As a response to liberalism and communism, they stressed the need for totalitarian racist and nativist dictatorships. The second wave of modern populism emerged from a Cold War defacement of fascism. After 1945, first in Latin America and then in other places, populist regimes reformulated democracy in a more authoritarian way that nonetheless rejected key ingredients of fascism.

Earlier populists left behind the four fascist pillars, instead engaging in more conventional lies, as well as relatively low levels of demonization, violence, and repression. This is essentially the main difference between historical populists and fascists. Twentieth-century populism was an attempt to return the fascist experience to the democratic path, creating an authoritarian regime that operated within democracy, stressing social participation combined with intolerance and the rejection of plurality. In populist regimes, political rights have been highly constrained but never eradicated, as they had been under fascism.

In recent years, there has been a resurgence of interest in fascism, which has become a threat to democracy across the globe. Simply put, fascism is no longer relegated to the past.

The aim of this book is not to discuss the uniqueness of Trumpism, its place in American history, its function within American politics, or the events of Trump's presidency. Several books already cover such topics in great detail. Instead, I offer a precise historical explanation of why Trumpism and its minions belong to a new political breed, a movement and sometimes a regime with a new type of autocrat that is the final outcome of the combined histories of fascism and populism: the wannabe fascist. It is puzzling that although fascism and populism are two historical formations that are contextually connected, they are rarely analyzed together. My work fills this gap and offers a new way to understand a new historical phenomenon: the morphing of right-wing populism into something closer to fascism.[12]

Fascism is knocking at our door and this book presents a guide for assessing the four pillars of fascism in our world today. Each chapter addresses one pillar. Chapter 1 addresses a key component of fascism: violence and the militarization of politics. Fascists see politics as a form of war involving enemies who shall be dealt with violently, often fatally. This fascist idea of politics, as driven by paramilitary formations, is first conceived internally as civil war by way of physical punishment and violence in the streets, and then later externally as total war. Fascism's methods against the enemy are persecution, imprisonment, torture, and elimination. In fascist ideology, violence and aggression are considered the best expressions of power, as embodied in the leader. Fascists attack political and ethnic minorities in the name of the leader, the nation, and the sacred. Fascism in its many transnational variations does not hesitate to kill its own citizens, as well as its colonial subjects. These gruesome acts of violence and repression define fascism's distinct form of political domination.

Chapter 2 addresses the second pillar of fascism: lies, myths, and propaganda. These three elements are part of a single process where myths are manufactured and falsely presented as the truth. The fascist way of lying is different from other forms of political lying. Fascists believe their big lies and try to transform reality to resemble their lies. Fascists lie in specific ways and their lies differ in both qualitative and quantitative terms from other political lies. Fascist political power is significantly derived from the co-opting of truth and the widespread promulgation of lies. Fascists defend a messianic cult of leadership based on manufactured myths and fantasies. They consider the leader to be sacredly linked to the people and the nation; the leader always knows what they truly want.

Chapter 3 deals with the third pillar: the politics of xenophobia. There is no fascism without racism, an extreme politics that demonizes enemies and hates diversity. Fascism denies rights for people who are ethnically or racially distinct or who behave, identify, or think differently. Fascists transform traditional binaries such as "us versus them" or "civilization versus barbarism" into an idea of the other as a total, existential enemy. Fascism always puts hatred and xenophobia at the very center of politics.

Finally, chapter 4 addresses the last pillar of fascism: dictatorship. Not all dictatorships are fascist, but there is no fascism without dictatorship. Fascist dictatorships fully eliminate political discussion and all opposition. They also enforce counterrevolutionary, ultranationalist, anti-liberal, and anti-socialist principles. These dictatorships initially took shape in the perfect storm of the interwar years, with the dual crises of capitalism and liberalism fueled by the depression and the widespread questioning and undermining of democratic practices and procedures that affected all levels of government, from voting rights to religious rights to economic rights. In fascism, the discretionary power of the dictator prevails over the rule of law, and this is facilitated by enablers, ambitious conservatives, and careerist officials who ingratiate themselves with their new masters. For example, in Nazi Germany, most jurists, prosecutors, judges, and public officials under Nazism accepted Hitler's transformation of the democratic system. The distortion of legality for the sake of the leader's legitimacy therefore becomes the rule, and human and political rights are pushed to the side. Fascists justify the most absolute illegality in legal terms. The primary aim of fascism then is to destroy democracy from within or without—via coup or autocoup, civil war and/or foreign invasion—and create a totalitarian dictatorship. Destroying democracy will in turn destroy civil society, political tolerance, and pluralism, followed by the gradual or rapid dismantling of the law, the separation of powers, electoral procedures, and the independent press. Fascism is formulated on the basis of a modern idea of popular power, but one in which political representation is eliminated and power is fully delegated to the dictator, who acts in the name of the people.

Well before January 6, 2021, Trump had already established (to some alarming extent) three of the four pillars of fascism: violence and the militarization of politics, racism, and lies. The element that Trumpism was missing was dictatorship. And then the attempted coup d'état happened. How else can you define the rule of a president who was determined to retain power despite losing reelection by seven million votes? Had his attempt succeeded, Trump would have become a dictator. In that scenario, it would have been more appropriate to think of him as a fascist. Because he wavered and failed, I call him a wannabe fascist. Trump behaved as a fascist up to the point that, for whatever reason, he backtracked and decided not to join his mob at the Capitol. Perhaps he feared that joining the insurrection would lead to personal or legal implications, but more importantly, he saw that his vice president, key players in the GOP, the armed forces, and the Supreme Court were not supporting his actions. An interwar-era classic fascist would not have backed down, but Trump did. Of course, it is not yet possible to predict how this is going to end, and this book concludes with unanswered questions about history and the future of global autocrats.

This book pays attention to how fascists and populists understand themselves vis-à-vis violence, xenophobia, propaganda, and dictatorship, but it is not the only dimension to be considered. Actions matter equally. Sometimes a leader's words meant the opposite of what they stated. Hitler always accused Jews of being what he actually was, namely, a master of lies. Similarly, Trump projected fascism and dictatorial wishes on his enemies, while he actively engaged in fascist behaviors. Regarding populism, Trump seemed to view himself as such a leader, as shown, for example, in this exchange on populism with his then-guru Steve Bannon:

> "I love that. That's what I am," Trump said, "a popularist." He mangled the word.
> "No, no," Bannon said. "It's populist."
> "Yeah, yeah," Trump insisted. "A popularist."

Ironically, perhaps, Trump was right in his erroneous self-proclamation as a "popularist." It is highly probable that his Freudian slip was pointing to the fact that his politics were not the classical kind of populism.[13]

Leaders like Trump and Bolsonaro are still experimenting with how to effectively destroy democracy. Trump has been continually trying out a combination of populist and fascist strategies and then repeating those that seem to appeal most to his base supporters. His natural instinct is to increase the danger to democracy while affirming his power and his cult. These basic tendencies make him almost fascist.

Despite Trump's praise for Hitler, and the fact that whisperers and speech writers like Steve Bannon and Stephen Miller can be considered fascist intellectuals, it is highly improbable that Trump has read the history of fascism (or populism) and planned to adhere so closely to the fascist playbook.[14] Like Hitler, wannabe fascist leaders like Trump and Bolsonaro are not fascist theorists, nor are they engaged in deep autonomous thought. It is their behavioral tendencies that put them close to fascism. Fascism has never been a deep intellectual enterprise anyway, but merely a radical form of subordination and repression, and a conscious form of racism, propaganda, violence, and dictatorial power. Fascist ideology is not a closed body of thought but rather the glorification of very basic and destructive ideas.

Fascists do not need to understand their history and theory, but they always act upon the premise that their leader is always right and that equality is essentially bad. It was Hitler who said, "One can die only for an idea which one does not understand."[15] Similarly, Trump famously told his followers, "What you're seeing and what you're reading is not what's happening."[16] Without knowing it, or even thinking about it, Trump is carrying on a long political tradition of fascist leaders who impose ideology onto reality. And yet, populist leaders like Trump are not yet fascists because they have not (yet) destroyed democracy. But they are not typical populists, in the sense that their threats against democracy go beyond the standard populist downplaying of democracy. We are living what could be a possible new historical transformation from populism to fascism. It is clear that Trump, Bolsonaro, and many others have deep admiration for dictators and autocrats, and also limited knowledge of their histories. In contrast with their myth of origins, I place the wannabe fascists in historical context. My point is to highlight how they constitute a dire threat to democracy.

There have been plenty of books that have tried to explain the reasons for the rise of Trump and Trumpism. This is not one of them. Instead, this book explains why and how Trump and others like him are behaving like fascists in the making.

1 *Violence and the Militarization of Politics*

On July 3, 2020, at Mount Rushmore, then-US president Donald Trump warned about the threat of a new kind of fascism: "In our schools, our newsrooms, even our corporate boardrooms, there is a new far-left fascism that demands absolute allegiance. If you do not speak its language, perform its rituals, recite its mantras, and follow its commandments, then you will be censored, banished, blacklisted, persecuted, and punished. It's not going to happen to us."[1]

We are living in confusing times when wannabe fascists depict themselves as democratic while falsely presenting fascism as an ideology of the left—as Trump did at Mount Rushmore and as Brazil's far-right former president Jair Bolsonaro has done for years.

As with the fascist leaders of the past, Trump's denunciation of tyrannical invisible forces is contradicted by his violent fascist leanings. In fact, Trump echoed a classic technique: fascists tend to deny what they are and ascribe their own features and their own totalitarian politics to their enemies. The first and foremost of these features is the threat of violence.

Along with radical lies, the politics of xenophobia, and dictatorship, violence is one of the four main pillars of fascism. Fascism presents violence as a beautiful, moral force—the source of greatness, purity, and power—and it practices violence through its militarization of politics, the ultimate consequences of which are war and genocide. The violence of fascism is extreme in terms of both its execution and its long-term effects and legacies.[2] Violence has been a key historical dimension of fascism as an ideology, as a movement, and as a regime.

It's no coincidence that fascist violence is always preemptive. As Trump and Bolsonaro portray it, violence is falsely presented as a necessary response to an imagined threat. This type of anticipatory violence is what jump-started the Holocaust and justified it in the minds of its Nazi perpetrators.

Think of Adolf Hitler's infamous self-fulfilling prophecy in his speech on January 30, 1939, two years before the Holocaust began: "Today I will once more be a prophet: If the international Jewish financiers in and outside Europe should succeed in plunging the nations once more into a world war, then the result will not be the Bolshevization of the earth, and thus the victory of Jewry, but the annihilation of the Jewish race in Europe!"[3] Hitler inverted the terms of the equation, accusing others of plunging the world into a war that he himself intended to launch.

At Mount Rushmore, Trump argued that "the radical ideology attacking our country advances under the banner of social justice. But in truth, it would demolish both justice and society. It would transform justice into an instrument of division and vengeance, and it would turn our free and inclusive society into a place of repression, domination, and exclusion."[4] Trump's own sense of urgency and his claims of an imminent threat to the nation—as he narrowly conceived of it—show how close he is to making a fascist argument, where the threat of imagined violence justifies its preemptive practice under the leader's command. Contrary to what he proclaimed at Mount Rushmore, it was Trump who was and is constantly undermining democracy and inclusion, promoting violence, repression, and coup attempts, and enabling domestic terrorists and mobs. His nativist right-wing populism echoes the fascist past.

The Centrality of Violence in Fascism

There is no fascism without extreme violence. Historically, fascism has been a radical violent revolt against widely held democratic values. Benito Mussolini created the first fascist movement in Italy in 1919 and the movement reached power in 1922, but its politics were shared by antidemocratic forces worldwide.

Fascism was an anti-left and anti-liberal counterrevolution, and while it appropriated the vocabulary of the left—it bears remembering that the Nazi movement's official name was the National Socialist German Workers' Party—it used this vocabulary in the service of right-wing domination and oppression. Hitler liked to tell a story about how he once lost an argument with leftists when they told him that if he continued speaking they would throw him off the scaffolding. In the story, Hitler had to stop arguing and leave. He concluded that violence always defeated reasoned arguments. In this context, as Hitler explained in *Mein Kampf*, winners in politics are those who resort to "the weapon which most readily conquers reason: terror and violence."[5]

Hitler first ascribed this terror and violence to his main enemies: Jews and the left. But he also advocated violence because "terror is not broken by the mind, but by terror." For Hitler, violence needed to go beyond self-defense; it needed to be elevated by an ideology. Hitler said that he personified such a "new spiritual doctrine."⁶ So did countless other fascists worldwide. In Italy, Mussolini grandiosely declared, "I have made the apology of violence for most of my life."⁷

Across the globe, antidemocratic ideologues made the apology of violence. Violence was not just the aim of fascism; it was also the starting point of its politics. Fascism had violence in its DNA. As the Portuguese Blue Shirts stated, "Violence is the essential and intelligent start of all good politics because without violence and in adversity, conquest is impossible." In fascism, violence became the outcome of blind faith in the leader. Spanish fascists talked of the "sacred violence of action." Egyptian Blue Shirts also stressed that "obedience and struggle" (*al-tcah wa al-jihad*) were rooted in faith. They pledged, "I swear by almighty God, by my honour and by the fatherland that I will be a faithful and obedient soldier, fighting for the sake of Egypt." Far from the Middle East, the Chinese Blue Shirts maintained that violence was at the center of politics: "There must be a determination to shed blood—that is, there must be a kind of unprecedented violence to eliminate all enemies of the people."⁸

Fascists regarded violence as a natural "cleansing" force.⁹ The Brazilian fascist leader Plínio Salgado explained "the sense of our violence" as entirely different from that of the left. Brazilian fascists did not have quantifiable ends but spiritual ones: "Our struggle, in Brazil, is not subordinated to the materialism of the 'struggle for life' applied to the class struggle, according to the Hegelian dialectic and the Marxist conception of history. Our violence must have a sense of the Spirit, of its intervention in the course of events, of the imposition of a new meaning of life."¹⁰

Inayatullah Khan Mashriqi, also known as Allama Mashriqi, the fascist supreme leader of the Khaksar movement in Punjab, said,

"We do believe in violence. Nonviolent people must be stamped out from the face of the world. Nonviolence is unnatural."[11] Similarly, Nicaraguan fascist Pablo Cuadra argued, "We are Fascist in our will to organize our disorganized lands in their truth and tradition. We use violence against those challenging the advance of our resurgence with their incomprehensible stupidity."[12]

Mussolini warned that enemies of fascism had no right to complain about "our violence" because it was a response to their violence, which was for him more extreme than fascist violence. The Duce, as Mussolini was known, insisted on the need for "our violence" to have "specific fascist dimensions." He repudiated the violence of all against one. He also condemned "the violence that is not explained." Mussolini identified those forms of violence with his enemies. He said that while fascist violence has a liberating power, socialist violence constrained the individual: "There is a violence that frees and a violence that chains; there is a violence that is moral and a violence that is stupid and immoral."[13] Mussolini made a "profound distinction" between forms of violence: on the one hand, those that were unacceptable because they were egotistical, individualistic, socialist, or liberal, and on the other hand, fascist violence, which was absolutely sacred and moral in nature.

Without specific ends, violence was potentially limitless and self-legitimizing. As historian Paul Corner argues, "Because of what was considered its moral function, violence was seen as totally legitimate—something essential to the cause of national transformation." Violence was the fascist path to power.[14]

In this way, fascism cannot be simply defined by what it stood against—liberalism, Marxism, and democracy—but also as a theory of violence with extreme practical consequences, including, in some cases, genocide. Fascism promoted violence to undermine the political tendency toward liberal conciliation. Fascists considered discussions fruitless. They saw no point in engaging with other traditions.[15] Violence defined all stages of fascism.[16] For these reasons, Norberto Bobbio, an Italian political scientist and a major interpreter of fascism and politics, said, "Violence was the ideology of fascism."[17]

But what is ideology? Ideologies are moralistic systems of common opinions and ideas intended to justify and motivate political action. They stress rhetorical points rather than logical arguments and are often resistant to evidence. They are often circular. Ideologies don't to need be complex; in fact, they are more successful when they are simple, or even simplistic. As Hannah Arendt noted, ideologies "can explain everything and every occurrence by deducing it from a single premise."[18] This is a needed frame of reference to understand why and how violence, and its appeal and glorification, was not a mere tool but a major foundation of fascist ideology and practice.

But what kind of violence? Was fascist violence different from the violence of other political systems? While most political ideologies regard violence, even extreme violence, as a means to an end, in fascism violence becomes an end in itself. For fascists, violence is transcendental, linking humanity to a heroic mythological world.

Across the globe, fascists equated political violence with the source of political power. While liberals and communists viewed power as the result of the state's monopoly on violence, fascists equated power with the exercise of political violence. Fascists saw the state's restriction of violence as the opposite of political power. They believed that unleashing violence created and increased their own power. They envisioned violence as the source of a new authoritarian society where nationalism, racism, and (centrally planned) capitalism could be integrated. For similar reasons, they also believed that a free press and an open public sphere were against their own interests. Fascism identified the pacification of national and international spaces with political weakness. At the same time, fascists conceived of their own violence as "sacred." Nationalist myths inspired and legitimized violence as a key dimension of the fascist political religion. According to fascist ideology, these myths preceded and transcended historical time. Central to this conception was a sacred contest against internal and external enemies. Fascism imagined an existential enemy that it subsequently identified and repressed. Brute force was considered necessary against those who were perceived to oppose the fascist trinity of people, nation, and leader.[19] Mussolini argued that fascist violence was the decisive solution for the "gangrenous" political situation that preceded him. He said that "our violence" is "extremely moral, sacrosanct and necessary."[20]

In India, fascists like M.S. Golwalkar argued that understanding "[our] history" would provide Hindus with an image of "ourselves" not as "the degenerate, downtrodden, uncivilised slaves that we are taught to believe we are today, but a nation, a free nation of illustrious heroes fighting the forces of destruction for the last thousand years." This imagined "history" implied a notion of mythical violence that was needed again in the present. National ardor and the "race spirit" called on Indians to "carry on the struggle to the bitter end." This struggle meant the elimination of all enemies: "National consciousness blazes forth and we Hindus rally to the Hindu Standard, the *Bhagawa Dhwaja*, set our teeth in grim determination to wipe out the opposing forces."[21]

In this view, fascist violence was a defense mechanism against the violence of the enemy, generally presented as a conspiracy of communists, liberals, and Jews. This fantasy was disseminated by fascists across the world. One of the most famous representatives of American fascism, Father Charles Coughlin, a radio personality who, according to the *New York Times*, commanded a weekly audience of ninety million listeners, stated in 1938 that "Nazism was conceived as a political defense mechanism against Communism." Those who fought against fascists were enemies of God. Coughlin included the president of the United States among these enemies. In an address before a National Union for Social Justice rally, he was quoted as having referred to President Roosevelt as "anti-God" and advocated the use of bullets "when an upstart dictator in the United States succeeds in making a one-party government and when the ballot is useless."[22] Another cleric—fascist radio personality Father Virgilio Filippo of Argentina—similarly believed that fascists, willingly or unwillingly, acted in the name of God against the existential threat represented by communist, Jewish, and secular enemies of the nation. He assured his followers that "God punishes his enemies with the methods they used to defile him."[23]

Fascists argued that violence was good when it was noble, sacred, and mythical. Words like *bloodbath* were meaningful to fascists insofar as they related the violence to a sense of regeneration and purification through violence. But whereas Mussolini especially liked the violence of "one on one," other fascists praised the idea of the unlimited bloodbath, the purification of an absolute and impersonal violence.[24]

This was the message that Heinrich Himmler, the leader of the SS, gave when he talked to a select group of Nazis at Posen in German-occupied Poland in 1943. In his secret speech, Himmler explained that the extensive number of victims was a cause for pride and their domination an opportunity for feelings of redemption and regeneration.[25] Himmler used explicit language: "I am referring here to the evacuation of the Jews, the extermination of the Jewish people. This is one of the things that are easily said: 'The Jewish people are going to be exterminated.'"[26] With these remarks, Himmler highlighted the difference between the discourse of victimization and the actual experience of victimizing others, between saying and doing. For him the latter was a privilege reserved for a select few. Referring to the first group of perpetrators, he said, "Of all those who talk like that, not one has seen it happen, not one has had to go through with it. Most of you men know what it is like to see 100 corpses side by side, or 500 or 1,000. To have stood fast through this and except for cases of human weakness to have stayed decent, that has made us hard."[27]

Decency was a key element of the Nazis' vision of an essential and moral genocide. Himmler believed that "this is an unwritten and never-to-be-written page of glory in our history, for we know how difficult it would be for us if today under bombing raids and the hardships and deprivations of war if we were still to have the Jews in every city as secret saboteurs, agitators, and inciters. If the Jews were still lodged in the body of the German nation, we would probably by now have reached the stage of 1916–17."[28]

In his novel *Kaputt* (1944), the maverick fascist writer Curzio Malaparte criticized this form of violence, even saying that one could find more humanity in the artificial eye of a German killer than in the real one. Similarly, Mussolini stated that "violence is immoral when it is cold and calculated but not anymore when it's instinctive and impulsive."[29] Nazism presented a more detached form of violence, one that led to further dehumanization and legitimized the Holocaust in the eyes of its perpetrators, but for most fascists, violence was entirely moral when applied to the cause.

Moreover, it was a "good" thing to "exterminate" enemies, as Himmler grotesquely put it in a speech in 1944.[30]

To sum up, in fascism, extreme violence was conceived as a way to preempt national disaster and was justified as a defense of the homeland against an imagined conspiracy of existential enemies. But fascists also thought that violence was the source of all power. In contrast with all other political traditions, they believed that the state monopoly on violence needed to be extensively used rather than restricted. Peace—internal or external—was anathema to fascists. This is one of the reasons why Hitler, after having established total domination at home, started the Second World War and the Holocaust. When he joined Hitler's war, Mussolini declared that it was "the logical development of our revolution." Fighting alongside Nazism was an obligation emanating from the "laws of fascist morality."[31] External war was a direct consequence of having finished the internal one. Fascism was rooted in the militarization of politics at home, but its idea of politics-as-war implied the need for total war. Just as the politics of fascism was conceived as the opposite of politics as usual, fascist war was the opposite of conventional war.

Violence and Terror

Hitler stated that "coercion is broken only by coercion and terror by terror." For Hitler, violence and terror were deep foundations of Nazism: "Political parties are inclined to compromises; philosophies never. Political parties even reckon with opponents; philosophies proclaim their infallibility."[32] This self-understood rising to the level of a philosophical, aesthetic, moral, and even transcendental status is what defines fascist violence and makes this pillar of fascism so unique.

Brutality per se—even in the most extreme forms, such as the Soviet Gulags or the American use of napalm in Vietnam and atomic bombs in Japan—does not make its users fascists.[33]

Violence is intrinsic to fascism, but, of course, it is not exclusive to fascism. The same applies to other thinkers of the left and the right. Karl Marx, for example, said that violence is the midwife of history and thus unavoidable, but at least as the story is told, in Marxism as well as in liberalism and conservatism, that violence is always a means to an end.[34] Bobbio thought that renouncing violence to achieve and exert power is a key feature of democratic politics. If democratic regimes, at least in principle, avoid producing violent outcomes to solve social conflicts, fascism actively promotes them. Fascism does not limit but actually expands institutional violence.[35] This is partly because it bases its legitimacy in violence and partly because its ideology and practice of violence are not separated; they are one and the same.[36]

In his "Doctrine of Fascism," Mussolini argued that fascism was born out of a need for action and it became action.[37] On another occasion he argued that "violence is decisive" and said that "by forty-eight hours of systematic, warrior violence we have obtained what we would not have obtained in forty-eight hours of preaching and propaganda."[38]

Fascism was violence incarnated. But we need to think more deeply about the historical reasons why its antidemocratic views were fused with racism, oppression, and mythology to create such a distinctive form of political violence. The context of World War I and the extreme brutalization of its trenches led to the idea that soldiers could form a "trenchocracy," as Mussolini and others put it. Once the war was over, it was not a great leap for former soldiers to view politics as another instance of the war they had just experienced. Colonialism and imperialism also served as "laboratories of fascism," with their extreme racialization and oppression in the forms of mass killings, "absolute destruction" warfare, and concentration camps.[39] Think of the German colonial extermination of the Herero in Namibia, or the words of the Kaiser when he asked his troops in China in 1900 to avenge injustice via the use of total violence: "When you meet the enemy, you will beat him; you will give no pardon and take no prisoners. Those whom you capture are at your mercy." The Kaiser presented his violence, in typically racist terms, as a response to the putative inferiority of the Chinese people and their supposed ignorance of the law. In this context, extreme violence was for him unavoidable: "As the Huns a thousand years ago under King Etzel made a name for themselves that has lasted mightily in memory, so may the name 'Germany' be known in China, such that no Chinese will ever again even dare to look askance at a German."[40]

In the few instances when fascism became a regime, it took a little more than a decade (Italy) or six years (Germany) to move from total internal war to absolute external war and empire. Fascist empires radicalized previous imperial traditions—including the idea of war as a civilizing mission, and the uses of violence and repression and racial hierarchies—and fused them with their own dreams of a homogeneous national regeneration. In this context the obliteration of the colonized was a foregone conclusion.[41]

What started in the colonies expanded to Europe. As Hannah Arendt explained, colonial administrators of violence soon formed a new bureaucracy that was ready to influence home politics with the idea that violence and power were intimately linked and represented the essence of every political system. Another major influence on the development of fascism's philosophy of violence was

WWI. Some members of the front generation displayed a combination of "antihumanist, antiliberal, anti-individualist, and anticultural instincts." They praised violence, power, and cruelty, linking these things back to the imperialist rationale. They equated terror with everyday politics.[42] These precedents opened the way for a total transformation of political language; the classic myth of the warrior was combined with a "new man forged by total warfare."[43]

The violence of fascism was conceived as the shell-shocking violence of the life-or-death situation experienced in the trenches. In short, fascists rooted their politics in the mythological tenets of violent sacrifice and violent death. They rapidly translated the world of external war into the world of internal politics.[44] After this internalization was complete, fascism once again externalized war.

The Fascist Militarization of Violence

The German Jewish anti-fascist thinker Walter Benjamin said that fascism regarded politics as spectacle, or as he put it, "The logical outcome of fascism is an aestheticizing of political life."[45]

Violence and the performance of violence were at the heart of all fascisms. But fascist violence was not merely performance. Street fighting, the assault on state institutions, and marching in costumes were seen as first steps toward the militarization of political life.[46]

Uniforms and other pseudomilitary regalia were important in ideological terms but not necessarily military ones.[47] All across the world, from Brazil to India, fascists paraded in military costumes or pseudomilitary uniforms, displaying guns as the central element of their politics. In Punjab, fascist leader Mashriqi argued that "the aim of the Khaksar soldier is to establish sovereignty over the whole world and to secure social and political supremacy through their fine conduct." His organization was fully militarized, with a clear chain of command, uniforms, and pseudomilitary titles.[48]

In 1935, Mashriqi defined his fascist organization as "a movement for men, lions, soldiers and belligerents, and never the movement for women, wives, eunuchs and boys." Violence was the only natural response to their situation because the nation was "in the throes of death and decline."[49] Similarly fusing politics and holy violence, Eugenia Silveyra de Oyuela, one of the most extreme Argentine fascist intellectuals, asserted that violence was legitimate as a result of God's war against the internal enemies. For her, this was the situation in Argentina: "red hordes" had invaded the country, and "we have the invaders in our midst, and we are, in fact, in a state of defensive war. This is a licit war for the Argentine who needs 'to defend the rights of the threatened homeland.'"[50] For fascists, war was the normal way for politics to work, and militarization was its logical consequence.

As Mashriqi also wrote, "Every principle and every action of the Khaksar movement is based on military patterns. . . . The Khaksar soldier is not a showy and toy soldier."[51] Brutalization was both intuitive and the object of cultivation.[52]

A concern for the weakness of the masses was shared across the globe; this is why the masses needed to be regimented. To achieve this aim, fascist violence projected a sense of über-masculinity. Pistols and other weapons, regimentation, uniforms, and militaristic rituals functioned as gendered attributes that helped reinforce the idea that fascist men ought to be respected, followed, and potentially feared qua men (patriarchs).[53] Manliness and violence were conceived as part of a fascist sense of "the supreme hierarchy of moral values." As Spanish fascist leader José Antonio Primo de

Rivera rhetorically asked, "Who said that when they insult our feelings, rather than react as men, we are obliged to be nice?" He answered his own question by stating that being respectful was cute, but real men reacted against offenses by adopting "the dialectic of fists and pistols."[54]

Fascism needed fit male bodies organized in militia formations. As Mashriqi eloquently put it, soldierly life corrected many of the democratic "tribulations" that his Khaksar fascists had to overcome.[55] If these "tribulations" were the outcome of pluralism, nonviolence, and the peaceful resolution of conflicts, then fascism provided homogenizing forces that affirmed a masculinity that was aggressive, active, and warrior-like. Spanish fascist Ernesto Giménez Caballero stated that masses were useless in and of themselves and were in need of a hierarchy and regimentation. He said that "life needs" to be militarized and the "militia is the organism that needs to be unleashed in our movement."[56]

Violence and Legality

The Spanish conservative philosopher José Ortega y Gasset observed in 1925 that a key difference between communist and fascist violence was that violence in fascism was more important than the law. He noted that the Soviet government used violence to ensure its right but did not make it "its right." In contrast, fascism did not intend to establish a "new law" because it "did not care about giving a legal basis to its power."[57] In short, while communists used extreme violence when it suited them, fascists elevated violence to a status higher than the law. For fascists, violence was more legitimate than legality, because while the former was the result of a cult of heroism and leadership principle, the latter was rooted in hypocrisy, treason, and artificial intellectuality. These enemies needed to be openly confronted. Fascist violence was "saintly and justifiable."[58]

Mussolini explained that a hierarchy was necessary to organize the masses, whereas legality was an open question that depended on the needs of the moment. Against an "imbecile" democracy that ruled in administrative and parliamentary terms, fascism put forward a military organization. Fascism had to be "swift and inflexible. Where there is a sick situation, it must be cured with iron and fire. When we say 'iron and fire' one must not believe in rhetorical amplification. We intend to speak of iron in the sense of a wounding weapon and of fire in the more specifically cauterizing sense of the word."[59]

As Brazilian fascist leader Salgado understood it, fascist violence was the outcome of a fight for the soul of civilization. It would save the nation from extinction by destroying those it regarded as different. As he saw it, one could not be impartial in the battle between "good and evil." Supporting fascism's violent march to power was the "only one attitude worthy of those who sincerely love Brazil and have enlisted for the fight against enemies of the country." Fascism was not organized to "show off" in "parades" but to destroy democracy. Fascism was against "degenerates and criminals." He argued that its violence should not treat them as subjects but as a living disease, in the way one deals with "cancer by cauterizing it."[60]

Similarly, Jorge González von Marées, the jefe of the Chilean *Nacis*, argued that what was at stake was the future of culture: "Violence is necessary when reason becomes powerless to impose sanity." This was a "counterattack" against those "who intend to destroy with blood and fire." This was a major task, a call to arms for "our young legions, whose martial footsteps will vibrate again." In other words, violence was the road to power.[61]

Recasting Fascist Violence: From Populism to Wannabe Fascism

To sum up, fascism identified the pacification of national and international spaces with political weakness and dubious legitimacy. At the same time, fascists imagined their own violence to be "sacred," a source of power and purification. Brute force was deemed a fundamental tactic in opposing those who were perceived to be against the fascist trinity of people, nation, and leader. On a global scale, this fascist brutalization of politics created and legitimized the conditions for extreme forms of political repression, war, and genocide. Fascism theorized an existential enemy that it would subsequently identify, repress, and eliminate.

Violence is often the outcome of an idea of victimhood. In this context, violent actors and oppressors recast themselves as victims. In populism, this violence remains rhetorical, whereas fascism constantly put it into practice.

Fascists connected the glorification of violence and the need to "conquer the world" with a notion of victimhood that they linked back to the divine. In the Punjab, Mashriqi linked fascism back to Islam.[62] While Mashriqi had no influence in Pakistan after 1945, Indian fascist ideology became a key source for the Bharatiya Janata Party (BJP) of Narendra Modi.[63] Thus, Hindu fascists were much more successful in provoking genocidal histories of violence that would have an impact on the present.

As formulated by Savarkar and Golwalkar, Hindutva ideology reinvented Hindu nationalism in ways that redeployed Western ideas of fascism, racism, and modernization. Mahatma Gandhi, the "recognized symbolic father of modern India, epitomized an oppositional relationship both to Western modernity and to Hindu nationalism.... Although he considered himself an orthodox Hindu, Gandhi rejected this form of nationalism because it channeled colonial subjugation as a form of mawkish innocence to authorizing violent expression, which he vehemently opposed." Gandhi was assassinated in 1948 by a member of the Rashtriya Swayamsevak Sangh (RSS), who would be incorporated into the pantheon of the current BJP populist party in India.[64]

The Indian case offers one of the most striking continuities between fascism and populism. The RSS, founded in 1924, had a later political offshoot in the Jana Sangh, which was launched in 1950 and later renamed the BJP. The BJP reformulated itself while never leaving behind key elements of fascism, especially xenophobia and the role of violence in politics. But radical propaganda and dictatorial aspirations only returned more fully in recent years with the wannabe fascism of Prime Minister Narendra Modi.

In contrast, most "classic" populists did change their fascist or pro-dictatorial ways after 1945. As a result of the defeat of fascism, populists attempted to reform and change the fascist legacy. They consistently renounced their fascist foundations, but they did not leave fascism entirely behind. Populism took the place of fascism as a new "third way" between liberalism and communism. However, unlike fascism, populism wanted to be a democratic choice. This populist intention to create a new political tradition, apart from fascism, explains the complex historical nature of populism as a varied set of authoritarian experiments in democracy. To be sure, eventually modern populism incorporated elements from other traditions, but its authoritarian origins shaped its signature tension between democracy and dictatorship.

Fascism idealizes and practices raw forms of political violence that populism rejects in theory and, most often, in practice. Talking about populism and fascism as though they are the same is thus problematic. After the fall of the fascist powers in WWII, early populists rejected not only dictatorial fascism but also high levels of political violence, racism, and anti-Semitism, together with total war and militarism. It's true that the first populist to come to power, Juan Perón, welcomed many Nazis and other fascists. However, Perón also allowed Argentine Jews to be full members of the nation as long as they declared themselves Peronist Jews, and Vargas's campaigns against minorities more closely resembled the contemporary illiberal trends of American democracy (for example, Franklin Delano Roosevelt's actions against Japanese Americans) than Nazi-fascist-style racist laws. Populism implied a rejection of fascist violence. Populists polarized their societies but did not engage in high levels of repression and political violence.[65]

Populism exemplified the first two elements of the fascist maxim "believing, obeying and fighting," but it clearly rejected the third. As Perón said in 1945 before he was elected, "One does not win with violence."[66] For Perón, a political leader did not need to be feared: "Fortunately, I have been always obeyed and respected. To be obeyed, I never commanded nothing that could not be done." He never asked for things that could not be easily accepted. He wanted his followers to believe in "logical things" and act "with pleasure, and not with violence."[67] Similarly, Getulio Vargas stated, "I don't need to urge the people to react or incite violence because the people always know when to react and against whom."[68] For populists, and in contrast with the fascists, violence was not a source of power and wisdom for the people and the leader. As Ecuadorian populist leader José María Velasco Ibarra explained, "If there is no understanding, there is hatred and the practice of violence is advocated. The practice of violence corrupts the governments, corrupts the youth, corrupts the people."[69]

Violence as a practice was anathema to populist politics. As Eva Perón put it in 1949, violence was "a phantom" hovering over the present world, a remnant left by the Second World War, and she was willing to identify it with the new geopolitical order of "the failed principles of liberalism" and those that "stick to violence as the only means of domination."[70] As Perón's wife and one of the key leaders of the Peronist movement, Eva Perón had a unique role as a mediator between genders, bearing witness to the equally unique Peronist rethinking of traditional gender relations. In this aspect, as in many others, Peronism *transcended fascism*. It was a movement of organized workers, not of paramilitary formations. Rather than identifying with communism or liberal democracy, populists put forward a third position beyond communism and what Venezuelan populist leader Rómulo Betancourt called the "decadent Western democracies."[71]

While fascism promoted war for its own sake, populists starkly differentiated themselves from the fascist militarization of politics. As Colombian populist Jorge Eliécer Gaitán explained, fascists "not only do not repudiate war, but love it." Fascism enshrined war and viewed it as a "constitutive element of society." In a famous speech in 1947, Gaitan stated that violence was a sign of weakness: "No one can conceive of violence as a way to create law."[72] As Perón put it, "Violence generally incarnates violence. Violence is blind. Violence—as Sartre says—is illiterate. It knows nothing."[73] Similarly, Brazilian populist Vargas argued for the rule of law instead of violence. Violence, its conception and more importantly its practices, divides the waters between fascism and populism. For fascists, violence generated power, although in reality, as Vargas put it, violence just generated more violence, and this was not what the people wanted.[74] Violence and its legacy of repression and extermination define the contrasting global experiences of fascism and populism as ideologies, movements, and regimes, as well as their subsequent reformulations in our new century.[75]

For populists, force and violence could not solve political problems. As authoritarian as populist leaders were, militarization was not central to populism. Like the fascists, Perón positioned himself as a law-and-order leader who could knit together a divided public balanced on a fragile peace. In doing so, he valorized the police and the armed forces against imagined enemies of the people, both inside and outside Argentina, who compromised not only the country's safety, but its identity. Referring to himself in a 1945 speech, Perón said, "Let Colonel Perón be the link of union that would make indestructible the brotherhood between the people, the army and the police. Let this union be eternal and infinite so this people will grow in that spiritual unity of the true and authentic forces of nationality and order."[76] And yet, this union did not lead to a full unification of the movement, the state, and the security forces. Perón said that victory would be won not with violence but with "intelligence and organization." But as the former fascist strongman in a military dictatorship, a leader who had turned to democratic procedures to become the elected president of the country, Perón believed that a mix of authoritarianism and consensus was better than terror.[77]

To be sure, Perón often threatened the opposition with radical violence. The nation had to be defended from "visible and invisible enemies of the homeland."[78] He warned that if the enemies wanted war, the Peronists would hang them with a rope.[79] His antagonism was so extreme that when Perón engaged in verbal fights with the absolute enemies (internal and external) whom he never or clearly identified, he said, "They should know that they will pay a high price, if they forget that in this land when it was needed to impose what the people wanted it did not matter how many Argentines should die."[80]

War was connected with these imaginary enemies of populism and the nation. Perón carefully delineated the notion of an absolute enemy, but he never actualized it. At one point he warned that political adversaries turned into "enemies of the nation." And yet, the populist leader's theory of the enemy remained distant from his practice. Populists displaced the total war of destruction to an imaginary future. Their positions were imaginary responses to the violence of the enemy, but they never came close to adopting war as an ideology. As Perón said, "If they want war they will get a war. And above all, they should know if they choose war, its outcome will be that they or us will disappear."[81]

In fact, violence was more typical of the practices of antipopulist enemies. In Colombia, it was the populist leader Gaitán who was assassinated in 1948. Perón went into exile in 1955 rather than face the prospect of internal war. Populists rejected the possibility of a fascist civil war. Internal violence was entirely avoidable.

Perón stated, "We have suffered and endured violence, but we have not exercised it, because we are against those methods. Because he who has the truth does not need violence, and he who has violence will never get the truth."[82] A former dictator turned populist, Perón relied on the votes of the Peronist masses to keep him in power (from the first time he was elected in 1946 until the coup that toppled him in 1955). In turn, he delivered for the masses, including paid vacations, more rights for peasants and farm and urban workers, fully funded state retirement, basically no unemployment, and substantial increases in state support for public health care and public education. Because of these gains, Perón never needed to crack down on his regime's critics. His popularity and these material gains built a consensus that neutralized critics without the need to resort to violence or the militarization of state and society. While Perón famously said that there was a moment when political adversaries became "enemies of the nation" and thus "snakes that one can kill in any way," this sort of statement was not coupled with the type of dictatorial repression that constitutes fascism.[83]

Fascism and populism presented clear distinctions in their uses and conceptions of political violence. If fascism understood power as firmly rooted in violence, populism shared with liberalism a more Weberian, and restricted, notion of violence, namely, that when power is achieved, violence is restricted. In fact, when populist forms of democracy were replaced by dictatorships in countries like Argentina in the 1970s, fascist forms of violence returned. This renewed fascist ideology was visible in the post-fascist and neofascist features of the Latin American "Dirty Wars" and in other "hot" war contexts of the global Cold War, from the Middle East to Africa and Southeast Asia. Many of these radical dictatorships represented a form of anti-populist ideology, in which violence reigned supreme. They presented continuities with fascist practices, and in some cases—such as Argentina, and to a minor extent Pinochet's Chile—with fascist notions. In contrast, populism put forward an authoritarian version of democracy that straddled democracy and dictatorship, leaving fascist violence behind.[84]

The Manufacturing of Violence

Fascism's idea of politics as a total war has consequences not only in conceptual terms but also in practice. We can see this in practice through the cult of the leader and his violent rhetoric and actions that sometimes resemble acts of war. The cult of the leader and his search for power warranted extreme violence. Although it was presented as spontaneous, this violence was, in fact, planned. Fascist leaders manufactured the conditions for civil war. Fascists "blackmailed their way into power," creating a fear of further terror and violence that they constantly fueled with ever-increasing terror and violence. This shared theory and practice of violence, and the complicity in illegality they engendered, created a fiction of security among the members of fascist nations. Only fascist violence protected members from the "outside world."[85]

As we will see in the next chapter, lies and propaganda are key elements of the promotion and dissemination of violence. In 1936, Spanish fascist dictator Francisco Franco, an unremarkable general, launched a coup and a gruesome civil war to destroy Spanish democracy while openly denying killings. Terror and total militarization were the foundation of his coup and his regime. This fascist war against constitutional democracy proceeded with the support of Hitler and Mussolini. The fate of the Spanish Republic was widely left unattended by Western democracy. In fact, it was an internal war. Franco rebelled against democracy and eventually turned the state against its own citizens. He regarded his war as a battle against the "anti-fatherland." He considered his enemies to be tools of a "Jewish-Masonic-Bolshevik conspiracy." Terror and the militarization of society were central to Franco's campaign to "purify" his country. His idea was that terror would lead to "redemption." Mass killings, rapes, and widespread economic expropriations were the clear effects of Franco's sacrificial violence. All in all, two hundred thousand people were assassinated, while four hundred thousand were imprisoned in two hundred concentration camps. Franco's sacred war against democracy was lethal.[86]

Italian fascists, for their part, are to blame for the premature deaths of around a million people, including thousands of political assassinations and innocent victims from the unprovoked Italian war against Ethiopia and the colonial war in Libya, where fascists used chemical weapons, as well as during the Second World War and the Holocaust.[87] As Franco did, the Italian fascists systematically denied their multiple crimes.

The Nazis also denied their Holocaust atrocities, stating that facts about them were part of a disinformation campaign by their enemies. Neofascists today continue to deny the Holocaust and even deny their own fascist behavior while they promote violence. In fact, the Nazis inherited a tradition of violence rooted in racism and discrimination, and they carried it forward. As historian Raul Hilberg brilliantly put it, "We have observed the trend in the three successive goals of anti-Jewish administrators. The missionaries of Christianity had said in effect: You have no right to live among us as Jews. The secular rulers who followed had proclaimed: You have no right to live among us. The German Nazis at last decreed: You have no right to live."[88] The same logic was often applied by other fascists toward their imagined and/or real enemies—for example, by Romanian, Italian, Hungarian, and Ukrainian fascists toward Jews, or Franco's total destruction of his enemies. To be sure, this level of extreme violence has not been met by the new aspirants to fascism in our century. But it is worth briefly analyzing the four stages of the Holocaust to assess whether these classic forms of fascist violence relate to the present forms of violence among populists and post-fascists.

Here, the Holocaust, which the Nazis justified as preemptive violence, remains the most extreme case of fascist violence. Hilberg distinguishes four fundamental stages that were chronological steps toward the final goal:

1. An initial moment of definition of the future victims, made up in nominal terms by the enactment of a specific legislation that defined who was a Jew.
2. A second phase of expropriation, characterized by the "aryanization" of properties, job dismissals, special taxes, and food rationing policies.
3. A third phase of deportation and concentration in ghettos and/or concentration camps.
4. A final phase of extermination in mobile killing operations or in extermination camps.[89]

It is clear that populism and wannabe fascism are nowhere near this level of systematic violence, but neither were most other cases of fascism between the 1920s and 1945. While populists denied the practical value of this level of violence even after they clearly constructed their enemies, wannabe fascists have often idealized it. It is important to remember that fascism is a specific form of politics where violence plays a central role, so the question is to what extent we can see continuities between past and present forms of extreme right-wing violence.[90] Despite wannabe fascists being more subtle or incompetent when it comes to glorifying violence and militarization, the connections are important and should not be ignored.

Even in countries where populism has predominated, many neofascist groups existed and continue to exist. Neofascist movements, which aim to invoke and replicate the fascist legacy, are on the rise in Europe and Brazil. The United States, with its organized paramilitary militias and racist gunmen, has provided its society with measured doses of the fascist political violence and death that so well define what neofascism stands for. Neofascists are the natural companions of populist wannabe fascists.

In 2020, one day after it was reported that law enforcement used force, including rubber bullets and tear gas, to clear peaceful protesters from outside the White House, the Trump campaign put out a statement claiming that it never happened, despite numerous eyewitness accounts and video of the scene.[91] The president's response to the uprisings across the United States after the killing of George Floyd featured several falsehoods and misdirection, including blaming antifa for the widespread protests. The same pattern of misinformation was often adopted to depict the Trumpist coup of 2021, whose outcome was violence. Trump's demonization of anti-fascism, Black Lives Matter, and critical race theory acted as the reason for the validation of violence against those who fight fascism and racism.

Misinformation has been a central feature of the current attempts to turn the history of the January 6 coup into its opposite: a manufactured myth. According to this myth, "Those accused of rioting were patriotic political prisoners and Speaker Nancy Pelosi was to blame for the violence." As the *New York Times* informed the public, these lies were voiced at the highest levels of the Republican Party.[92]

Trump used a health crisis of major proportions (the COVID-19 pandemic) and a failed coup to promote his brand of violent authoritarianism, positioning himself not as an elected official but as a leader who permanently owns the truth and whose authority is total. Once out of power, Trump increased the fascist patterns of his behavior, even warning that people would be exterminated and the country would be destroyed if nobody acted. He said, "The Green New Deal, going to destroy our country, this Green New Deal. It's green new bullshit. That's what it is. It's bullshit." As he stated in Arizona in July of 2021, "These people are crazy. Whatever happened to cows, remember they were going to get rid of all the cows? They stopped that, people didn't like that. Remember? You know why they were going to get rid of all the cows? People will be next."[93]

Bolsonaro, who is also known as the Brazilian Trump, was advised by Steve Bannon in his electoral campaign in 2018. The Brazilian populist combined promises of austerity measures with self-fulling prophesies of violence and the literal militarization of his government (with a record number of military men in key positions of the administration). In addition to military men, Bolsonaro's government was made up of disciples of "philosopher" Olavo de Carvalho, whose idea of violence was clearly fascist. For de Carvalho, violence was not a noun but an "adjective" that became legitimate when acting against criminals and "predators."[94] Bolsonaro's campaign and his time in power (2019–2022) were marked by racism, misogyny, extreme law-and-order positions, and criminal mismanagement of the COVID-19 pandemic.

For Bolsonaro, the left represents the antithesis of democracy—what he calls the "Venezuelanization" of politics. But left-wing populists in Latin America do not usually engage in racism or xenophobia. They do not seek to destroy democracy with violence, lies, and racism. To be sure, left-wing populist leaders like the Néstor and Cristina Fernández de Kirchner administrations in Argentina (2003-2015), the Rafael Correa administration in Ecuador (2007-2017), and Hugo Chávez in Venezuela (1999-2012) corrupted democratic institutions, but they still accepted the results of elections when they lost. Even on the right, there have been plenty of traditional populists, including Carlos Menem in Argentina, Fernando Collor de Mello in Brazil, and Silvio Berlusconi in Italy, who are not antidemocratic by way of the glorification of violence.

This is not what Bolsonaro stands for. Unlike previous forms of populism (on the left and right) that embraced democracy and rejected violence and racism, Bolsonaro's populism hearkens back to Hitler's time. Bolsonaro has endorsed the "militarization" of education.[95] A former captain in the Brazilian army, he sees politics and history in military terms. "If need be," Bolsonaro said at an election rally in June of 2022, "we will go to war."[96]

Latin America has experienced these fascist-inspired politics before, most notably during Argentina's "Dirty War" in the 1970s, when the government killed tens of thousands of its citizens, and during the Pinochet regime in Chile (1973-1990). Bolsonaro famously declared in 1999 that the Brazilian dictatorship also "should have killed 30,000 persons, starting with Congress as well as with President Fernando Henrique Cardoso."[97] Like his fascist predecessors, Bolsonaro has argued that this sort of dictatorial regime was a true democracy—just without elections. What is new about Bolsonaro is that, unlike those military dictatorships, he wants to market fascism as democracy.

Some Brazilian observers argue that strong opposition from women and minorities has boosted his power. A similar dynamic played out in 1930s Germany. The more repressive Nazi extremism became, the more public support Hitler gained.

The same can be said of India, a country that offers a striking example of strong continuity between fascism, populism, and wannabe fascism. Inspired by the bloodthirsty aspirations of India's fascist political traditions, Modi has a long history of promoting and enabling violence. Genocidal calls to turn India into a Hindu nation were at the center of Indian fascism in the interwar years, and this pattern progressively changed from talk to action.

It is no coincidence that Modi was the chief minister in Gujarat when his followers launched a pogrom that began on February 28, 2002, and killed one thousand people while driving one hundred and fifty thousand from their homes. This pogrom expanded and solidified Modi's reach among his fanatic nationalist followers and in broad segments of society.[98] Indian nationalists have, in fact, replicated the Kristallnacht playbook, which used an attack against a Nazi officer in Paris as an excuse to attack and destroy German Jews: after a bloody incident in Godhra railway station when two train wagons ignited, killing fifty-nine Hindu passengers, Indian nationalists launched a pogrom of sweeping proportions.[99] Joseph Goebbels recalled Hitler's reaction in 1938: "He decides: demonstrations should be allowed to continue. The police should be withdrawn. For once the Jews should get the feel of popular anger." Similarly, Modi declared that "every action has an opposite reaction" and the violence was a "natural reaction." Like Hitler, Modi gave explicit orders to the security forces during the pogrom that people "should be allowed to vent their anger."[100]

Trump, too, has embraced the notion of certain types of mob violence. As a response to the protests regarding the police assassination of George Floyd in 2020, Trump tweeted that indiscriminate military violence was the only possible answer: "These THUGS are dishonoring the memory of George Floyd, and I won't let that happen. Just spoke to Governor Tim Walz and told him that the Military is with him all the way. Any difficulty and we will assume control but, when the looting starts, the shooting starts. Thank you!" Critics accused this tweet of glorifying violence, but the White House said the opposite was true. This idea of the legitimacy of angry men with guns was emphasized when paramilitary followers of the president breached the state capitol in Michigan. Trump tweeted, "LIBERATE MICHIGAN!; LIBERATE MINNESOTA!; LIBERATE VIRGINIA, and save your great 2nd Amendment. It is under siege!" This was a dress rehearsal, a harbinger of the way Trump symbolically ended his government on January 6 of the following year. This politics of paranoia that leads to fascist violence always begins with the justification of anger. In fact, Trump defended these armed men in Michigan in a way that was similar to his infamous defense of neo-Nazi marchers in Virginia: "These are very good people, but they are angry."[101]

The strong connection between the ideology and practice of violence in fascism and in the populism of wannabe fascists goes against a more general trend of low levels of violence in populism. In the case of BJP, once they reached power in 2014 at the national level, and before that at the regional level, the glorification of violence hastened Modi's journey toward wannabe fascism. The paramilitarization of the state served as the intimate link between sacrificial violence and the cult of the leader. On the internet, armies of trolls dedicated themselves to inciting and justifying violence.[102] As in fascism, and in contrast with the violent rhetoric of most twentieth-century populism, in India, gaining power increased raw practical violence.[103]

Although Narendra Modi's rise to power in 2014 was a turning point in the history of Indian populist nationalism, the main policies of fascist-inspired violence and the militarization of politics did not change at all. Once in power, the BJP's long-standing demonization of Indian Muslims and "liberals" and the promotion of violence against them became government policy. Modi adopted a moniker that carried an inference of menial service and pushed the idea of selflessness—"Chowkidar" (watchman, or sentinel)—and described his followers in paramilitary terms, just like historical Indian fascists did. The similarities with the Punjab Muslim fascism of Mashriqi are striking, even if Modi's tradition is more in line with that of Golwalkar. Modi's politics encouraged a cult of personality in which emulation was prioritized above reflection.[104]

As with Bolsonaro and Trump, whose fellow travelers included far right and neo-Nazi groups (the Michigan militias, the Proud Boys, and the Oath Keepers in the United States; vigilante and integralist groups in Brazil), Modi's links with "fringe elements" (terrorists and pogromers and vigilante groups) were extremely porous.[105] Modi's glorification of violence and militarization had more in common with fascism than populism, and this led to high levels of illegality in a regime that was supposed to be devoted to law and order. As one of Modi's loyalists said, "Might is the only law I understand. Nothing else matters to me. In India it is a war-like situation as between Rama and Ravana."[106] This idea of politics as an all-or-nothing war between good and evil defines the theory and practice of the wannabe fascism that is affecting populism.

The leadership of Rodrigo Duterte in the Philippines (2016–2022) is a clear example of the new populist rapprochement with the violent logic of classic fascism. Unlike most populist leaders, Duterte placed violence at the center of his politics from the time he got his start as mayor of Davao City. In law-and-order fashion, he promised death to criminals, telling them in 2009, "For as long as I am the mayor, you are a legitimate target of assassination." Like Trump, Bolsonaro, and others, Duterte linked his actions to toxic masculinity, the phallus, fantasies of violence, and the vindication of dictators past and present.[107] Homophobia, misogyny, and praise of rape were key elements of his macho-populism, as was the case with Trump's "grab them by the pussy" comment.[108] In the context of public dissatisfaction with the elitist and technocratic dimensions of Philippine democracy, Duterte combined the glorification of violence with his dubious claim of being a political outsider (he has been in politics since the 1970s) and the intimidation of his critics. Once in power in 2016, Duterte unleashed antidrug campaigns that resulted in at least twenty-nine thousand deaths, including thousands of extrajudicial killings of alleged drug users and pushers.[109] He explicitly drew comparisons with fascism and the Holocaust: "Hitler massacred 3 million Jews . . . there's 3 million drug addicts . . . I'd be happy to slaughter them." While obscuring the fact that Nazism was responsible for the death of six million Jews, he linked his actions to both the precedent of fascist violence and its apocalyptic connotations. In 2016, he told reporters that his critics presented him as "a cousin of Hitler." Duterte said that "if Germany had Hitler, the Philippines would have" him: "You know my victims. I would like (them) to be all criminals to finish the problem of my country and save the next generation from perdition."[110]

The Real Fascists

The new wannabe fascists have not demonstrated the willingness to reach the mass killing stage of traditional fascism. But they are not typical populists, either. Think of the Holocaust, genocidal campaigns in Africa, the Spanish Civil War, or more recently, the genocide perpetrated in Guatemala and the thousands killed by Latin American dictators throughout the 1970s and 1980s.

Duterte and Modi have approached these patterns of violence without getting anywhere close. But the wannabe fascists push ideological state violence to a new level, as the Brazilian scholar Conrado Hubner Mendes has explained about Bolsonaro's shift from police lethality to the massive "violation of human rights in prisons, under judicial, political and social approval."[111]

A similar impulse is behind Trump's policies of law and order, mass incarceration, anti-abortion, the legitimization of white power groups, the radicalization of the "deportation machine," and the repression and concentration of immigrants. And let's not forget his mismanagement of the COVID-19 pandemic, which had deadly consequences, as in Brazil.[112] This mix of symbolic violence with possible practical outcomes could also describe wannabe fascists such as the Vox party in Spain, José Antonio Kast in Chile, Keiko Fujimori in Peru, Marine Le Pen in France, Javier Milei in Argentina, and countless others. What makes this vocation for violence different from long-standing structural violence in society is that it is reframed within the ideological glorification of violence and the militarization of politics. The lethal dimensions of wannabe fascism are no longer typical of populism but not yet fascist.

So, despite key differences, the first pillar of fascism—the glorification of violence and militarization—still relates to the wannabe fascists. The violence of the wannabe fascists represents an enduring threat to citizens and is intimately linked to fascist techniques of persuasion. We will now turn to these techniques: lies and propaganda.

2   *Fascist Lies and Propaganda*

"Is it the influence of the tremendous propaganda—films, broadcasting, newspapers, flags, ever more celebrations (today is the Day of the Nation, Adolf the Leader's birthday)? Or is it the trembling, slavish fear all around?"[1] This is the question that German Jewish professor Victor Klemperer asked himself in his private diary on April 20, 1933, less than two months after Adolf Hitler came to power in Nazi Germany. Klemperer was witnessing the rapid disintegration of German democracy and could not yet grasp how propaganda and lies worked in tandem with violence, fear, and terror. In fact, it was the combination of the lies and the fear that justified the perpetrators' actions and dealt deep, numbing blows to victims and bystanders alike.

Like many others, Klemperer fell into resignation: "I almost believe now that I shall not see the end of this tyranny. And I am almost used to the condition of being without rights. I simply am not German and Aryan, but a Jew and must be grateful if I'm allowed to stay alive."[2] But Klemperer never completely lost "hope" that German fascism's state of "boundless tyranny and lies" would collapse at some point. Klemperer himself survived Nazism and managed to write a major work, *The Language of the*

Third Reich, which presented German fascism as turning "everything it touched—like some Midas of lies—into an untruth."[3] This turning of reality into untruth marked a key element of fascism.

There is no fascism without big lies. Fascists not only believe their lies but also want to transform them into reality. Only if the universe resembles their lies does the universe make sense to them. This inverted sense of reality defines the logic of fascist propaganda, a logic that determines what is true and what is not, a logic that insists the emperor is not naked. Lies are a key pillar of fascism. Not only are they different from other types of propaganda, they are also distinctive in quantitative and qualitative terms. Fascist lies are political false information that are intended to turn the world upside down. Fascist politicians lie, and believe their lies, and want to impose them on others.

Projections and Repetitions

The repetition of lies has been a powerful tool for fascist leaders in the past, as it is for would-be fascists in the present. Both types of leaders ascribe the manufacturing of lies to their enemies. "There's a word [called] 'disinformation.' . . . If you say it enough, and keep saying it, just keep saying it, they [people] will start to believe it." Donald Trump shared this revealing observation in Florida on July 3, 2021. Trump claimed it was his enemies who "say it again and again and again and after months and months of hearing, people begin to believe the Democrats' claim."[4] This could not be further from the truth.

When Trump repeatedly lied about the election, his failed coup, or the COVID-19 pandemic, he was creating a false sense of the "truth," of his own grandiosity and invincibility. In 2018, Trump told his followers that "what you're seeing and what you're reading is not what's happening."[5] According to this mindset, what the leader says and does matters more than facts, science, and even the followers' own perceptions about the world.

Fascist lies often project what fascists do onto others. In fact, the most famous fascist propagandist, the Nazi leader Joseph Goebbels, is often misquoted as stating that repeating lies was central to Nazism. He never said that. This misquotation has led to a perception of fascist leaders being fully conscious of the extent of their deliberate falsehoods. But the relationship between truths and lies in Nazism is more complicated. When Goebbels said that Hitler knew everything and that he was "the naturally creative instrument of divine destiny," it wasn't mere flattery or spin.[6] He actually believed it. Similarly, Hitler deeply believed that he could win a war on all fronts because he was invincible. Goebbels and others serving the regime came to believe it, too.

Goebbels was a master of creating an alternative reality that justified Nazi rule and violence. As his biographer, the historian Peter Longerich, noted, having once faked and then published news about an assassination attempt on himself, Goebbels then "published" it as fact in his diaries.[7] In these diaries, not written for public consumption but published many years after his death, he also noted the "success" of his speeches after they were celebrated by the media he controlled.

Was Goebbels lying to himself, or did he believe in a form of truth that transcended empirical demonstration? Both. For fascists like Goebbels, knowledge was a matter of faith, and especially a deep faith in the myth of the fascist leader. Fascists believed in a truth that transcended facts. They did not see a contradiction between truth and propaganda.

As philosopher Jason Stanley explains, propaganda can be sincerely believed when it is justified by ideology. Committed believers will take it seriously even when it is evidently false and outrageous.[8]

In the 1930s and 1940s, fascists around the world saw truth expressed in anti-Semitic myths, as well as myths of a golden past that was going to be reinstated and expanded—what the German Jewish philosopher Ernst Cassirer called "myth according to plan." Fascists fantasized an alternative reality—for Hitler this was a world where Jews had lied their way to prominence and brought economic collapse for the German people—and then changed the actual reality to reflect their ideas.

Concrete policies aimed to reshape the world according to these fascist lies. For example, if anti-Semitic lies stated that Jews were inherently dirty and contagious and therefore ought to be killed, the Nazis created conditions in the ghettos and concentration camps where dirtiness and widespread disease became reality. Starved, tortured, and radically dehumanized, Jewish inmates became what the Nazis had planned for them to become and were, accordingly, killed.

In their search for a truth that did not coincide with the experienced world, fascists conceived that what they saw and did not like was *untruth*. They believed in a form of truth that transcended common sense and observation.

Italian dictator Benito Mussolini stated, "At a certain moment in my life I risked being unpopular with the masses to announce to them what I thought was the new truth, a holy truth [*la verità santa*]."[9] This idea of a sacred truth that displaced empirical truth is key to understanding how lying operated in fascism.

Hitler, and also Goebbels, insisted that propaganda needed constant repetition, but they never said they were telling lies. In fact, they believed that what they said was true. In 1942, Goebbels wrote in his private diary that "the essence of propaganda is simplicity and repetition."[10]

The propaganda playbook was often more important than the content of the lies. Klemperer argued that form, rather than content, was "the most powerful Hitlerian propaganda tool." He stressed that "the most powerful influence was exerted neither by individual speeches nor by articles or flyers, posters or flags; it was not achieved by things which one had to absorb by conscious thought or conscious emotions. Instead, Nazism permeated the flesh and blood of the people through single words, idioms and sentence structures which were imposed on them in a million repetitions and taken on board mechanically and unconsciously."[11] This is why simply repeating messages can be incredibly dangerous, particularly when they are based not on facts but on antidemocratic ideology.

Fact-checking President Trump and leaders like him has become a full-time job. Their comments are peppered with inaccuracies and lies. As we have seen, these lies have deadly consequences. But there is a deeper problem than simply lying, that is, coming to believe that these lies are in service of the truth.

This was particularly dangerous when it came to the US response to the COVID-19 pandemic under the Trump regime. Trump alternated from downplaying its deadly nature to repeating promises of a "miracle," which he used to argue for lifting restrictions designed to slow the spread of the virus. His rhetoric pitted the "real people" against experts, scientists, and especially the media in an attempt to shift the blame for the resulting economic catastrophe.[12]

Trump believed his opinion was superior to that of doctors, scientists, and local officials. At first he did not wear a mask to protect himself and others from COVID-19, he promoted fantasy cures, and he demanded that governors and mayors follow his blueprint for addressing outbreaks. Even more dangerously, he pitted public health precautions against economic reopening, as though an economy could be turned on like a light switch while thousands died daily from coronavirus. Millions were unemployed, he argued, not because of a legitimate health crisis, but because his political enemies were punishing him by insisting on closures, stay-at-home orders, and other mitigation efforts.

Once out of power, Trump constantly repeated that the United States was facing destruction. He argued that he was persecuted by "maniacs," "perverts," and "lunatics."[13] Trump fantasized about ongoing economic destruction and the end of border security. But above all, Trump pretended that America lived in a totalitarian reality where extremists ruled.

In this sense, his message on Mother's Day in 2023 was highly symptomatic. Trump wrote, "Happy Mother's Day to ALL, in particular the Mothers, Wives and Lovers of the Radical Left Fascists, Marxists, and Communists who are doing everything within their power to destroy and obliterate our once great Country. Please make these complete Lunatics and Maniacs Kinder, Gentler, Softer and, most importantly, Smarter, so that we can, quickly, MAKE AMERICA GREAT AGAIN!!!" Thus, he proposed that every problem could be corrected by following him and his MAGA movement.

Previously, at Easter, he had celebrated the resurrection of Jesus with the following message: "HAPPY EASTER TO ALL, INCLUDING THOSE THAT DREAM ENDLESSLY OF DESTROYING OUR COUNTRY BECAUSE THEY ARE INCAPABLE OF DREAMING ABOUT ANYTHING ELSE."[14] Trump's meaning of salvation was related to a reality that did not exist. And yet many of his followers saw the leader himself as suffering the same fate as Jesus. As Congresswoman Marjorie Taylor Greene, a Trumpist representative from Georgia, stated in April 2023 when Trump was arrested in one of the many trials he faced, "Jesus was arrested and murdered by the Roman government. . . . There have been many people throughout history that have been arrested and persecuted by radical corrupt governments, and it's beginning today in New York City."[15] Only blind ideological followers could believe these arguments, which disturbingly conflated the sacred with the most profane, instead of seeing them as a departure from the world as we know it.

As Hannah Arendt explained, fascist propaganda presents a closed body of thinking and argumentation that produces a complete explanation. It is aimed at the "emancipation of thought from experience through certain methods of demonstration. Ideological thinking orders facts into an absolutely logical procedure which starts from an axiomatically accepted premise, deducing everything else from it; that is, it proceeds with a consistency that exists nowhere in the realm of reality."[16]

Big Lies

Fascist lies are not all the same and change over time. Their reach and content have no limits, but their simplicity and simplifications remain the same. Fascist propaganda relies on the idea of a credulous public. As Goebbels explained, "Our propaganda is primitive [because] the people think primitively. We speak the language the people understand."[17] The fascist attempt at "primitive" propaganda results in words that are mesmerizing to believers while being revulsive, unreal, and even idiotic to critics.

Why do people believe fascist lies? Klemperer observed that "the extraordinary thing was the shameless transparency of the lies revealed by the figures; one of the fundamentals of Nazi doctrine is the conviction that the masses are unthinking and that their minds can be completely dulled."[18] But this dulling of the minds required fascist propaganda techniques. Arendt explained that lies and propaganda were "self-generated" but also took a few elements from reality, transforming them into exaggerated circular arguments that eventually made them virtually unappealable. Lies may have had grains of truth, but propaganda moved them far away from reality. The unbelievable became a matter of belief. Once this happened, evidence and critical thinking were rendered meaningless. Fascists used these lies as weapons that destroyed reason. This is why Klemperer stated that it was "undeniable that the propaganda exposed as bragging and lies still works if you only have the audacity to continue with it as if nothing had happened; the curse of the superlative is not always self-destructive, but all too often destroys the intellect which defies it; and Goebbels had much more talent than I gave him credit for, and the ineffective inanity was neither as inane nor as ineffective."[19]

Big lies always include the accusation that it is the enemy who is lying. The Big Lie turns the world upside down and presents itself as a Big Truth.

When Hitler talked about big lies and big truths, he wanted to flip the world of true and fake. His fascist take on reality relied on a notion of truth that did not need empirical verification. In other words, what is true for most of us (the result of demonstrable causes and effects) was potentially fake for him. What most of us would see as lies or invented facts were for him superior forms of truth. Much like populist media claims today, Hitler inverted reality by projecting onto his enemies his own dishonesty regarding the truth, falsely stating that the Jews were liars, not him. The fascist liar acted as if he represented the truth. He accused Jews of engaging in "colossal distortion of the Truth." But Hitler identified this real truth with the anti-Semitic myths that he believed and propagated.[20] He said,

> The foremost connoisseurs of this truth regarding the possibilities in the use of falsehood and slander have always been the Jews; for after all, their whole existence is based on the great lie, to wit, that they are a religious community while actually they are a race—and what a race! One of the greatest minds of humanity has nailed them forever as such in an eternally correct phrase of fundamental truth: he called them "the great masters of the lie." And anyone who does not recognize this or does not want to believe it will never in this world be able to help the truth to victory.[21]

In his Arizona speech in the summer of 2021, Trump similarly turned his big lies into an alternative truth, a dumbed-down alternative reality manufactured for him and his followers: "The big lie they call it, you know what is the big lie? The opposite was the big lie. The election was the big lie."[22] This speech made it clear once again that Trump is a vocational fascist. He represents a return to key elements of fascism: a style and substance steeped in political violence, a leader's cult, dictatorial aims and practices (remember the coup attempt), a politics of hatred, religious fanaticism, militarization of politics, denial of science, and totalitarian propaganda.

Fascists believe their lies and try to transform reality to resemble their lies. This is what Trump expected of his public in Arizona;

it's also what he expected of his fellow wannabe fascists worldwide. Bolsonaro was the most consequential liar of his cohort. When asked about the storming of the US Capitol, Bolsonaro stated, "I followed everything today. You know I'm connected to Trump, right? So you already know my answer. . . . There were lot of reports of fraud, a lot of reports of fraud." Bolsonaro even believed that there was fraud against him when he won the election in 2008; he thought he should have won without the need for a runoff.[23]

After his own electoral defeat in 2022, in a failed bid for reelection, Bolsonaro first remained silent while his supporters (including many members of the police forces) attempted to create the conditions for a coup. During the election, the federal highway police had actively engaged in voter suppression efforts by creating roadblocks, especially in states that voted for the opposition. Like Trump, Bolsonaro created what the *New York Times* called the "myth of stolen elections." At a rally in 2022, as his followers chanted his nickname—"Myth"—"he told them there was no way his opponent could feasibly win."[24] This assertion was reinforced by the idea of his own infallibility as a heroic warrior, meaning he could not really be rejected by the majority of the people. In this fantasy, the mythical death of the warrior was the alternative to defeat or prison. In 2021 Bolsonaro said, "I have three alternatives for my future: being arrested, killed or victory."[25] This turned out to be just another lie.

During his meteoric rise to power, Bolsonaro had normalized lies such as "fake news is part of our lives. Who never told a little lie to their girlfriend? If I didn't, the night wouldn't end well." But he distinguished between his own lies, which were rooted in a form of repressive masculinity, and the lies of his enemies (especially independent journalists), which were basically evil. He argued that he was the ultimate victim of fake news and he had "suffered" the most.[26]

In casting blame on others for the pains that resulted from their destructive policies, Trump, Bolsonaro, and other wannabe fascists were echoing what Goebbels did. And, like him, they believed their own lies. The results are already part of the historical record, and they are catastrophic.

Fascists identified truth with the sacred, and in turn conflated the leader's lies with God's will. Those that did not accept these sacred beliefs were the real liars. As Nicaraguan fascist Pablo Cuadra stated in 1940, "Lies are always vile imitators of the truth," and in the context of the enemies' lies, "God was denied worthy worship" and what remained was "cowardice and effeminacy."[27]

This fixation on "truth" as an emanation of an ideology, which also defined the empirical reality that others clung to as the "untruth," was central to the emergence of fascism and more recent developments, including the lies about disease, elections, and White Replacement.

Lies and the Manipulation of the Media

How should a democratic society and its independent media respond to fascist propaganda? As the history of fascism shows, news organizations have long battled with fascist leaders over control of information, balancing the demand to present different perspectives with the need to inform based on facts, not falsehoods.

Totalitarian leaders manipulated the independent media to gain power, only to crush their operations once they did so. Why? Because dictators and authoritarians trade on the repetition and amplification of big lies. To them, the media is both a tool for manipulation and also a potential threat to their propaganda efforts.

There is an important lesson to be learned from the history of fascist lies. Independent journalists, and citizens as a whole, cannot assume that propagandists are honest actors. They need to recognize that propagandists are dishonest players who want to promote their lies rather than inform the public.

Adolf Hitler understood the importance of propaganda—and thus control over the press—in achieving, and then maintaining, political power. In *Mein Kampf* he wrote, "Propaganda must be adjusted to the broad masses in content and in form, and its soundness is to be measured exclusively by its effective result." This is why he also argued that the state "must particularly exercise strict control over the press. . . . It must not let itself be confused by the drivel about so called 'freedom of the press.'"[28]

Once in power, the Nazis destroyed the independent media, closing down more than two hundred newspapers, which collectively had a circulation of 1.3 million readers. And they put thousands of journalists in jail. As historian Richard Evans explains, "The Editors' Law of 4 October 1933 gave the Nazis total control over the press." Once in power, "[Joseph] Goebbels [the Nazi propaganda minister] issued instructions to the papers every day, outlining what they could or could not print."[29] Fascists especially hated journalists because their line of work represented the opposite of what fascism stood for: truth, transparency, and freedom of thought.

In 1932, one of the few American journalists to interview Hitler, Hans Kaltenborn, explained that "Adolf Hitler has an intense instinctive aversion to interviews. This man, whose 'hunches' on what to do and whose uncanny sense of when to do it astound the world, thinks best and decides most shrewdly when he is alone. He dislikes talking to strangers because they intimidate him. He compensates for his timidity by raucous self-assertion in their presence. Instead of answering an interviewer's questions he makes excited speeches, thus seeking to create for himself the atmosphere of the public meeting in which he is at home."[30]

Kaltenborn hoped the interview would shed light on Nazi operations, particularly its leaders' racist and antidemocratic mentality. But his questions about Hitler's anti-Semitism and his views on dictatorship conflicted with a central element of the fascist playbook, that is, *Führerprinzip*, the idea that leaders are correct all the time, and others, including journalists, should accept their explanation without questions.

This is why, as Kaltenborn explained, "From the beginning of his public career, Hitler has avoided personal contact with men who disagree with him. He is as conscious of his inability to persuade individuals as he is sure of his skill in mass appeal. Not more than a dozen foreign newspaper men have had individual access to him in as many years."[31]

Kaltenborn felt he was able to ask Hitler critical questions. But when Hitler became unhappy with the questioning, he merely affirmed his anti-Semitism, his fascist alliance with Mussolini, and his dictatorial vision. In other words, he repeated his big lies.

This is why dictators like Hitler preferred doing interviews with those who idolized them—not independent, professional journalists—so they could avoid critical questions and extend their cult following. The first Argentine dictator, José Félix Uriburu, was "interviewed" to legitimize the coup of 1930 by framing it as a heroic "revolution."[32] The interview helped reinforce his myth as a leader, crystallizing a fictitious narrative that became part of the history of authoritarianism in Argentina.

In 1931, the German Jewish writer Emil Ludwig interviewed Benito Mussolini at the height of his dictatorship. Initially, Mussolini saw this as an opportunity to disseminate his lies abroad, while Ludwig saw it as an opportunity to distance Mussolini from Hitler and critique Nazi racism and anti-Semitism. Perhaps it was Ludwig's congratulatory, even admiring tone that led Mussolini to drop his guard and openly ridicule Germanic theories of anti-Semitism.[33]

But then Mussolini changed his mind, ultimately halting the dissemination of the interview and allowing it to be republished only after important changes were made, for fear of appearing weak with journalists and to avoid damaging his relations with Hitler. The published interview appeared across the world in multiple languages, helping normalize Mussolini's image abroad, while being silenced within Italy itself. Eventually, Mussolini passed his own racial laws in the fall of 1938, and as historian Simon Levis Sullam has shown, fascists became key perpetrators of the Holocaust in Italy some years later.[34]

Former president Donald Trump abruptly ended an interview with NPR after he was asked about his "big lie" that the 2020 election was "rigged" against him.[35] But the interview itself provided yet another opportunity for him to amplify his baseless propaganda—and reminds us why it is dangerous for journalists, especially broadcasters, to continue to interview these wannabe fascists.

Historically, fascists and populists have spurned debates and open access to ideas, while seeking to downplay the relevance of key democratic institutions like the free press. Wannabe fascist leaders have often blamed the existence of a free press for the criticism they receive, but they often make these complaints through the free press. This is why Trump, Bolsonaro, Orbán, Milei, and others have come to view the independent press as a key adversary of their own politics but also as a tool of manipulation. The independent media's "both sides" framework leaves it vulnerable to being used to amplify dangerous lies. As history shows us, fascist dictators have long understood that the role of the free media is incompatible with their antidemocratic propaganda. But if they can exploit it, they will.

Fascist Martyrs Then and Now

A central fascist lie is that people who decide to sacrifice themselves for their leaders' ideology are not blind and reckless followers, but martyrs.

Fascists rooted their violence in myths about past warrior-leaders and their all-or-nothing battles against alien invaders. From Roman emperors to Spanish invaders to Hindu warriors, fascists imagined a history of violence as the mythical foundation for their present. They believed that the past resounded in their present, and they distorted history because of a perceived need to correct their enemies' "distortion of history." These distortions of the past became a rationale for absolute violence in the present: "Rise for the cause of the Hindu Nation in the North, and I, too, with my brave spearsmen, shall rush down from my mountain throne, like a torrent, sweeping out the enemy from the land and join you in the plains, where we shall amalgamate our forces and create such a blaze of power, that we shall wholly destroy and root out the least vestige of the foe, and re-establish the Hindu Empire in Hindusthan."[36]

Acts of violence were incorporated into the mythological corpus of fascism. Perpetrators who died while engaged in full-blown fascist brutalization were welcome into the pantheon, while no mention was made of their drug-induced euphoria. As Ruth Ben-Ghiat explained, there was a link between the internal violence of fascist squads and their "practices of violence initiated twenty years earlier—the forced ingestion of oil, beatings with clubs, and burning and sacking of public and private buildings—[to] recreate the collective ecstasy and transgression that marked *squadristi* when sacking and raping expeditions went on for several days, fueled by cocaine and drink."[37] What made this behavior diverge from other wartime practices was that it was consciously rooted in fascist origin myths. Colonial wars and the Second World War provided fascism with new opportunities to return to its fabricated mythical past.[38] These fabrications justified Indian fascists' actions against Muslims and Burmese fascists' persecution of their racial enemies.[39] Internal repression and domination were subsumed in the glorification of violence and the militarization of politics.

This is what happened to Ashli Babbitt, who was killed by police at the US Capitol while she was participating in the anti-constitutional attempt to seize it. Fascists behave as if they are trying to anticipate what the leader might order them to do, or what he expects from them, even when his words are unclear. In their head they are having a constant conversation with the leader. Babbit might have thought she was defending the law, but she was actually subverting it.

The so-called MAGA bomber, a fifty-seven-year-old Florida resident whose own lawyers called him "a Donald Trump superfan," followed the same logic. In 2018, he illegally mailed explosives intended to kill Trump's enemies. Prosecutors said Cesar Sayoc's crimes represented a "domestic terrorist attack." The MAGA bomber lived alone in decrepit conditions, estranged from his family. He suffered from anxiety and paranoia. His lawyers wrote that "in this darkness, Mr. Sayoc found light in Donald J. Trump." He "religiously" followed Trump on social media and at rallies. "He became obsessed with 'attacks' from those he perceived as Trump's enemies. He believed stories shared on Facebook that Trump supporters were being beaten in the streets. He came to believe that he was being personally targeted for supporting Trump."[40] In Nazism, what happened to Babbit and the MAGA bomber was called the *Führerprinzip*, which meant that everything Hitler wanted was legitimate and beyond the rule of law. This was the rationale for Trump's and Bolsonaro's failed coup attempts. Followers of fascist cults act as scapegoats for their leader, providing support and deniability.

Nationalist myths inspired and legitimized violence as a key element of the fascist political religion. According to fascist ideology, these myths preceded and transcended historical time. Central to these myths was the idea of a messianic warrior who would lead the people into holy contests against internal and external enemies.[41] As Hans Frank, the Nazi theorist and criminal governor of occupied Poland, put it, "The categorical imperative of the Third Reich: Act in such a way that the Führer, if he knew your action, would approve it."[42] The cult works as categorical imperative for fascist followers, and later, populists and wannabe fascists. Followers are expected to act as if the leader would like their actions if he was aware of them. Thus, they pretend to anticipate what the leader wants.

Fascists often conflated their political cult with institutional religion. In Argentina, fascists compared the suffering of Christ with the suffering of their martyrs and their dictator, General Uriburu.

Fascists always believed violence and death were inextricably linked with their autocratic politics. If Spanish fascists looked to the mythical past to affirm their cult of "the legitimate sacred violence [*la santa violencia legítima*]," the Spanish wannabe fascist leader of Vox, Santiago Abascal, affirmed with similar sacralizing language that he was not going to allow his followers to be "stoned." Promising preemptive violence against imagined attacks by his enemies (anti-fascists and children of immigrants who acted like "dogs"), Abascal vowed that he was going to grab "street terrorists" by the "neck."[43]

The Cult

There is no fascism without the cult of the leader. Cults are rooted in the big lie that a leader is not like other people. All governments that present a cult of the leader eventually feel the need to give themselves a doctrinal framework. They need a way to define their movement and make it seem serious. They want to inscribe themselves in the great history of political ideologies. In short, they want to dress a leader's momentary leadership in transcendental clothing. This is necessary because, after all, an ideology based on the opinions of a single person presents limits to its own national and international legitimacy. Fascist groups must find a way to give some amount of gravitas to the leader's tantrums, narcissism, and instances of flip-flopping.

For most followers, this doctrinal moment does not contradict the cult of the leader; instead, it comes across as the moment when the leader decides it is time to use the trappings of political theory to disguise a set of simple notions about power, obedience, and violence. In general, the doctrinal occasion is nothing more than an ornament decorated with the ideas and whims of a given moment. But it can also be a telling sign of the ideal world that the leader and his followers envision. In the past this happened when leaders felt comfortable enough in power to risk tying themselves to a few specific phrases. This moment came to Italian fascism in 1932, when, assisted by the philosopher Giovanni Gentile, Mussolini wrote his "doctrine" of fascism. Argentine Peronism, the original form of populism in power, which was so often influenced by the Duce's thinking, gave itself a doctrine in the Mendoza Philosophy Congress in 1949 with the canonization of the slogan of the "organized community."[44]

Other fascist and populist leaders used books, radio, and later television advertisements to try to canonize their rather banal anecdotes and thoughts, but in Mussolini, Perón, and Trump there is a desire to link their personal actions with an array of transcendent achievements. When this is not evident in reality, they appeal to fantasy.

When we think about ever-expanding lies, from "classic" propaganda to Trumpism, it is important to remember how fascist propaganda is received differently by the cult's believers. Followers never cease to believe the propaganda, even when it becomes shocking or foolish. This sets them apart from other ideologies. As German anti-fascist Siegfried Kracauer explained, "Unlike its communist counterpart, fascist propaganda does not have the disappearance of the mass and therewith its own disappearance as its goal. It has—and this is its peculiar feature—no goal." For him, the idea of fake reintegration is key: people achieve a feeling of belonging that is not based on any real gains, just the fascist pretense of being superior to others. Fascist propaganda produces an "illusion." Kracauer explained, "Fascism can just as little do without propaganda as it can without terror. It subsists through propaganda."[45] This is why wannabe fascists like Trump can't stop telling lies. Trumpism is propaganda.

This prevented his followers from opposing the Biden administration by offering any realistic alternative measures. Instead, they supported Trump and his utterances about things that did not exist. For instance, Trump insisted that Biden is anti-science and undemocratic, and that he is against the rule of law and against women. All of these attributes (or rather defects) belong to Trump himself, but in attributing them to Biden, he characteristically followed the projective nature of the authoritarian personality studied by the philosopher Theodor Adorno and his collaborators.[46]

For this kind of follower, believing in the leader as a force of light was more important than respecting the lives of others or even self-respect. In 2016 when Trump said, "I love the poorly educated," nobody among his uneducated followers felt insulted. And in 2019 when he insulted a supporter he mistook for a protester for being overweight, the supporter later said he was not insulted: "Everything's good. I love the guy."[47] These expressions of love should be concerning. They echo the love of political cults that has often manifested in dangerous ways.

Historically, idolizing the "leader" is a key dimension of fascism. In the 1930s and 1940s, different fascist leaders inspired cults of personality, which came in different colors across the globe. In China, supporters of Chiang Kai-shek wore blue shirts, while Brazilian supporters of Plínio Salgado wore *integralista* green shirts. Argentina's dictator, José F. Uriburu, Romania's Corneliu Codreanu, and Spain's Francisco Franco similarly inspired loyal followings. Supporters of fascism fervently believed in the heroic, even godlike nature of their leaders. Joseph Goebbels, the Nazi propaganda minister, wrote in his diaries about his feelings for Hitler: "I love him . . . I bow to the greater man, to the political genius."[48] Such devotion ultimately allowed leaders to insulate themselves from criticism and accountability.

Instead of seeing idolization as a natural expression of grassroots support, we should examine more closely the ways leaders cultivated this particular form of loving devotion to distract from their obvious limitations and failures, and to sustain their dangerous ideologies.

As Hitler's biographer, the British historian Ian Kershaw, first explained, Hitler made Christian religious images and metaphors of adulation central to his cult.[49] A sense of divine infallibility had once belonged exclusively to the history of institutional religion, but in twentieth-century fascism, it was applied to the leader, with supporters cultivating a sacred faith in him. Benito Mussolini equated his fascist ideas with the sacrosanct "truth" and stated that when thinking about the historical destiny of the nation, he was able to "see" the work of a sacrosanct will, "the infallible hand of providence, the infallible sign of divinity" in the unfolding of events. Hitler made his own link with the divine even more explicit, asserting, "I hereby set forth for myself and my successors in the leadership of the Party the claim of political infallibility. I hope the world will grow as accustomed to that claim as it has to the claim of the Holy Father."[50]

Applying the language of sacred ritual to secular politics helped create a cult of leadership that motivated followers, leading them to persecute and even exterminate others in service of the leader. For Mussolini, the "sovereignty of the people" existed only if they delegated all power to the leader, who ruled by force, not consensus. Hitler took it even further. By claiming "I am acting in accordance with the will of the Almighty Creator: by defending myself against the Jew, I am fighting for the work of the Lord," Hitler used religious faith in his leadership to provide a rationale for many Nazi perpetrators of the Holocaust.[51] Fascists thus tortured and killed with the understanding that their leaders sacredly embodied the will of "the people."

Another consequence of this cult was that it led followers to take the heat for their leaders. They absorbed blame for the leaders' failures, leaving the leaders' images intact for the rest of their followers. The cult of personality was so strong that it took extreme economic hardship and military defeat to pierce the belief that leaders were infallible, sent by God to renew the country.

Such a dynamic may be at play in the United States, India, and Brazil, and in many other places with wannabe fascist politics.

For followers, the attachment to the leader seems so secure that it transcends transgressions or failed promises and justifies the leader's most offensive and illegal acts. Fanaticism and feelings of deep political love can replace critical thinking. Some supporters seem unconvinced that their leaders have done any of the things they are accused of; when presented with irrefutable evidence, they say whatever he did wasn't wrong. Followers are not meant to ask questions.[52]

Fascist and wannabe fascist leaders demand their followers' faith and use symbols and language from religion to depict themselves as modern-day saviors, crusaders, and warriors. This is one reason why perceptions of persecution embolden them, feeding the savior or warrior-martyr image they are constructing. Trump repeatedly deemed himself the most persecuted leader in history, and he seems to relish the opportunity to complain that any investigation into his alleged crimes is a "witch hunt." In 2023, he linked his old claims about embodying the people with the image of the military avenger: "In 2016, I declared, 'I am your voice. . . . Today, I add: I am your warrior. I am your justice. And for those who have been wronged and betrayed, I am your retribution."[53]

These beliefs are widely shared by his followers, including a belief in his unique connection to God. In this sense, Trumpism shares features with the fascist history of crowd manipulation and propaganda, which often involved shared fantasies and an expectation of redemption. "A Trump rally," as writer Carl Hoffman writes, "is a sensual assault that hijacks your soul."[54] The Trumpist political religion works from the top because it involves feedback from below.

To attend one of these events is to experience belonging to a group of people who look and think and eat and hate in the same way. There is euphoric dancing and singing before the leader appears. Village People hits such as "YMCA" and "Macho Man" play before Trump reaches the stage. The hype turns to fury when the leader himself tells the crowd how he is constantly persecuted. He shows them an alternative world without complexity, where "all of their hopes, and dreams and resentment" are addressed.[55] Within this echo chamber, the combination of racism and misogyny, with a profound antidemocratic ethos, builds toward a mystical moment as the crowd witnesses of the passion of the leader. The narrative is that the leader has been vilified by enemies both secular and demonic, which makes them not just enemies of the people but also enemies of God.

Lies of Persecution and Civil War

We are living in strange times when far-right enemies of freedom can refer to themselves as conservatives, liberals, and decent people. They can even call their enemies fascists. They can denounce dictatorships and dictators when their own politics are antidemocratic. This level of distortion and fantasy has its roots in the past.

Fascists denounce persecution while unleashing persecution. They warn about civil war while jump-starting it. They ascribe lies to their enemies while becoming masters of lies.

The idea of being persecuted is central to messianic fascist and wannabe fascist leaders alike. Hitler said in *Mein Kampf*, "If an idea in itself is sound and, thus armed, takes up a struggle on this earth, it is unconquerable and every persecution will only add to its inner strength."[56] Fascists linked their paranoia to the history of religion in order to justify a world of pain and suffering. The Brazilian fascist leader Gustavo Barroso talked about a time of "persecution" that prompted people to be close to "Christ." For him, the left was persecuting the Brazilian *integralistas* in the same way that "Christians had been persecuted by Nero."[57] A feeling of near-religious persecution allowed fascists to embrace the most fanatic and intolerant responses.

Hitler explicitly praised intolerance: "The future of a movement is conditioned by the fanaticism yes, the intolerance, with which its adherents uphold it as the sole correct movement, and push it past other formations of a similar sort." This was "religious fanaticism" of a movement zealously convinced of "its own right," and thus "it intolerantly imposes its will against all others."[58]

This fanatism converged with a belief in the purifying qualities of civil war. Hitler stated, "It should have been borne in mind that the bloodiest civil wars have often given rise to a steeled and healthy people, while artificially cultivated states of peace have more than once produced a rottenness that stank to high Heaven. You do not alter the destinies of nations in kid gloves. And so, in the year 1923, the most brutal thrust was required to seize the vipers that were devouring our people. Only if this were successful did the preparation of active resistance have meaning."[59]

The fantasy of a civil war was incongruously framed as both (a) an existing reality of the present, and (b) a continuous aim of the enemy. In 1919, the year fascism was founded, Mussolini stated that its politics were informed by a civil war that had started in Italy in 1914.[60]

And yet the glorification of civil war was based on the lie that any such war would be a response to the desire for it by left-wing or liberal enemies. Lies about civil war were a key part of fascist politics. They justified preemptive responses against the left, even though they were presented as an unavoidable reality. Mussolini stated, "The imminent fatality of the civil war hangs over the electoral war."[61]

Other fascists preferred the notion of internal war rather than civil war. For them, the idea of civil war gave too much legitimacy to foreign traitors who did not belong to the nation in the first place. This was, of course, a lie. German Jews were obviously Germans, and the same applies to the children of immigrants in countries like Argentina, Brazil, or the United States, or to Muslims in India. But fascists did not care about the realities of diverse nations.

Other fascists promoted the falsehood that internal war was a synonym for national history. One could not exist without the other. For Indian fascists, their war against "the forces of destruction" had lasted a thousand years. Their intention was to "wipe out the opposing forces."[62]

Argentine fascist intellectual Leopoldo Lugones argued that in a diverse country like Argentina, internal war was the work of foreigners (i.e., immigrants) who did not want to be part of the country. When masterminded by global communism, it was civil war, but when fought by Argentine patriots, it became a "national war."[63] For Lugones and many other fascists, civil wars were promoted by "Marxists" and their "propaganda," while the civil wars of fascists were a natural response to the presence of aliens within the nation. In this context, fascists projected their own civil war as the goal of their enemies, arguing that their enemies were lying about their supposed "pacifism."[64] Brazilian fascist leader Plínio Salgado amplified this by arguing that capitalism and communism were a single "monster with two heads." Liberal democracy was a means of national destruction; this was the reason why "integralism, with God, fatherland and family, declares war on the slavers of humanity, the arsonists of temples, the destroyers of homes, the murderers of Nations, the oppressors of the working class, and the animalizers of humanity."[65]

As was most often the case with fascist lies, a secret cabal was invented as an excuse for taking action. Enemies were manufactured and assigned responsibility for the real civil war that fascists promoted and yearned to launch. In politics, whenever we hear words likes *cabal* and *replacement*, and especially when they are presented together, fascism is not far behind. We should be especially worried when these fascist key words are linked to racist fantasies about "civil wars" and the "persecution" of national majorities, or to racist slogans like White Lives Matter. Fascists appropriate vocabularies from their victims and indulge in fantasies of suffering the same forms of oppression they are so keen to engender and intensify.

Narendra Modi in India has represented these fascist affinities to the core. In 2013 he proposed an India "free" of the opposition, and in 2017 he stated that "an election is a war, and I am the commander." As Christophe Jaffrelot argues, this a classic "Hindu nationalist tactic: finding excuses to legitimize their violent reactions (never action)."[66] Thus, victims are turned into culprits of the genocidal actions perpetrated against them. This monstrous logic can only exist by and through conspiracy theories.

Lies about internal war and the need to destroy the opposition often lead to an autocratic project of replacing a diverse civil society with the idealized homogenous world of the leader. In this alternative universe, the leader appears as the redeemer of a country on the edge of destruction. This is a world that does not exist in reality, but the leader wants to achieve it.

When Trump told his most fanatic followers, in his speech before the assault on the US Capitol on January 6, 2021, "If you don't fight like hell, you're not going to have a country anymore," there was no actual danger that the country might disappear, but his followers acted as if it was true. Even more explicitly, Marjorie Taylor Greene said in 2022 that "Democrats want Republicans dead" and that "Joe Biden has declared every freedom-loving American an enemy of the state." One of the most fascistic people in the Trumpist populist-fascist coalition, Stewart Rhodes, a leader of the paramilitary group the Oath Keepers, wrote to his associates in 2020, "We aren't getting through this without a civil war." Trump often used civil war as an imminent outcome of what he saw as the historically unprecedented persecution of his persona.[67]

Like Trump and his fascist predecessors, Bolsonaro saw civil war as a political goal. The idea of politics as the site of an all-or-nothing pseudoreligious war between the sacred truth and the lies of a demonic enemy explains why political violence comes so easily to Bolsonaro. In 1999 he stated, "Through voting you will not change anything in this country, nothing, absolutely nothing!

Things will only change, unfortunately, the day you set off for a civil war, and doing the work the military regime didn't do. Killing about 30,000 . . . not letting him out, killing! If some innocents are going to die, it is all right. In war innocent people die."[68]

From Fascist Lies to Populist Lies

Fascists want to change the world in order to make it resemble their lies. Their truth is based in the mythical, not the empirical. For them, the myth that cannot be empirically demonstrated is the real truth. We do not see this form of lying in most twentieth-century populists. In this regard, there is a break between fascism and other political traditions, including populism. Populists in power throughout the twentieth century, especially after 1945, have lied like more typical politicians: they lie without believing their lies. Juan Perón and Silvio Berlusconi, for example, were liars like everybody else. They promised things that they cannot and will not do. Wannabe fascist liars like Trump, Bolsonaro, Orbán, Modi and many others are different.

Fascism ascribes total legitimacy to the leader by fusing him with the concepts of the people and the nation. This logic is based on the notion of popular sovereignty, but it turns the leader into a totalitarian. In contrast, in populism the panorama is more complex. Populist leaders combine the dictatorial notion of popular sovereignty—the idea that a particular person can be fused with the people and the nation—with electoral procedures. The people are understood to be two mutually exclusive things at once. On the one hand, they are identified with the leader, as in fascism, but on the other hand, the people need to confirm by elections that this leader is the embodiment of the people and the nation. Here we find the most democratic—and also the most authoritarian—dimensions of populism. Both fascism and populism believe in personification as representation: in effect, achieving the will of the people is fully delegated to the leader. This myth of representation rests on the propaganda fantasy that somehow a single leader is the same as a nation and its people.

In fascism, this personification did not require any rational or procedural mediation, such as electoral representation. But in populism, elections are important for confirming the truth of the divine supremacy of the leader, and spreading lies about elections is a crucial part of maintaining the leader's idea of his place in history. By winning plebiscitary elections, populist leaders confirm the dual nature of their power: they are both elected representatives and quasi-transcendental conductors of the people's will.[69]

The idea of incarnation led, in fascism, and leads, in populism, to the proclamation of the leader's infallibility, even to the extent that the selection of the leader represents the nation's last hope. This sense of urgency and imminent danger to the nation and the people is a result of the way the leader has characterized his opponents. As then-candidate Trump claimed, referring to the upcoming presidential election of 2016, "For them [his enemies] it's a war, and for them nothing at all is out of bounds. This is a struggle for the survival of our nation, believe me. And this will be our last chance to save it on November 8th—remember that."[70]

Here, fascism presents important differences from populism and other autocratic regimes. The radical cult of the leader sets it apart. To be sure, populists build a cult around the leader, but this never becomes a cult of the dead, of violence and the actual destruction of enemies. Fascists' kamikaze belief in making sacrifices for the sake of the leader presents the starkest contrast between fascists and populists.

Populism, as a movement, even if it does not renounce democratic electoral procedures, becomes wannabe fascism when it switches from generic rhetoric about the enemy (the elites, traitors, deep state, outsiders, etc.) to the specific naming of racial, political, and/or sexual, and/or religious foes who are then met with political violence. People are killed or sacrificed in the name of the leader. In his name, followers die for the cause. Only in a fascist bizarro universe can this idea take hold. This is why, when you are a scholar of fascism, it is hard not to worry about the would-be fascism of Trumpism and its global acolytes. To this list of warning signs of Trump's vocation for fascist politics, we must also add the politics of fallen soldiers. The idea that the January 6 coup attempt had martyrs is neither new nor original. And it has fascist precedents.

This was typical during the dictatorship that I grew up with in Argentina. In Argentina in 1982, it was dictators against reality. They decided to go to war against the United Kingdom. I remember as a young kid listening to the TV and they were insisting on lies every single day—lies that were typical of totalitarian dictatorship, but not of democracies. In Argentina, the dictatorship that ruled between 1976 and 1983 was inspired by fascist ideology and turned against many of its citizens. When these victims—citizens—were put in concentration camps and tortured, the conspiracy-ridden questions they were asked were fascist questions. They were asked to confirm things that actually reinforced the lies and propaganda of the dictatorship. This is how fascist torture works. There is an idea that needs to be confirmed and people are subjected to extreme violence in order to confirm it. This is the ideology of propaganda, not the actual truth. Because when these dictators and fascists lie, either they believe their lies are the truth, or they believe their lies are the servant of the truth, or—and this is the worst part of it—they believe that if reality doesn't conform to this ideological "truth," then it is this reality that needs to be changed.

When modern populism gained power after 1945, it turned fascism into something more democratic. Now, the new populists of the contemporary right are drifting back toward the fascist dream of the destruction of history and its replacement with the myth of the infallible leader and the eternal nation. Early populist leaders had a certain hesitation about radically changing the historical record, as the fascists had done. Not anymore.

As with violence, terror, racism, and dictatorship, fascist lying is different from that of other political ideologies. This is not a matter of degree, even if the degree is significant, but a qualitative difference between fascism and other political ideologies.

Violence, History, and Memory

To defend democracy, it is necessary to put a stop to the attacks on history that attempt to redefine our present with fantasies about the past. Many actors on the extreme right want to turn history into a myth and then use it as a model to distort the present. In the United States, Donald Trump devoted part of his presidency to the idea of returning the United States to the time before the civil and democratic reforms of the 1960s, presenting himself as a defender of "truth" in American history that had been abandoned by a supposed new national orthodoxy. With this objective, he promoted a "patriotic education" to undermine the importance of the 1619 Project (presented in the *New York Times* in August 2019 with the aim of focusing attention on the foundational violence of slavery as the cause of so many evils of the past and the present). In criticizing this project, and in seeking to replace history with self-congratulatory myths, Trump clashed with numerous professional historians, whom he accused of promoting "anti-Americanism."[71] In October 2020, he took on "radical activists" who wanted to unfold a "revisionist history" that was trying to "erase Christopher Columbus from our national heritage."[72] This revision of history is not a phenomenon limited to the United States; Europe, Asia, and Latin America have practiced it extensively. In each case, this revisionism is linked to the politics of xenophobia and hatred. Using this framework, wannabe fascist Spanish leader Santiago Abascal sought to turn old fascist lies into new myths of the past by falsely claiming that the conquest of the Americas "ended a genocide among indigenous peoples." Numerous post-fascist right-wing leaders greeted him enthusiastically, including Peru's Keiko Fujimori, Brazil's Eduardo Bolsonaro, Argentina's Javier Milei, and Hungarian strongman Viktor Orbán. American Trumpist Ted Cruz sent a message that said, "We face an emboldened global left that seeks to bring down cherished national and religious institutions, in too many cases, violently."[73]

While Bolsonaro's guru Olavo de Carvalho defended the legacies of slavery and the inquisition, Bolsonaro has located the legitimacy of violence in the more recent past. He endorses the legacy of Latin American dictatorships and their Dirty Wars and is an admirer of Chilean General Augusto Pinochet and other strongmen. Like the Argentine Dirty War generals of the 1970s and Adolf Hitler himself, Bolsonaro sees no legitimacy in the opposition, which for him represents tyrannical powers. He said in 2018 that his political opposition, members of the Workers' Party, should be executed. This idea of violence as the solution to politics-as-usual was first articulated by Mussolini, who presented it as a model of heroism and a playbook for political action.[74]

This violence was a key part of the fascist idea of politics as warfare. In Argentina, after General José Uriburu's fascist coup in 1930 and his premature death in 1932, Argentine fascists fantasized about the coup as a conventional military conflict. Some of the participants who were killed in that coup were repackaged as fallen soldiers in a great war. Near the Recoleta Cemetery in Buenos Aires, the curious tourist can see the monument to the fallen of the Uriburista "revolution." Fascists in Germany, Japan, and Italy presented similar fantasies of war and fake martyrdom. They organized a variety of rituals (recitations, marches, gatherings) to commemorate things that either never happened or did not happen as they were remembered. But none of this mattered to fascists, who blindly believed in the myth of their leaders.

These fake memories served the purpose of elevating the leaders above politics and beyond history. Memories of "martyrs," "wars," "persecutions," and "witch hunts" are ornaments of political religion.

Fascist leaders connected power to the glorification of violence and death. Fascism stressed the idea of regeneration and the salvation of its warriors through death as sacrifice. For them, as "God wanted" it, "the germ of a renewal can grow only out of death, of suffering." Romanian fascists claimed to "love death." Death was for them "our dearest wedding among weddings."[75] Hitler exterminated millions of European Jews because he believed it would bring about a new historical era for the Aryan race. Pinochet tortured, imprisoned, and killed thousands of his opponents in Chile, arguing that acts of extreme repression were at the service of saving Chile from civil war. He claimed that it was via a state of exception that Chile had regained its "freedom" and avoided the "triumph of totalitarianism" and "the end of every human right."[76]

Both propaganda and repression have evolved in our new century, becoming less conspicuous and more overt. If raw violence was the mark of dictators during the eras of fascism and the Cold War, as historian Ruth Ben-Ghiat argues, the new-era strongmen like Bolsonaro and Trump have adopted more selective forms of repression and violence. Violence becomes more targeted and less organized (no mass killings or summary executions in the thousands). Deeply repressive acts such as the operation of detention camps in the United States, the policy of child separation, and the enabling and celebrating of police brutality become structural dimensions of strongman rule. Although state violence is more difficult to carry out in a country with a free press, in the new media landscape populist leaders can bypass the press and communicate directly with their followers without scrutiny. Changes in media—from radio and cinema at the time of Hitler and Mussolini, and Perón; to television at the time of Silvio Berlusconi, Ecuadorian populist Abdala Bucaram (1996–1997), and Argentine populist Carlos Menem (1989–1999); to social networks and media today with Trump, Modi, and Bolsonaro—have affected the production and reception of propaganda. Unlike in past eras, when people relied on a few media outlets, more recent populists communicate using "niches and information silos in which citizens share information directly." They use WhatsApp or Telegram and other media, and tend to restrict communication to those who share their points of view. This is why there is no need for censorship, and perhaps no need to create media monopolies or semi-monopolies, as fascists and classic populists did in the past.[77] The media and the context have changed, but not the patterns of violent strongman behavior. As Ben-Ghiat observed, Twitter was for Trump "what newsreels were for the fascists: a direct channel to the people that keep him constantly in the news."[78]

Nazism as Insult and Reality

"Why can't you be like the German generals?" Trump asked his chief of staff. He expected his own generals to be "totally loyal to him," as he imagined the German military had been to the Führer.[79] This was a private comment. In fact, in public Trump did not use the Nazi dictator as a model but rather as an insult against his enemies. This was a global trend: act like a fascist and accuse others of being Nazis.

In the United States, Brazil, and elsewhere, right-wing populists are increasingly acting as the Nazis did and, at the same time, disavowing this Nazi legacy or even blaming the left for it. For almost fascists, acting like a Nazi and accusing your opponent of being one is not a contradiction at all. Indeed, the idea of a leftist Nazism is a political myth. This idea enables fascists' most fanatic followers to engage in acts of sedition and domestic terrorism. Think of the five hundred detainees from the assault on the Capitol who are falsely presented by Trumpist propaganda as freedom fighters and as the "political prisoners" of an authoritarian order.

According to Brazilian right-wingers and Holocaust deniers, it is the left that threatens to revive the violence of Nazism. Similar accusations are presented by Trumpist ideologues in the United States, who falsely state that Democrats and the left are fascists. This is, of course, a falsehood that comes straight out of the Nazi playbook. Fascists always deny what they are and ascribe their own features and their own totalitarian politics to their enemies. As we saw with his Reichstag speech of 1939, while Hitler accused Judaism of being the power behind the United States and Russia, and said Jews wanted to start a war and exterminate Germans, it was he who started World War II and exterminated the European Jews. Fascists have always replaced reality with ideological fantasies. This is why Bolsonaro presents the left's leaders as latter-day emulators of Hitlerism when in fact he is the wannabe fascist, intimately closer to the Führer in style and substance.

In Germany itself, some far-right protesters perform the Nazi salute in demonstrations, yet their leaders in the Alternative for Germany, which is now one of the largest parties in the country, explicitly disavow Nazism. At the same time, they use Hitler's infamous insults and propaganda strategies to attack independent media. Just as the Nazi leader did, they call the media "the lying press."

In the United States, then-president Donald Trump infamously said in 2017 that some neo-Nazis and white nationalists were "very fine people."[80] Trump also, at one point in his presidency, accused the CIA of acting like Nazis. Following Nazi doctrines of propaganda, many in the contemporary far-right (often white nationalists and neo-Nazis) deny links to their ideological predecessors and even argue that those standing against them are the real Nazis. Latin America's new right-wing populists are following suit.

In 2018, when another presidential candidate accused Bolsonaro of being a "tropical Hitler," Bolsonaro responded that it was not him but his enemies who praised the Nazi leader. (In 2011, Bolsonaro said he would rather be called Hitler by his critics than be perceived as gay.)[81] In the new populist era of fake news and outright lies, a particular falsehood about Nazism stands out—the twisted idea that Nazism and fascism are left-wing violent phenomena.

In an era when the contemporary far-right and the populist leaders who excuse its racism and extreme violence are closer to Nazism than ever before, many of them are trying to distance themselves from Hitler's legacy by using simplistic arguments to blame the socialist left for Nazism. This is a notorious propaganda tactic that resembles previous fascist campaigns and enforces new waves of would-be fascist violence.

In Hitler's early days, Nazi propagandists repeatedly stated that Hitler was a man of peace, a moderate when it came to anti-Semitism, racism, and the personification of the nation and its people. In short, he was a peaceful leader above the pettiness of politics. As historians of fascism know so well, these were egregious lies that generated long-standing support for Nazism despite the fact that Hitler was exactly the opposite of how he was described—he was one of the most radical warmongers and racists in history.

As in Nazi times, repetition has replaced explanation. Only ignorance or conscious oversight of the historical legacy of Nazism can lead propagandists to mislabel an explicitly right-wing nationalist appropriation of left-wing concerns.[82] Despite the mischievous moniker "national socialism," which was intentionally misleading to confuse workers and make them vote for fascists, the Nazi Party soon renounced any possible socialist dimension.[83] Those who simplify history to argue that fascism is socialism intentionally forget that fascism was about violently fighting socialism (and also constitutional liberalism), while displacing concerns for social justice and class struggle and replacing them with nationalist and imperialist aggression.

Fascist forms of propaganda represent an inspiration for wannabe fascists worldwide.[84] As Kracauer explained in 1936, unlike other forms of propaganda that have fixed goals, fascist propaganda "breeds itself anew time and again." In fascist propaganda, people become ornaments who are fused with the leader. The cult of personality "weakens the sense of reality." The result is the triumph of a kind of charlatanry that displaces any real solutions.[85] If we are to defend democracy, we must pay attention to and denounce these lies and propaganda. About reading Nazi propaganda, Klemperer wrote, "Every time I read it I feel sick; but the tension is now so great one must at least know what lies are being told."[86]

3   The Politics of Xenophobia

There is no fascism without its enemies. There is no full-fledged fascism without their subsequent repression and persecution. Fascist dictator Benito Mussolini explained this fascist logic of enmity when he stated, "In every society there is a need for a part of the citizens who must be hated."[1]

Fascism is created and sustained by demonizing others. Projecting extreme hatred onto the enemy represents a pillar of fascist ideology. Only when the dissent, difference, and resistance of enemies can be misrepresented as an example of the need for preemptive action is fascism unleashed. Adolf Hitler explained this need when he said that the movement "must not fear the hostility of their enemies, but must feel that it is the presupposition for their own right to exist."[2]

Only when people are turned into "mortal enemies" does true fascism emerge. Making these enemies living subjects that can be victimized becomes its practice. Thus, when the concept of the enemy is projected onto the victims, when it becomes a concrete manifestation of the fascist politics of extreme hatred and xenophobia, fascism is able to turn propaganda into reality. Enemies are no longer an idea; they become real people, victims of fascist ideology.

There is no fascism without extreme victimization, but racism, domination, and demands for inequality among people are never absent from the picture, either. Fascism cannot exist without creating its enemies, and these enemies are always conceived of as the ultimate "other" that must be controlled. This type of persecution has become a transnational enterprise with global antecedents. As Aimé Césaire explained in his "Discourse on Colonialism," fascists applied racist techniques of colonialism to European victims. Hitler said, "We aspire not to equality but to *domination*."[3]

Domination, of course, needs demonization, but the identity of the enemies can vary. In historian Zeev Sternhell's formulation, fascism was "neither right nor left" in the traditional sense but rather an extreme right-wing appropriation of both. Indeed, when the Nazis talked about their social concerns, they had in mind a racist society with a sort of social equality among the members of the master race. Building this society meant excluding all others, which is why we can see so many resonances of the past in our present.

Fascism was first and foremost about politics as violence, politics as domination. If the left claimed to want rights for all, fascism wanted no rights for people who were ethnically or racially distinct or who behaved or thought differently. In other words, fascists attacked political and ethnic minorities in the name of the leader, the nation, and the sacred. Fascism in its many forms did not hesitate to kill its own citizens, as well as its colonial subjects, in its search for ideological and racial supremacy.

Millions of civilians perished across the world during the apogee of fascist ideologies in Europe and beyond. Fascism outdid the old reactionary right by adding leftist themes to produce a new racist and nationalist approach to social, economic, and political problems—an approach to politics that has resurfaced with more traction today, from Europe to Brazil to the United States.

In fascism, destroying democracy would in turn destroy civil society, political tolerance, and pluralism. But none of this could happen without the fear that a few people who behaved differently or were perceived as different would destroy the leader and his ethnic national community first. The new legitimacy of the fascist order was rooted in the power of the leader, the people, and the nation but also in the threats represented by powerful enemies. The fascist dictatorship of the people, with its will to create a new man and a new world order, relied on its dialectical other, the existential enemies, the antipeople. These links between the enemy, the dictatorship, and the people were central to fascists around the globe. As the Argentine fascists put it in the 1930s, "The day of final reckoning is close in the future, we will make disappear all the unworthy for the sake of the fatherland."[4]

Hatred Defines the Fascist Self

In fascism, enemies cannot be feared, but they must be hated. This fascist projection of hatred, in turn, breeds more hatred. Nazism "must not shun the hatred of the enemies of our nationality and our philosophy and its manifestations; they must long for them. . . . Any man who is not attacked in the Jewish newspapers, not slandered and vilified, is no decent German and no true National Socialist. The best yardstick for the value of his attitude, for the sincerity of his conviction, and the force of his will is the hostility he receives from the mortal enemy of our people."[5]

How does a simplistic idea that the self only exists through the enemy's hatred work? Victor Klemperer asked "whether this endless assertion of Jewish malice and inferiority, and the claim that the Jews were the sole enemy, did not in the end dull the mind and provoke contradiction." His answer was that Hitler considered his followers stupid: "With great insistence and a high degree of precision right down to the last detail, Hitler's *Mein Kampf* preaches not only that the masses are stupid, but also that they need to be kept that way and intimidated into not thinking."[6]

The idea of not thinking allowed fascists to present the ultimate binary between "us" and "them." The enemies were an existential threat, constantly menacing the well-being of the nation: "There is no more major Enemy than the parasites who live hanging around their prey."[7]

As philosopher Jason Stanley explains, this creation of a "dangerous them" that aims to destroy everything of value is central to the fascist aim to unify people against objectionable ends while presenting hatred as a virtuous preemptive reaction.[8] In this context, racism and xenophobia helped cement the formation of fascism's enemies. A famous anti-Semitic Argentine fascist leader, Enrique P. Osés, claimed in 1940, "All those who go against the Homeland are our enemies. And all, if it is in our hands, will perish or we will perish. This is the demand. This is the fight we are engaged in."[9] For Osés and many other Argentine fascists, the main enemy of Argentina were the Jews.[10]

The idea of self-defense against imagined racial threats became a motif for demonizing and persecuting others. Once this racist propaganda was presented as factual, it ceased to be shocking or reprehensible and became a need for the community. Mexican fascist José Vasconcelos stated that "many people are astonished that, suddenly, racial persecutions are unleashed. And although no one approves of them in his heart, it is a fact that the tension that has been contained for a long time explodes sooner or later in a violent form. And perhaps the only way to avoid this violence is to denounce the causes that have provoked them in other peoples."[11]

Thus, racism and persecution were misconstrued as emanating from a factual critique. Fascism featured racist forms of hatred and it misrepresented its reactions against enemies as being genuine. These actions became a kind of self-victimization, since they were based on lies presented as facts. At the core of these lies were extremist pseudoscientific ideologies. As Hannah Arendt explained,

> An ideology is quite literally what its name indicates: it is the logic of an idea. Its subject matter is history, to which the "idea" is applied; the result of this application is not a body of statements about something that is, but the unfolding of a process which is in constant change. The ideology treats the course of events as though it followed the same "law" as the logical exposition of its "idea." Ideologies pretend to know the mysteries of the whole historical process—the secrets of the past, the intricacies of the present, the uncertainties of the future—because of the logic inherent in their respective ideas. Ideologies are never interested in the miracle of being. They are historical, concerned with becoming and perishing, with the rise and fall of cultures, even if they try to explain history by some "law of nature." The word "race" in racism does not signify any genuine curiosity about the human races as a field for scientific exploration, but is the "idea" by which the movement of history is explained as one consistent process.[12]

While Arendt correctly pointed out how fake scientific claims were central to totalitarian ideologies, there was an oversight in her powerful critique of Nazism. For example, one of the most rabid anti-Semites within the Nazi movement, Julius Streicher, stated, "If the danger of the reproduction of that curse of God in the Jewish blood is finally to come to an end, then there is only one way open—the extermination of that people whose father is the devil."[13]

Beyond Nazism, fascists did not exclude religious fanatism as fuel for their hatred. They actually conflated pseudoscience and pseudoreligion. One of the most infamous examples of this clerico-fascism was the American fascist Father Coughlin, who argued that self-defense meant going on offense: "Why, then, should I be on the defensive against this highly organized irreligious Jewish onslaught? I am not on the defensive—I am on the offensive for God and country."[14]

This strategy of using imagined enemies of God and country to explain reality led to extremes of projection. Typical in this sense was the fascist tendency to accuse the victims of racism of being the actual racists.

Father Gustavo Franceschi, who was director of the significant Argentine Catholic journal *Criterio* in the 1930s and 1940s, maintained that the necessary exclusion of the Jews was owed to their political and cultural behavior and not their racial character.[15] For Franceschi, this was enough to explain the persecution of the German Jews during the Holocaust and marked as an obvious consequence the necessity of rejecting the new refugees who tried to enter the country. These thoughts were accepted and shared by those in power and enabled countries like Argentina and the United States to contribute (like many other countries but with an insidious combination of racism and apathy) to the deaths of millions of Jews. They were not the main culprits, but their racism contributed by default.

By the end of the 1930s, fascists all over the world fantasized that the cause of anti-Semitism lay in the very actions of the Jews—inseparable from their existence as a group.[16] Blaming the victims opened up new possibilities for action, new solutions to the "Jewish problem," and Father Franceschi did not reject them outright because they were "reactions" against the "catastrophe" that the Jews were bringing to the country: "What until very recently was judged to be impossible in Argentina, an assailant antisemitism . . . that demands the elimination of the Jew by whatever means, is manifested with each step and gains day by day new and enthusiastic supporters. Let's be real: a great pogrom is no longer improbable among us."[17]

In this way of thinking, Judaism, as a millenarian race, tried to dominate the world through the secularization of Christian societies. Another Argentine cleric-fascist priest, Father Julio Meinvielle, established a historic dichotomy in which Christianity and Judaism represented an eternal battle between the spiritual and the ethereal nature of the former, and the low, the secular, and the carnal qualities of the latter. Christians represented God; Jews represented the Antichrist.[18]

Similarly, the Brazilian fascist *integralista* leader, Gustavo Barroso, stated in 1936, "The Integralist State is profoundly Christian, a strong State, not in Cesaristic terms but in Christian ones." He claimed that it had the "moral authority" as well as the "strong men" to go on the offensive. Somehow, he convinced himself and others that "defending unity" and "Brazillianness" meant that their racism was anti-racism. He said that their *integralista* state "fights Jews, because it fights racism, and racial exclusivism, and Jews are the most irreducible racists in the world."[19] Not all fascists embraced the word *racism*, but this was indeed the case with Italian fascism, which in 1938 presented to the world the decalogue of the "Manifesto of the Race." The ten points of fascist racism stated that

1. Human races exist.
2. There are great races and small races.
3. The concept of race is purely biological.
4. The population of Italy today is Aryan, and its Civilization is Aryan.
5. The contribution of huge masses of men in historical times is a legend.
6. There is a pure Italian race.
7. It is time Italians clearly proclaim themselves racist.
8. It is necessary to make a clear distinction between the European Mediterranean (occidentals) on one side and the Orientals and Africans on the other side.
9. Jews do not belong to the Italian race.
10. No hybridism should alter the pure Italian race.[20]

The Nazis also wanted people to "learn to think like a racist." But the explicit politics of xenophobia in fascism does not mean other ideologies, movements, or regimes were not racist in theory and practice. For example, the Nazis regarded the American "one drop rule" as too extreme. As James Whitman noted, it was a Nazi doctor, Dr. Möbius, who said, "I am reminded of something an American said to us recently. He explained, 'We do the same thing you are doing. But why do you have to say it so explicitly in your laws?'"[21] This American racist failed to see the fascist logic of racism. Fascism was about stating the quiet part out loud.

Fascist Racism and Xenophobia

There is no starting point for fascism without the creation of absolute foes, but these can be imagined and targeted in different ways.

There is a misconception that certain fascisms were neither racist nor extremely discriminatory. This is historically wrong. Most historians of fascism present racism as a key element of transnational fascisms, and before them many anti-fascists and victims observed the centrality of racism to fascism. Minorities were often the first to see and suffer the consequences of fascism. For example, in the United States, and as historian Matthew F. Delmont explains, "For Black Americans, the war started not with Pearl Harbor in 1941 but several years earlier with the Italian invasion of Ethiopia and the Spanish Civil War."[22] And when Hitler took power in 1933, Black Americans clearly recognized the threat and similarities between Nazi and American forms of racism. As the prominent African American journalist Langston Hughes said, "Yes, we Negroes in America do not have to be told what Fascism is in action. . . . We know. Its theories of Nordic supremacy and economic suppression have long been realities to us."[23]

It is clear why all those who perceived what fascism really meant quickly became anti-fascist. Worldwide, anti-fascists highlighted these global fascist-racist connections.[24] In 1923 in Argentina, social democratic representative Alfredo Palacios noted that the racist and anti-Semitic Ku Klux Klan was the American version of fascism, so well represented by Mussolini in Italy and by Leopoldo Lugones in Argentina.[25]

Fascists themselves pointed out these connections between deep hatred, racism, persecution, and extermination. As Lugones had stated, even before he became a fascist, racial considerations shaped considerations of law and justice in Argentina, Latin America, and beyond: "If the extermination of the Indians is beneficial to the white race, it is already good for it; and if humanity benefits from its triumph, the act also has justice on its part, whose base is the predominance of interest."[26] Not all fascists agreed with the idea of excluding Native American populations from the fascist project of racial nation building. Chilean *Nacis* argued that the Chilean race was "united and homogenous" because it had fused Spanish and Araucanian blood over three centuries.[27] Chinese fascists also highlighted the cohesion of the Chinese of "the yellow race" and how enemies wanted to force the Chinese to "become a different race."[28]

Old racist notions worked to confirm a fascist hierarchy of peoples. Ideas of racial superiority, racist laws, and fears of miscegenation shaped the emergence and development of fascism. To put it simply, one cannot understand fascism without the history of racism that preceded it.

Eugenics set a key precedent in this regard. In Sweden and the United States, the dubious idea of improving the race via segregation and forced sterilization led fascists to mistakenly believe their racism had a scientific basis.

Admirers of fascism, like the Egyptian Salama Musa, saw Nazism as a great example of the need to strictly separate races. As historians Israel Gershoni and James Jankowski explain, Musa saw "the mixing of different races, such as 'the black with the white and the yellow with the brown'" as leading, at best, to "the adverse mixture of races in which the qualities of the more superior race would be polluted by the inferior."[29]

Fascists typically linked this idea of contamination of the self with conspiracy theories. Egyptian fascist and Green Shirt Ahmad

Husayn saw Jews behind every bad thing that happened to the Middle East: "They are the secret of this cultural squalor and these filthy arts. They are the secret of this religious and moral decay, up to the point where it has become correct to say 'search for the Jew behind every depravity.'"[30] Similarly, Hitler presented the fantasy of an attempt to make Germany less white as something ultimately devised by the Jews. He warned against a future European "mulatto state."[31] For the Führer, France was the example of a state dominated by Jews: "The French people, who are becoming more and more obsessed by negroid ideas, represent a threatening menace to the existence of the white race in Europe, because they are bound up with the Jewish campaign for world domination." The actions of Blacks and Jews were one and the same in Hitler's mind. The corruption of the race was at the center of "the contamination caused by the influx of negroid blood on the Rhine, in the very heart of Europe . . . in accord with the sadist and perverse lust for vengeance on the part of the hereditary enemy of our people, just as it suits the purpose of the cool calculating Jew who would use this means of introducing a process of bastardization in the very centre of the European Continent." Hitler claimed that Jews wanted to destroy the white race "by infecting the white race with the blood of an inferior stock, [which] would destroy the foundations of its independent existence."[32]

Fascists were obsessed with the idea of the degradation of a racially conceived pure national community. Precedents for these deranged ideas varied and included the Spanish fifteenth-century statutes of "purity of the blood" (a clear precedent for Nazi thinking) and, more recently, the history of American racism.[33]

As the Nazis saw it, racism was a response to liberalism, which was the ultimate culprit. As fanatical Nazi propagandist Streicher put it, "The emancipation of the Jews and the liberation of the black slaves are the two crimes of civilization committed by the plutocrats in the last few centuries."[34] In this context, for Nazis, the Jim Crow South was an inspiration. Nazis mined American race law as a key example for their own racist policies of persecution.[35] But they were not the only ones to see American racist and fascist traditions as connected to their own. As early as 1923, an article published in the most important fascist magazine, *Gerarchia* (directed by Benito Mussolini), stated that "around the world, various political movements are shaping themselves or they try to model themselves on Fascism." They had in "common the nationalist ideological foundation." While nationalism was "unique and equal in all countries in its philosophical substratum, in its praxis, it must inevitably adapt to different needs and different aspirations of each people and every race." The fascist writer concluded that "this is why the 'awakened Magyars' are royalists and anti-Semites, while the Bavarian National Socialists attempt to unite dynastic and military sentiment with the economic aspirations of the very troubled Germanic proletariat. That's why in America the powerful and mysterious sect of the Ku-Klux-Klan performs all sorts of harassment against black men." This violence was warranted for fascists because "in fact, the ever greater increase in the black population, who is the enemy of the whites by tradition of race and for the contempt that still surrounds it today, represents a terrible unknown for the future of the United States."[36]

Fascist racism was inseparable from the idea of radical enmity toward the left and secularism. As a leader of the Colombian fascists, the Leopards, explained, there "are no enemies to the right." What he meant is that fascism represented the violent edge of a larger right-wing alliance of conservatives and fascists against "internal enemies" and the "ambitions of other races."[37]

Nazi racism represented both an alluring model and an extreme example, as recalled by the Syrian Nazi admirer Sami al-Jundi (later a Baath party leader): "We were racialists. We were fascinated by Nazism, reading its books and the sources of its thinking."[38] Racialism or racism were used to describe a profound rejection of difference. Fascination, however, did not mean imitation. How could one possibly imitate Hitler if "racism was created by the French," asked Brazilian fascist and anti-Semite Gustavo Barroso.[39] Many fascist intellectuals also warned that Nazi racism was a problem if they wanted to lead an international movement against democracy.[40]

To be sure, not all fascists were deeply connected to the Nazi model. But all forms of fascisms were rooted in a radical politics of xenophobia. The important question is, who did different fascists define as their enemy? For Peruvian fascists, for example, the enemies were immigrants from China and Japan. Brazilian fascists would say that what made Brazil better than other nations is that Brazil had a combination of races—the European white races, black African races, and indigenous races. And yet in this conception the Jews had no place in Brazilian society, so their racism was anti-Semitic as opposed to the anti-Asian racism of the Peruvian fascists.[41] The initial forms of anti-African racism in Italy were also different from anti-Jewish racism in countries like Hungary, Argentina, or Germany.

Fascism imagines its enemy by fomenting and expanding on structural forms of racism. As political scientist Terri Givens explains, in Europe and in countries like the United States, slavery led to the "development of a structure of racism" that still plays out in current politics: "Norms around the idea of Whiteness are embedded in our societies. The groups who are the targets of racism and violence may be different in these countries, but the impact on equality is the same. Whether it's people of Muslim background, African descent, or newly arrived Asian immigrants, the norms around White supremacy and political power come into play."[42] Indeed, American fascists from the Ku Klux Klan to Father Charles Coughlin to scores of Nazi sympathizers played with these racist norms, appropriating and cementing them.

The most important anti-Semitism promoter in the United States was Henry Ford. Between 1920 and 1927 he ran wide anti-Semitic attacks in his personal news media outlet (which was second in circulation in the country). His series "The International Jew" lent the legitimacy of modern cars, money, and power to racist ideologues the world over. Ford was a millionaire car entrepreneur and technology innovator who also dabbled in media and propaganda. His talent for business was confused with wisdom and intelligence, of which he had none. He was a person ready to believe and promote reckless anti-Semitic fantasies. Red scare tactics and racism were at the center of his paranoic hatred of Jews. Among the many fascist admirers of Ford was Hitler, who "kept a picture of Ford on the wall of his office in Munich, praised the automobile magnate in *Mein Kampf*, and later told a Detroit News reporter, 'I regard Henry Ford as my inspiration.'"[43]

Ford's ideas were highly influential but not original. Ideas of white-hood, Aryanism, and other clumsy claims about the superior races were present in earlier stages of fascism worldwide.

Eventually, most fascisms joined the movement in full-fledged racism, as when Mussolini stated in 1938 that "also on the question of race we shoot straight."[44] What he meant was that fascists were racists without hesitation. But some hesitation had existed before then. In 1921 Mussolini had claimed that fascism was not merely an outcome of the Great War, but it was born out of a "deep perennial need of our Aryan and Mediterranean *stirpe*."[45] He had also argued that same year "that fascists need to care for the health of the race with which history is done."[46] And yet, before the 1930s, fascists did not radically emphasize the race of the enemy. What changed was a combination of factors, such as the influence of Nazism in fascist Italy and, more importantly, the mixed practical and ideological implications of imperialism.[47] As Mussolini explained in his famous speech in Trieste in 1938, "The racial problem did not break out suddenly as some people think who are used to sudden awakenings because they are used to long lazy sleep. It is related to the conquest of the Empire. History teaches us that empires are conquered with weapons, but they hold on with prestige. And for prestige you need a clear, severe racial conscience which clearly establishes not only difference, but superiority." For Mussolini, the need for a racial hierarchy between white Europeans and Black Africans affirmed fascist power over its enemies. Fascism and racism were part of the same will to dominate others. Thus, for Mussolini, "the Jewish problem is therefore only one aspect of this phenomenon. Our position has been determined by indisputable data. World Jewry has been, for sixteen years, in spite of our politics, an irreconcilable enemy of fascism."[48]

Fascism relied on the creation of its "irreconcilable" enemies to define itself. In their racism, and more generally in their construction of a radical other that cannot be fully integrated into society, fascists and other extremists replicated and amplified a cultural code that was widely shared in politics and society.[49]

The Internal and External Enemies

The idea of the internal enemy was intrinsically connected to a notion about the inferiority, impurity, and treasonous nature of those who were considered different from the majority. Fascists disputed the idea that citizenship defined the community. They linked ideas of internal enmity to their fantasy of a racially homogenous community that was constantly threatened. The enemy as a traitor to the national race was also presented as having a symbiotic relation with external enemies.

Historically, the internal enemy evolved with the repression of political difference and dissent at home and abroad. Global contexts such as transatlantic trade, world colonization, leftist revolutions, and the First World War provided justification to the need to link internal opposition to a form of treason inspired and planned by external enemies. Fascism was an ideal home for the bestialization and racialization of enemies. Demonization, of course, had a long history, and it was refashioned by the emergence of modern propaganda in the early twentieth century.

But there were important precedents. For example, in the Middle Ages, as historian Angelo Ventrone explains, demonization of others was traditionally done by representing them as beings with monstrous features:

> In medieval times, so it was with the Jew, painted in yellow, with a pointed headdress and usually while gesticulating in a vulgar way. Physically and morally similar to the devil, then, or to a witch, with a pointed hat and a lumpy nose, perhaps while eating children. In England, in the modern age, the French were often described as emaciated, because absolute monarchy was linked to poverty and

oppression; in the nineteenth century the Irish were represented both in British cartoons and in the American ones as monkeys or subhuman beings. During the French Revolution, Louis XVI was often represented as a pig, substantially anticipating the stereotype of the fat, stocky and vulgar capitalist, so common in socialist and then communist propaganda. Political propaganda, therefore, very often divides reality into good and evil, friend and foe. This division leads to a connection between morality and physicality. In this context, enemies are rendered ugly and deform. Their depravity becomes dual: an internal moral one and an external physical one.[50]

Eventually democracy came to be represented as foes disguised as friends. For Indian fascists, who conflated the fight against colonizers with the need to persecute religious minorities within India, "wrong notions of democracy strengthened the view and we began to class ourselves with our old invaders and foes under the outlandish name—Indian and tried to win them over to join hands with us in our struggle. The result of this poison is too well known. We have allowed ourselves to be duped into believing our foes to be our friends and with our own hands are undermining true Nationality. That is the real danger of the day, our self forgetfulness, our believing our old and bitter enemies to be our friends."[51]

As Goebbels explained regarding the Nazi destruction of democracy from within, "We do not come as friends, nor even as neutrals. We come as enemies. As the wolf bursts into the flock, so we come."[52]

As historian Robert Paxton argues, the "diabolized internal/external enemy—Jews or others—" was "an essential ingredient of fascism."[53] Enemies were central to the anxieties that helped inflame fascist paranoia: "Fascists saw enemies within the nation as well as outside." The fears generated by the Bolshevik revolution and the traumas of the First World War contributed to a context where ultranationalism and white supremacy thrived in tandem with economic and social conflicts. As Paxton noted, "The discovery of the role of bacteria in contagion by the French biologist Louis Pasteur and the mechanisms of heredity by the Austrian monk botanist Gregor Mendel in the 1880s made it possible to imagine whole new categories of internal enemy: carriers of disease, the unclean, and the hereditarily ill, insane, or criminal." The urge to purify the community from enemies led to the "forcible sterilization of habitual offenders (in the American case, especially African Americans), but Nazi Germany went beyond them."[54]

In Germany, Argentina, the United States, and India—but not only in these countries—the internal enemy was conceived as part of a race war. Typically, fascists presented themselves as ideal types of real men. As historian George Mosse noted, the Jew was conceived as a countertype "whose conspiratorial activities could beguile foreign powers and turn them into the enemy of the superior race."[55]

The internal enemy defined what ideal manhood was not. Fascism exacerbated prejudices and ideas of masculinity and femininity that were predominant in society. As Mosse explained,

> The Nazis once again sharpened and made more absolute modern society's apparent need for an enemy. Either as internal or external enemies, Jews, blacks, and Gypsies were all singled out as the sworn enemies of the health and well-being of the Aryan race. Following the passage of the Nuremberg racial laws, which defined

who was or who was not an Aryan, semiofficial commentaries on these laws classified Gypsies, Jews and Blacks as people with "alien blood." But even here there was a clear-cut hierarchy that made the Jews the root of all evil. Others who did not necessarily belong to a so-called inferior race also helped to undermine Aryan society, and they were established as countertypes as well: homosexuals, vagrants, habitual criminals, beggars, the handicapped, and the feebleminded—all those who were unable to do so-called productive work or who had no established place of residence. These the Nazis called "asocials," and defined them broadly as people who could not be integrated into the community of the *Volk*, and who lacked the generally accepted norms that guaranteed so-called productive work within a settled community, be it the family or the state.[56]

Jews and other ethnic minority groups were targeted because they could be turned into a symbol. Once they were no longer considered human beings, they became a living metaphor of what fascists considered to be wrong with society. But everyone and everything could be turned into the proverbial enemies—journalists, members of the opposition, external actors, independent women, and all those whose sexual identities were different from the repressive fascist norm.

As the Indian fascist Inayatullah Khan Mashriqi explained, "We, Khaksars, are sworn enemies of, and shall take severe revenge even at extreme personal sacrifice upon, treacherous and dishonest leaders who have harmed the national cause and are exploiting the masses, upon the mercenaries of hostile nations, upon anti-national editors and journalists, upon misleading propagandists, upon betrayers of the country's interests, and upon miscreants, to whatever community they may belong, who have stirred up sectarian animosities among the various communities of India or among the various sections or groups of Muslims."[57] Internal and external enemies conspired together and were often fused, or even indistinguishable.

Thus, for Brazilian fascist leader Plínio Salgado, the enemy was defined by everything that was foreign to Brazil and Latin America. Drawing on the intellectual history of anti-Americanism, Salgado stated that the mythical image of Caliban defined the enemy, and this enemy also lived within the national body. It was internal and external at the same time: "Caliban lives in the body of society." Caliban was the "materialistic spirit" and the "denial of God." Caliban represented communists and "plutocrats." It represented a society "ruled by sex."[58]

Fascism displayed a fascination with pornographic images and caricatures of the enemy. In the pages of the Italian fascist journal *Difesa della razza* (*Defense of the Race*), the combination of pseudo-science with multiple images of naked (or semi-naked) bodies of Jews, Blacks, and other minorities cemented the idea of a direct racist link among deformity, abnormal sexuality, liberalism, and communism. Fascist bodies, on the other hand, were displayed as being "normal." The journal's front pages displayed a hierarchical superposition of three faces, presumably Aryan, Jewish, and Black. As you would expect, Aryan whites appeared measured and Olympian, while Jews and Blacks were represented by bare bodies that were meant to describe a degenerated, or even an absence of, culture. As one writer put it, "Racism therefore does not impede, on the contrary it comforts and specifies and circumscribes the moral responsibility and freedom of the individual; on the other hand, however, it ascertains and recognizes the inequality of human races, an inequality which is not only of somatic characteristics but, more importantly, of psychological attitudes."[59]

For fascists, racial determinism included religion. In the Argentine fascist journal *Clarinada*, traditional Catholic images of Jews as God-killers were fused with representations of them as naked, sick, and lubricious; their bodies tottered forward as their erect sexual organ threatened the environment with contagion.[60] *Clarinada* presented the image of a concentration camp where Jews and communists were surrounded by wires and a soldier pointing a machine gun at them asking, "When we will see this in our fatherland?"[61]

Argentine fascists presented the Jews as the "enemies of the people." They conceived of them as "active conspirators" against "Christianity" and the nation. A writer in *Clarinada* stated, "We have many enemies but we first need to annihilate the Jew." Jews represented the "anti-fatherland" and fighting them was "a holy fight." He argued that the elimination of the Jews would lead to "world salvation."[62] *Clarinada* was quoted by the Nazis of *Der Stürmer* as an ideal example of anti-Semitism because it proposed to bury the Jews alive in their graves.[63] The idea of contamination was depicted as a Jew kissing an Argentine flag: "With a kiss, Jews sold and betrayed Christ; that is why today they are not ashamed to kiss the flag of the Homeland, to sell and betray her while in their pockets they finger the dollars of treason."[64]

In another caricature, a "Jew" tried to rape a woman with the word *Argentina* written across her dress, who exclaimed that there appeared no "man to free her from this filth."[65] For Argentine fascists, women needed to be "on par with men" without abandoning their "natural" subordinate position. Women could also become internal enemies. Women who thought like men were disqualified as "*marimachos*," and men who agreed with them were presented as "*los feministas*" and "*maricones*."⁶⁶

As historian Ruth Ben-Ghiat explains, a "misogynistic cult of virility" was central to fascism. The fascist dictatorship was a "haven" for men who hated women. As she explains, the fascist idea of manhood relied on the need to dominate men and women, but with respect to women, strongmen like Mussolini and Hitler, as well as many other leaders, "presented by personality cults as the ideal blend of everyman and superman authoritarians make ordinary men feel better about their own transgressions." In the case of Mussolini, over two decades in power, "thousands of women" became "part of his state-assisted machine of libidinal gratification." The women who participated in these "brief and violent encounters" of fifteen to twenty minutes became persons of interest to his state repressive apparatus. As Ben-Ghiat argues, "His fixers and secret police stood ready to force an abortion, pay for silence, or make life difficult for the women's boyfriends and husbands."⁶⁷

The fascist view of women was that they should be subjugated within a male-dominated society. This was not original, but it was extreme. Women were expected to be passive wives and mothers of fascists, confined to the domestic sphere. Fascism imagined itself as having a reproductive and "family"-oriented mission for women. Domination once more reigned supreme. Fascists regarded abortion as a crime against the race (*stirpe*).⁶⁸ Fascist politics toward women regarded them as subordinate agents of fascist ideology. As historian Patrizia Dogliani explains, these politics were based on the idea of women's biological inferiority to men.⁶⁹ There was nothing new in the fascist notion of women, but the antifeminist politics of fascism cannot be dissociated from a wider totalitarian system based on various forms of discrimination and xenophobia.

The search for autonomy and equal rights for women, sexual minorities, and ethnic minorities was perceived as a threat. For fascists the idea of feminism was anathema. Peruvian fascist Santos Chocano warned against "the masculinization of women" that democratic politics created.[70] Others were even more extreme in their demonization of women who were politically active. Chinese fascists imagined Hitler as literally corralling women into the kitchen. As historian Maggie Clinton noted, for Chinese fascists, women who "exuded sexuality" were denigrated and "had to be corralled and contained."[71] Female agency was viewed in opposition to domesticity, the fatherland, and the "family." This is why Bolivian fascists claimed that "everything that tends to dissolve the family or corrupt it is contrary to the laws of nature and is only possible in states that, directly or indirectly, are getting closer to communism."[72]

Feminism was a particular source of animosity for fascists. Argentine writer Leopoldo Lugones accused feminists of being a key "agent of social dissolution" that precipitated major crises of civilizations. The social crises for which women and feminists were to be blamed included the fall of the Roman Empire, "the great anarchy of the renaissance and the formidable crisis of the 18th century."[73] Feminists were blamed for revolution and "unisexualism." Lugones equated feminism with "prostitution" and warned, "If women were equal to men, there would be only one sex, and the human species would have become sterile. Now then: sterile love (because love subsists within the feminist doctrine) is the supreme corruption, constituting a pleasure without compensation for the result that it normally produces, that is, the procreation of children." Gender equality created monsters: "The woman and the man, unified by equality, would form a monster, the androgyne, that is, the typical product in which the sick imagination of decadence indulges."[74]

Fascists defined their enemies in terms of very traditional gender roles and critiques of so-called abnormal sexuality. Racial enemies were depicted as "feminine," naked, old, nervous, and sexually degenerated, demonstrating moral disorder as well as physical disarray. Central to this ideology was the notion that the external (physical aspect) was a reflection of the internal (being and emotions). For fascists, the physical disorder of the enemy was a result of the old democratic system that the enemy embraced.[75]

Fascist Demonization and White Replacement Theory

Who is white, and who is not, is a question that has a long history in fascisms. The fascist killer who committed a racist massacre in Buffalo in 2022 stated in his "manifesto," "I believe I am ethnically white since my parent's nationalities are from north-western Europe and Italy."[76] But during the Italian immigration to America, Italians were often not considered fully white. Similarly, Adolf Hitler had warned in his racist fantasies that Germany was at risk of becoming "Southern Italy," a place he identified with racial mixing and the replacement of the white world. More than fifty years later, Ugo Bossi, founder of Lega Nord, would make similar xenophobic assumptions about Southern Italy.

Benito Mussolini disagreed with the Führer on Italian whiteness, but in 1934 he issued a "warning cry about the demographical decadence of the white race." This warning cry anticipated the racism and segregation that Italians imposed against Ethiopia in 1935, as well as the racist and anti-Semitic laws of 1938.[77]

These deranged fantasies and fears about racial pollution and "white" decline also appear in the Buffalo terrorist's 180-page "manifesto." He adheres to the so-called "great replacement theory," whose origins date back to late-nineteenth-century ideas of social degeneracy and scientific racism. According to these ideas, Western civilizing superiority had to be maintained biologically and culturally to avoid chaos and social collapse. This ideology was widely accepted by political elites in various countries on both sides of the Atlantic and gave rise to eugenic, segregationist, anti-immigration, and finally fascist and genocidal policies.

In the 1930s, the Nazis radicalized the lie of a Jewish conspiracy whose purpose was to organize the mixture of races, leading to an extermination of white populations worldwide. From then on, the idea of "white genocide" was used by fascists and related organizations during the Cold War to justify political violence in the name of defending ethnic nationalisms. In the 1970s, the Latin American Anticommunist Confederation introduced notions of "genocide and white supremacy" that influenced the doctrines of the agencies responsible for Operation Condor. The plan involved the coordination of Latin American dictatorships in a transnational plot of kidnapping and murder that operated throughout the Southern Cone, including Argentina, Brazil, Chile, Paraguay, and Uruguay.[78] The dictatorships of Bolivia, Chile, and Paraguay were very receptive to such ideas, partly because of the presence of former Nazis and former *Ustaše* in high positions. The Latin American military juntas saw themselves as warriors in a historic crusade to defend Western Christian civilization against a global conspiracy. During the 1970s and 1980s, there was strong transatlantic cooperation between operatives of the junta, European neofascist paramilitary organizations like the Italian P2, the apartheid governments of Rhodesia and South Africa, and elements of the American far right. These relations bore fruit during the genocidal wars and massacres in Central America, in which Argentina participated directly by sending "advisers" who were experts in illegal repression.

All of this gives us a historical framework for thinking about current delusions: white replacement and the defense of the West.

These are the global echoes of fascism. In internet forums, neofascists admire the Argentine dictatorship and Augusto Pinochet as actors to be emulated. One of the founders of Argentine fascism, Leopoldo Lugones, defended Argentine imperialism for its "white" superiority over other Latin American nations, and the generals of the last military dictatorship (1976–1983), who killed tens of thousands of citizens in a "Dirty War" launched in the name of the "Christian West," used a similar logic. In 1976, General Videla underlined the global nature of the conflict: "The fight against subversion is not exhausted in a purely military dimension. It is a worldwide phenomenon. It has political, economic, social, cultural and psychological dimensions." The ideas of replacement and invasion are central to the transnational fascist tradition, along with paranoid fantasies about the expansion and migration of nonwhite Europeans. The infamous statements of General Albano Harguindeguy, minister of the interior under the Argentine dictatorship, can be understood only from this historical perspective. In 1978, Harguindeguy spoke of the need to encourage European immigration. For him, this was urgently necessary so that Argentina could "remain one of the three whitest countries in the world."[79]

This explicit racism took the form of an open acknowledgment of the need to eradicate other "non-European" elements from the nation. The depth and scope of this desire manifested itself, once again, in concentration camps, where racism and anti-Semitism took center stage. The fight against the enemy had no limits. International cooperation between fascists and white supremacist organizations continued after the Cold War. In the past they fought to defeat communism in Angola, Chile, or Nicaragua; now the enemy was Islam in Croatia or Afghanistan, or multiculturalism (which they, in their anti-Semitic delirium, believe is financed by Judaism). The attacks in Utoya (2011), Munich (2016), Pittsburgh (2018), El Paso (2019), Christchurch (2019), and Buffalo (2022), among others, are the continuation of fascist violence against minorities to whom fascists attribute the future destruction of Western civilization and Christian values. Italy has not been immune to these kinds of attacks. In 2011, a neofascist killed two Senegalese migrants in Florence, and more recently, another neofascist and former member of Lega Nord shot several Nigerian immigrants in Macerata. In both cases, they were driven by delirious notions of invasion and replacement.

Fascism is and was transnational. We cannot treat these national histories as being exceptional because almost nothing in Italian, French, American, or other fascist traditions is exceptional. It is understandable that much attention has been paid to the local dimensions of the phenomenon, but what has been ignored until now are the global histories of fascism behind these attacks.

This type of terror distorts truth in order to promote an alternative reality. In this context, the idea of replacement as a form of corruption and contamination is key to understanding the history of fascist ideology. In *Mein Kampf* Adolf Hitler wrote, "This contamination of our blood, blindly ignored by hundreds of thousands of our people, is carried on systematically by the Jew today.

Systematically these black parasites of the nation defile our inexperienced young blond girls and thereby destroy something which can no longer be replaced in this world."[80]

In the United States, these fantasies are intermingled with conspiracy theories and with histories of slavery and racial injustice, which provide a context for right-wing violence and the delusion that the oppressed want to replace the ethnic majority. Neo-Nazi marchers in Charlottesville in 2017 infamously chanted, "Jews will not replace us." In his last sermon, just four days before he was assassinated, Dr. Martin Luther King Jr. warned that violence would "bring only a rightist takeover of the government and eventually a fascist state in America."[81]

As Cynthia Miller-Idris explains, "The Great Replacement is a white supremacist conspiracy theory about demographic change. It claims that there is an intentional, global plan orchestrated by national and global elites to replace white, Christian, European populations with non-white, non-Christian ones. Great Replacement-type theories seek to create a sense of urgency and call whites to action. They foster transnational inspiration and a sense of shared mission among global white nationalists and white supremacists, who see themselves as facing a common demographic threat."[82] France is one of the centers of white replacement theory, where ideologues like Jean Raspail and Renaud Camus have used nineteenth-century anti-Semitic and racist traditions to provide theories for anti-immigrant, wannabe fascist politicians like Éric Zemmour and Marine Le Pen.[83]

In fascist ideology, true national consciousness is pitted against domestic "enemies," who oppose national policies that are racially, ethnically, or religiously homogeneous. These domestic "enemies" are invariably institutions and individuals who champion democracy and its ideals. The Hindu nationalist ideologue M.S. Golwalkar, the founding father of BJP, the right-wing Hindu party of Narendra Modi, argued against the idea that a nation was composed of all its inhabitants and rejected the idea that every citizen of India had an equal right to freedom. Like American racists, Golwalkar regarded democratic ideals as a clear threat to his vision of the nation.[84]

If enemies are people who simply look, think, or behave differently, and their mere existence poses a threat to the imagined homogeneity of the nation, it is not surprising that radicalized believers would carry out mass murders, as has happened in the United States, Europe, and New Zealand, and pogroms, as in India.

The link between white replacement theory and fascism is not accidental, just as the mutual influence between, for example, the Ku Klux Klan (KKK) and Nazism is too important to be ignored. As historian Linda Gordon notes, Nazi leaders were knowledgeable "about American racism toward Blacks, and about the violence that maintained white supremacy. In fact, the KKK influenced the Nazi program. Alfred Rosenberg of the Nazi Party's Office of Foreign Affairs published a speech by KKK Imperial Wizard Hiram Wesley Evans, arguing that the white race had to be protected from 'lower blood.' The Nazi *Handbook for Legislation* cited U.S. immigration law as a model for Germany. American eugenics influenced Nazi 'race hygiene' policies. In fact, Walter Schultze of the Nazi euthanasia program called on German geneticists to 'heed the example' of the U.S." As Gordon suggests, "The Klan contributed considerably to international racism, even to the Holocaust."[85]

The idea of white replacement is a relatively recent label for traditional fascism. Through their propaganda, wannabe fascists are rebranding long-standing fascist paranoias and delusions about conquest and racial and political substitution. When they become normalized, these fantasies pose a real threat to democracy.[86]

On Populist Victimization

The politics of hatred, racism, and xenophobia are central to fascism but not populism. Populists invent an ultimate enemy, but they do not make the fascist move toward a practice of repression, imprisonment, and elimination. This distinction is an important one.

This is why, in terms of xenophobia, the wannabe fascists sound much more fascist than the populists who emerged after 1945. Wannabe fascists regularly define people in racial terms, and the antipeople are often defined in racist or anti-religious terms, but wannabe fascists do not physically persecute or fully eliminate these people as fascists would. It's veering toward fascism, but it's not fully there.

In postwar Latin America, former fascists like Perón decided that if dictatorship would no longer be successful or globally accepted, democracy could still be undermined, stripped of its liberal features, and repackaged as an authoritarian populist regime. In the populist formulation, electoral results delegate all power to a single figure who incarnates the people and constantly speaks for them. While constitutional democracies treat elections as discrete moments when politicians are elected to represent the citizens' will, populism envisions the people as one, and their will is embodied in the figure of the leader. Those who vote against the leader are enemies of the people. They represent a democratic diversity that cannot be legitimate, since only the leader knows what the people really want.

This is why populists hold elections as referendums against diversity, seeking to transform diverse societies into the old fascist trinity of one people, one nation, and one leader. But historically they have done this *without* establishing high levels of political repression and violence. Populists demonize their enemies, but they don't imprison, torture, and exterminate them in high numbers.

To put it differently, populists need enemies to play the role of eternal losers. As in fascism, these enemies can be both internal and external.

For example, in his successful campaign for the presidency in 1945 and early 1946, Perón accused the United States of supporting the elites against him and the people. For Perón, politics was a war between the real Argentine people (whom he personified) and the "enemies of the people," foreign and domestic. Peronist posters around Buenos Aires framed the dilemma as "Braden or Perón," pitching Spruille Braden, the US ambassador to Argentina, against Perón. This was a classic fascist argument—that powerful outsiders, allied to enemies from within, must be prevented from oppressing the country's authentic, common people—but one now shaped in electoral terms.

Perón also positioned himself as a law-and-order leader who could unite a divided public hanging on a fragile peace. In doing so, he valorized the police and the armed forces against imagined enemies of the people both inside and outside Argentina, who compromised not only the country's safety but its identity.[87]

Perón viewed his enemies as enemies of popular sovereignty. He stated, "The world is divided into two tendencies: the People and the anti-people. We the men of the People worship only one goal: the People. The anti-people worship only one thing: what they have in their pocket, and they hate the people."[88]

But these enemies were not foes to be eliminated. In fact, they had a central role in populist politics.[89] They were there to continually affirm how great the populists were.

To accomplish this, a big divide between the leader and the enemies needed to be created. According to Perón, "That is why I have always been a 'dangerous individual' for the interests of our enemies who are, in reality, the real enemies of the people. This legion of parasites, made up of politicians from different professions and trades, which to be leaders simulate a service that is in reality a form of treason."[90]

For Perón, the enemies included international press like the *New York Times*, as well as the national media and communists who worked on behalf of treasonous foreign interests. But despite some rhetorical excesses, populist leaders like Perón almost never named religious or ethnic minorities as their enemies. In fact, in 1954 he argued, "We are simply Peronists and within that we are Catholics, Jews, Buddhists, Orthodox, etc., because to be a Peronist, we don't ask anyone what God they pray to."[91] In populism, citizens became enemies because of their political opinions, not their identities.

To be a Peronist, one had to follow and obey the leader's command. This was the only thing that mattered for populists in the second half of the last century. Populists opposed those who were against the "national unification" of leader, nation, and people. An "organized community" could not have dissent; dissent was deemed the "anti-fatherland." Even while the enemy was part of a "confabulation," its identity remained political.[92] Populism divides the world into the people and the elites, but membership in the latter group is fluid. Anyone who is against the leader of the people and the nation becomes a member of the elites who have taken power from the people. Enemies were often construed as members of the oligarchy. These include professional politicians, journalists, and all those who criticize the leader. Still, despite the rhetorical excesses, populists didn't put their warnings and apocalyptic thoughts about political war into practice, unlike fascists.

Colombian populist Jorge Eliecer Gaitán (who had been an admirer of fascism early on) reflected that fascism was fundamentally different from other doctrines. In fascism, the political underdog had to be defeated, dispossessed, and banished from politics. In 1942 he stated, "Fascism assumes, or believes, that life is essentially a struggle and that in that fight it is not wrong for the weak to perish at the hands of the strong, because this corresponds to biological reality. This is the fundamental basic principle of fascism and Nazism. Both are the same doctrine."[93]

In contrast, for populists these pseudobiological considerations of fascism were out of the question. Vargas contrasted justice, love, and fraternity with force, hatred, and violence.[94] Enemies were not defined by their identity and did not need to be permanently eliminated.

After 1945, the populist leaders who gained power in Latin America and other places demonized the opposition, but racism and xenophobia have not been the main axis of populist politics—not until recently, that is, with the emergence of the new populism of the wannabe fascists.

Across the Atlantic and beyond, racist statements have already been matched by real actions, and the number of xenophobic attacks has increased dramatically. As the heirs of Mussolini, the wannabe fascists are using fascist dog whistles even more effectively than their predecessors, especially when they talk about elections and immigrants.

The linguistic and philosophical affinities between the wannabe fascists and the fascists powers of the past are strong. In Hungary, Viktor Orbán has created what historians Javier Rodrigo and Maximiliano Fuentes Codera aptly called an "ethnocracy."[95] Orbán presents a mix of paranoia about immigrants, sexuality, and "illiberalism," while defending racial forms of nationalism with coded anti-Semitic language. For example, borrowing from classic anti-Semitic tropes, he stated in 2018, "We are fighting an enemy that is different from us. Not open, but hiding; not straightforward but crafty; not honest but base; not national but international; does not believe in working but speculates with money; does not have its own homeland but feels it owns the whole world."[96] Orbán was clearly suggesting that George Soros (whom the *New York Times* described as "a Jew from Hungary, survived the Holocaust, fled communism and became one of the single largest funders of democracy promotion, anti-Communism and liberal education around the globe") was an expression of the global enemies faced by his country. In fact, he was using the paranoiac image of a powerful Jewish culprit to deny the real problems that his administration created. Similarly, Trump explained that he was the first American president to be indicted because of Soros's activities. In Trump's view—as well as in that of Trumpists like governor of Florida Ron DeSantis and racist representative and conspiracy theorist Marjorie Taylor Greene of Georgia—Soros, the Democrats, and the judiciary were one and the same enemy. In 2023 Trump stated, "The Radical Left Democrats—the enemy of the hard-working men and women of this Country—have been engaged in a Witch-Hunt to destroy the Make America Great Again movement." He said the Manhattan district attorney, Alvin Bragg, who brought charges against him "was hand-picked and funded by George Soros."[97]

This was one xenophobic trope among many. When Trump talks about the "infection" of immigrants, the loss of culture, and his longing for a golden past, or when Matteo Salvini in Italy suggests a "mass cleaning" to be made "street by street," they are actually referring to the defense of the (imagined) ethnic and cultural purity and homogeneity of their nations. As we have seen, in the late 1930s and early 1940s, Italy's fascist magazine *Difesa della razza* was similarly advocating for the unity of the race, saying religious and ethnic minorities could not be part of the nation.

Also excluded were those deemed race traitors (internal enemies), namely, members of the national race who embraced their enemies. As Indian fascists explained, "Consequently only those movements are truly 'National' as [they] aim at re-building, revitalizing and emancipating from its present stupor, the Hindu Nation. Those only are nationalist patriots, who, with the aspiration to glorify the Hindu race and Nation next to their heart, are prompted into activity and strive to achieve that goal. All others are either traitors and enemies to the National cause, or, to take a charitable view, idiots."[98]

This fascist logic imagines all enemies as traitors, while populists prefer to consider them as either traitors or just misguided individuals, in terms of their political opinions and their refusal to listen to their leaders. Fascists and populists shared a notion that the people were threatened by the ultimate enemies, which led to alarmist ideas about the onset of an apocalypse and crises that only their leaders could resolve. In fascism, this notion of the people was radically exclusionary and eventually racist, in most if not all cases, whereas most populist notions of the people, even when they were xenophobic and racist, tended to be more indeterminate and rhetorical.

The Enemies of Wannabe Fascism

One should not conflate the fascist anti-Semitism of the past with the anti-Semitism of wannabe fascists in the present. Fascists change their enemies according to context.

Historian Robert Paxton wrote in 2004, "While a new fascism would necessarily diabolize some enemy, both internal and external, the enemy would not necessarily be Jews. An authentically popular American fascism would be pious, antiblack, and, since September 11, 2001, anti-Islamic as well; in western Europe, secular and, these days, more likely anti-Islamic than anti-Semitic; in Russia and eastern Europe, religious, anti-Semitic, Slavophile, and anti-Western. New fascisms would probably prefer the mainstream patriotic dress of their own place and time to alien swastikas or *fasces*."[99] To be sure, anti-Semitism is still a big part of the picture. It has become normal for key Republican politicians to get away with deranged denunciations, such as when Representative Marjorie Taylor Green blamed "a space laser" controlled by Jewish financiers for starting a wildfire in California.[100] But unlike the Nazis, the wannabe fascists have widely varied enemies. And national histories matter. Thus, Sinclair Lewis astutely wrote in his classic novel from 1935 *It Can't Happen Here*, "In America the struggle was befogged by the fact that the worst Fascists were they who disowned the word 'Fascism' and preached enslavement to Capitalism under the style of Constitutional and Traditional Native American Liberty."[101]

This is the context for Donald Trump's wannabe fascist politics of xenophobia. A big divide between actual fascism and Trump's fiery rhetoric on Muslims, minorities, Democrats, and the press is that once fascist politicians reached power, they switched from racist statements and other forms of rhetorical demonization to the physical elimination of their foes. Fascism not only talks about its enemies but eliminates them from the political process.

Throughout his election campaign in 2016, Trump was regularly and strongly criticized for being a fascist and a racist, but after the election the discourse softened drastically. Early in his presidency, many newspapers hesitated to brand him a misogynist and a racist despite mounting evidence, and the f-word (fascism) was often dropped from the lexicon. Many people believed that institutions, the law, and the tradition of legality would force the new president to behave presidentially and respect the country's core liberal values. Of course, the opposite happened. Trump never became "presidential." Wannabe fascists never do.

The Trump administration unapologetically pursued a xenophobic agenda based on the complete abandonment of basic human decency toward minorities and immigrants. As many Americans waited patiently for the office to which he was elected to tame Trump, his xenophobia was gradually normalized and his calls for violence and the elimination of perceived threats increased.

Trump has mixed racist alarmism, jingoistic statements, and the idea of law and order with the fiction that he is the "messenger" of the people. In his inauguration speech in 2017 on "American carnage," he said the American people had defeated a minority of politicians: "For too long, a small group in our nation's capital has reaped the rewards of government, while the people have borne the cost." Trump also claimed that the country was beset by crime, stating falsely on the campaign trail that the "murder rate" was the highest it had been in almost half a century and the police "are the most mistreated people" in America.[102]

When George Floyd was assassinated by a police officer in Minneapolis in May of 2020, Trump tried to appropriate the legacy of the victim. He stated, "George is looking down right now and saying this is a great thing that is happening for our country." He also said, "I think I've done more for the Black community than any other president, and let's take a pass on Abraham Lincoln, 'cause he did good, although it's always questionable."[103]

This is an old trick in the history of racism. For racists, the victims of racism simply fail to appreciate the leader's power or refuse to believe in the leader's cult and thus undermine him. In *Mein Kampf*, Hitler said that Jews "destroy faith in the leadership." Trump complained in 2022 that Jews were not sufficiently "appreciative" of him and warned American Jews to "get their act together . . . before it's too late." For Trump, the proper role for minorities is one of subordinate acclamation.[104]

By representing himself as the embodiment of the American spirit and its everyday people (despite the fact that he lost the popular vote in 2016 and the election in 2020), Trump manufactured a popular mandate to turn the country upside down.

Political systems can be corrupted without being replaced by fascism. In Perón's case, this meant vastly altering the character of Argentina's democracy without eliminating it. In contrast with fascism, Perón's Argentina remained an authoritarian populist democracy that expanded social and economic rights and never violently repressed critics. Under Perón, Argentina experienced a strong redistribution of income, with wages rising and jobs increasing. Thus, Perón did not have to install himself as a dictator; instead, he relied on the votes of the Peronist masses to keep him in power.[105]

Enemies of the People

Never subtle, Jair Bolsonaro said to the press in 2021, "Fuck yourselves, shitty press!," while ministers in his cabinet were clapping and laughing.[106] Among the enemies of fascists, populists, and wannabe fascists, the free press and those who study the past are primary targets. The reasons for this are clear. In contrast to propaganda, an independent press provides empirical data that enables people to develop an interpretation of reality. That is why authoritarians inevitably have a problem with the free press: more free press means more empirical analyses, which work against their propaganda and myths.

The same happens with the work of historians because history is supported by facts. History is, after all, an interpretation of facts, whereas political myth involves the repetition of fantasies and propaganda. The latter serves the purpose of dividing society into followers of the faith and unfaithful traitors. Myths are not related to and do not necessarily rely on facts. As we have seen in the previous chapter, authoritarians always have a problem with an interpretation of the past supported by facts—what we call history.

In Trump's case, one of his slogans was Make America Great Again. A historian would ask, what was so great about America before civil rights that he is referring to? What was supposedly great in Trump's eyes was that minorities were strongly repressed, and there was something close to apartheid in the United States. In this sense, it is fair to compare US democracy to other young democracies, such as, for example, Spain. How could you call the United States fully democratic before its civil rights reforms? This is what the myth of the past as enabled and reenacted by Trumpism provides—a story about the US past that does not correspond to the reality of that past.

But racism, xenophobia, and hatred of journalists, historians, and history teachers are not the only tools of fascist demonization. As we have seen, there is no fascism without misogyny and homophobia. Toxic masculinity is a central facet of wannabe fascists as well. Wannabe fascists target religious and sexual minorities. The same goes for criminals and drug addicts, who are blamed for the social problems that create their situation in the first place. The most extreme and unabashed example of this recalibration of the fascist politics of hatred can be seen in Philippine president Rodrigo Duterte's pro-Nazi positions.

The Nazi connections behind this violence is clear, if not always explicit. India has a tradition of genocidal violence that goes back to the fascist origins of the current ruling party, the BJP. In Delhi in February 2020, during Trump's visit to India, an anti-Muslim pogrom was unleashed by movement members who were enabled by a lack of police and political interference.[107] At that time, Trump praised Modi for defending "religious freedom." While Modi enabled and defended this Kristallnacht-style pogrom, he was cautious not to talk about the Nazi inspiration behind it, as his Indian ideological fascist predecessors had done in the past. In contrast, Philippine Foreign Affairs Secretary Teddy Locsin Jr. stated, "I believe that the Drug Menace is so big it needs a FINAL SOLUTION like the Nazis adopted. That I believe. NO REHAB." Locsin stated that Hitler did some things "right." Similarly, Trump is said to have told his chief of staff that Hitler "did a lot of good things."[108] Like the Nazis, Trump has singled out immigrants and minorities as the sole reason for crime and disease.

The influence of historical fascism on contemporary wannabe fascists goes beyond admiration; it extends to the dehumanization of others. The Nazis believed their enemies were inherently criminal and that political ideologies like communism were promoting a race war against the Aryan race. Hitler argued that his enemies wanted to shatter "the personality and the race," and once this happened, "the essential obstacle is removed to the domination of the inferior being and this is the Jew."[109] Talking about adversaries in this way meant that they could be attacked without hesitation. Chinese dictator Chiang Kai-shek, leader of the Blue Shirts, said the communist enemies "are exactly like animals" and asked, "How can they count as people?"[110]

In describing his internal enemies, Mussolini distinguished between conscious and unconscious criminals: "Whoever believes or appears to believe the suggestions made by the enemy as part of the war of nerves, is a criminal, a traitor, a bastard." For Argentine fascists, the confluence of democracy, immigration, and socialism created more criminals and represented a major threat to "national security." Argentine fascist Lugones said that a great number of immigrants were "abnormal" and "vicious criminals" and their presence was "intolerable."[111]

This link between criminals, racial enemies, and ideology was central to fascist ideology. In *Mein Kampf* Hitler stated, "Never forget that the rulers of present day Russia are common bloodstained criminals; that they are the scum of humanity . . . do not forget that these rulers belong to a race which combines, in a rare mixture, bestial cruelty and an inconceivable gift for lying, and which today more than ever is conscious of a mission to impose its bloody oppression on the whole world. Do not forget that the international

Jew who completely dominates Russia today regards Germany, not as an ally, but as a state destined to the same fate." Hitler believed these enemies were outside of politics. He could not make pacts "with anyone whose sole interest is the destruction of his partner." Enemies "do not live in this world as representatives of honor and sincerity, but as champions of deceit, lies, theft, plunder, and rapine." He regarded these criminals as "parasites."[112]

This dehumanization of adversaries made it easier to victimize them. The next steps were deportation, concentration camps, and extermination. Similarly, Indian fascists argued,

> RACE: It is superfluous to emphasize the importance of Racial Unity in the Nation idea. A Race is a hereditary Society having common customs, common language, common memories of glory or disaster; in short, it is a population with a common origin under one culture. Such a race is by far the important ingredient of a Nation. Even if there be people of a foreign origin, they must have become assimilated into the body of the mother race and inextricably fused into it. They should have become one with the original national race, not only in its economic and political life, but also in its religion, culture and language, for otherwise such foreign races may be considered, under certain circumstances, at best members of a common state for political purposes; but they can never form part and parcel of the National body. If the mother race is destroyed either by destruction of the persons composing it or by loss of the principle of its existence, its religion and culture, the nation itself comes to an end. We will not seek to prove this axiomatic truth, that the Race is the body of the Nation, and that with its fall, the Nation ceases to exist.[113]

As French scholar Christophe Jaffrelot argued, once these ideologies of hatred are ingrained in the logic of radicalism and in the ruling party, they cannot be easily detached from politics. In fact, the opposite happens. The current form of Hindu populism under Modi advanced the legacy of Indian fascist predecessors. The nation is currently conceived in exclusionary terms that conflate the leader with the people, while blaming whatever happens in society on the leader's enemies. As with the fascist pogroms and persecutions of the past, the consequences can be extreme. In India,

> The key role played by the RSS also shows that, contrary to the moderation thesis, political parties playing by the rules of party politics cannot turn their backs on the radical movements that spawned them. In this case, such emancipation from extremist elements was all the more difficult to achieve given that practically all the party's leaders and cadres received their training in the RSS. All things considered, the BJP as it stood in 2014 had lost none of its original ideology and, on the contrary, wielded its Hindu nationalism to win an absolute majority that would release it from the compulsions of coalition politics. Once in power, it pursued the same path to win one regional election after another, playing on the same politics of fear that targeted both Muslims and the alleged Pakistani threat.[114]

Like Duterte and Locsin in the Philippines, Bolsonaro in Brazil wants perceived enemies such as criminals to be summarily shot rather than face trial. Bolsonaro's enemies have varied across time, including external and internal enemies. He called indigenous people "parasites" and advocated for discriminatory, eugenically devised forms of birth control. Similarly, Trump's racist statements, as when he complained about immigrants from "shithole countries" in the Caribbean, Central America, and Africa, were a form of extreme demonization. Trump protested the lack of immigrants from Norway and asked, "Why do we need more Haitians? . . . Take them out."[115] In 2023, in reference to immigrants, Trump warned of the racial risks involved: "It's poisoning the blood of our country. It's so bad, and people are coming in with disease." Trump considered these immigrants to be sent "from prisons. We know they come from mental institutions and insane asylums. We know they're terrorists." Trump returns to his sources. In one of many instances when Hitler made references to blood poisoning, he also denounced the "influx of foreign blood" in the context of open borders: "The poisonings of the blood which have befallen our people . . . have led not only to a decomposition of our blood, but also of our soul." He also said in *Mein Kampf*, "All great cultures of the past perished only because the originally creative race died out from blood poisoning."[116]

Bolsonaro has also warned about the danger posed by refugees from Haiti, Africa, and the Middle East, calling them "the scum of humanity" and arguing that the army should take care of them. He has regularly made racist and misogynistic statements. For example, he accused Afro-Brazilians of being obese and lazy and defended physically punishing children as a way to prevent them from being gay. He has equated homosexuality with pedophilia. During his political life, the former military man has bluntly defended dictatorship and has taken his racist, homophobic, and misogynist arguments mainstream. He stated that he had four sons and a daughter, who was born last: "The fifth time I was careless and a woman came." Bolsonaro is especially obsessed with sexual difference. He argued in 2002, "I'm not going to fight or discriminate, but if I see two men kissing in the street, I'm going to hit them." Like Trump, Bolsonaro defended sexual aggression against women, telling a representative in Congress, "I wouldn't rape you because you do not deserve it."[117]

Duterte, who defined the members of the opposition as "cunts," has made similar statements regarding rape. He celebrated the gang rape of an Australian woman, saying he would have liked to participate. When he was mayor of Davao City, he gave the following order: "Tell the soldiers. 'There's a new order coming from mayor. We won't kill you. We will just shoot your vagina.'"[118] Bolsonaro, Trump, and many others present misogyny as being normal for men.[119]

Bolsonaro has embraced the politics of misogyny that defines this generation of would-be fascist leaders. They have been returning to their fascist roots and the politics of xenophobia. For fascists, the internal enemy was fused with prejudices about weakness, pollution, and betrayal. Wannabe fascists are giving these notions a new chance. In 2022, Bolsonaro stressed the particularity but also the broad dimensions of the foe: "Our enemy is not external but internal. Our fight of the left versus the right. It is the fight between good against evil."[120] Similarly, Trump stated in 2023 that "the biggest problem is from within. It's these sick radical people."[121] But for Trump and wannabe fascists as a whole, these were not true members of the real people.

In these and other statements, the vocabulary of wannabe fascists recalls the rhetoric behind Nazi policies of persecution and victimization, specifically, the way that rhetoric imagined the enemy and then substantiated enemies in real people. For example, neofascist leader Giorgia Meloni, who as a young neofascist militant expressed her view that Mussolini was a "good politician," and in 2022 became Italy's prime minister, made a list of enemies for the benefit of her like-minded followers: "Yes to the natural family. No to LGBT lobbies. Yes to sexual identity. No to gender ideology. Yes to the culture of life. No to the abyss of death. Yes to the universality of the cross. No to Islamist violence. Yes to secure borders. No to mass immigration."[122] Migrants, Muslims, women who were pro-choice, and sexual minorities were used to define the authoritarian self.

The fascist approach to unifying some people requires excluding a lot of people. These enemies can include anybody who disagrees with or is critical of the leader—even you or me. In fact, "Carluxo" and Eduardo Bolsonaro (Bolsonaro's sons, one of them a Brazilian representative in Congress) insulted me by stating in anti-Semitic terms that my real name is Frankstein (*sic*) and by issuing homophobic slurs.[123]

The idea of other people being semi-human monsters goes back, of course, to Hitler, who promised that the elimination of physical enemies would end all problems. But Hitler also took a completely different tack and promised that Jews would somehow self-destruct: "The end is not only the end of the freedom of the peoples oppressed by the Jew, but also the end of this parasite upon the nations. After the death of his victim, the vampire sooner or later dies too."[124]

Victor Klemperer observed that anti-Semitism was Nazism's most effective lie: "For what do the German masses know about the danger of '*Verniggerung*' and how detailed is their personal knowledge of the supposed inferiority of the peoples in the east and south? But everybody knows a Jew. For the German masses anti-Semitism and racial doctrine are synonyms, and all the excesses and demands of the national arrogance, every conquest, every act of tyranny, every atrocity, and even mass murder, are explained and justified by this scientific, or rather pseudo-scientific, racial theory."[125] Personalizing an utterly indemonstrable theory was exactly the point.

In fascism, there was a constant need to feed paranoia about differences and plurality. Anyone could become the enemy that symbolized these fears.

4 *Dictatorship*

There is no fascism without dictatorship. This pillar of fascism was absent from classic populism after 1945, but it has returned with the emergence of the extreme new populism of the wannabe fascists.

Fascism rests on the assumption that democracy is weak and does not represent the will of the people. It also presents dictatorship (sometimes in theory, but always in practice) as the only political solution that would make the nation great.

The fascist notion of dictatorship differs from previous historical forms. It is neither legal nor liberal nor socialist. It does not involve a transition to something else, but the unleashing of permanent and absolute power incarnated in one person. It relies on a dual claim about popular sovereignty and political theology. In other words, it pretends to be substantiated by the will of the people, while elevating the dictator to the category of an almost divine being. Fascist claims about dictatorship are disparate, and even contradictory, but they are unified by this faith in the leader and the idea that ruling without checks is a sacred mission of the dictator. Defying logic, fascists assert that their dictatorial rule is not a deliberate act but the natural consequence of historical evolution.

They also insist that it is "democratic," revolutionary, foundational, personalistic, and popular. Finally, they falsely pretend that their dictatorships are legitimate when in fact, historically, they have typically been the result of the destruction of democratic institutions from within and illegal takeovers via coups, civil wars, and foreign invasions.

A History of the Concept of Dictatorship

In 1934, French fascist Pierre Drieu La Rochelle stated, "Fascism does not emerge from dictatorship; it is dictatorship that comes out from fascism."[1] Fascist dictatorship represented a new form of politics in the sense that it combined unlimited power and unlimited duration, but it also was part of a long genealogy of dictators.

Historically, dictatorship emerged as a legal dimension of the Roman Republic.[2] In ancient Rome, dictators were called in special circumstances, for a limited period of time, during a serious internal or external crisis, to impose order—sometimes including by extra-legal means.[3] With Sulla and then Julius Caesar (who was named dictator for life), Roman dictatorship morphed into something closer to what fascist dictatorship later became: absolute permanent power without restraints. Mostly abandoned in the Middle Ages, the idea of dictatorship reemerged in the Renaissance and found in Machiavelli its first modern champion. But even Machiavelli, like the Enlightenment philosopher Jean-Jacques Rousseau after him, still thought of dictatorship as a form of transition—a regulated momentary tyranny, a remedy rather than an end in itself. The same notion of transition, at least in theory, was later promoted by Lenin before, during, and after the Russian Revolution of 1917. Lenin was rehabilitating a concept briefly presented in 1850 by Karl Marx: "the dictatorship of the proletariat." He presented it as power without restrictions, but unlike his predecessors (from Dionysius of Halicarnassus to Machiavelli to Rousseau), he did not consider dictatorship to be grounded in a legal framework. It was the origin of a new sociopolitical system: communism. Lenin conceived of "the dictatorship of the proletariat as the destruction of bourgeois democracy and the creation of proletarian democracy."[4] It was a new foundation, an unregulated form of transition that created its own legitimacy and eventually its own legality. Following Marx's barely used term, Lenin claimed that this dictatorship should be the first step toward the creation of a society without classes and without a state. This dictatorship was supposed to last, and it indeed lasted, but in theory it was still transitory.[5]

Like Lenin and his binary approach to dictatorship, Carl Schmitt, the famous German right-wing thinker who embraced Nazism in 1933, wrote that there are two types of dictatorship, one that presents itself as transitory—the "commissarial" form—and the other, which Schmitt called "sovereign dictatorship," that wants to change the political system. For him, it was clear that parliamentary constitutionalism was a thing of the past and the future would be a contest between dictatorships.[6]

This argument was anticipated in 1849 by the Spanish reactionary thinker Juan Donoso Cortés in his famous speech on dictatorship. Donoso presented the future of the world as a contest between a self-appointed dictatorship of the just and the despotism of modern revolutionary politics. The choice was between "the dictatorship of the dagger and the dictatorship of the saber; I choose the dictatorship of the saber, because it is more noble."[7] Fascists later used this idea of a noble sovereignty of violence to argue for their legitimacy.

Fascism was anti-theoretical, and the same is true of dictatorship. In 1923 Mussolini said, "There is no doctrine on dictatorship. When dictatorship is necessary, it must be implemented."[8] And yet, fascists constantly thought about the whys and hows of dictatorship. They developed their own concept of dictatorship. Of course, they also borrowed from enemy traditions and concepts. A fascist fellow traveler, Indian leader Subhas Chandra Bose, stated that "in spite of the antithesis between Communism and Fascism, there are certain traits common to both. [They] both believe in the dictatorship of the party and in the ruthless suppression of all dissenting minorities."[9]

Even when they represented the opposite of communism, fascists emulated the majoritarian arguments of their enemy. As Hans Kelsen, a leading Austrian Jewish legal thinker, put it in 1936, there was a distinction between old forms of dictatorship and a new type—that of the "party dictatorship of Bolshevism and Fascism."[10] In this dictatorship there was no difference between party and state. In fascism this led to extreme forms of militarization. Differences between fascist and Bolshevik dictatorships were also visible at the ideological level. Communists claimed to represent the "true" form of democracy, while fascists openly rejected it.[11]

Although in practice communist dictatorship is far from being transitory, in theory it remains so, in the sense that is supposed to be part of the transition to a future of communist democracy. This dissonance between practice and theory does not appear in the fascist concept of dictatorship.[12]

Fascism created a new form of dictatorship, distinct from the classic juridical one and the revolutionary ones. The fascist dictatorship was meant to embody a trinity of leader, people, and nation. For fascists dictatorship is perpetual, not a transition to something else. As German Jewish thinker Franz Neumann noted after the Second World War, there was a difference between a dictatorship that was intended as education for democracy and a dictatorship conceived as the negation of democracy.[13] This negation was permanent, which is why, in fascism, dictatorship never ends.[14]

The Fascist Permanent Dictatorship

Fascists believed they represented the first and best example of a new era of revolutionary dictatorship. In 1926 Mussolini stated, "We have made the real, only, profound revolution."[15] By that time, all other parties but fascism were permanently banned. The fascist insurrection had eventually defeated its enemies—namely, all political actors from the previous political system.

Fascism emerged as an outcome of a long reactionary process that renewed the old idea of dictatorship by presenting it as a new moment in the history of politics. A fascist dictatorship was not transitory but revolutionary and constant. It was not a state of emergency in the traditional, constitutional sense, but one endless emergency.

Fascists worldwide explained the need for dictatorship as the only way to correct, appropriate, and reformulate the combined threat of revolution and dictatorship. Their response was one that discarded liberalism and was at the same time "revolutionary" and "reactionary."[16] For them, the past success of the democratic revolutions, and later the communist ones, meant a need for a new revolutionary dictatorship. This was a clear sign of the times.

Some months before the fascists came to power in Italy, a Latin American fascist poet, the Peruvian José Santos Chocano, presented a plea for dictatorship in "tropical nations." Drawing upon the history of the concept of dictatorship from Cicero to Robespierre, Chocano approvingly stressed the arguments by Sismondi and Donoso Cortés. The dictator represented a revolutionary spirit, but dictatorship set the proper limits to revolution.[17]

Many European fascists agreed with Chocano that in Latin America dictatorship was a "native and ancestral product." As French fascist Jacques Bainville put it, Latin America had always been the "happy hunting ground for dictators." It was the original place of "democratic Caesarism."[18] Anachronistically relocating the origins of fascist dictatorship to Latin American republicanism, Nicaraguan fascist Pablo Cuadra imagined a dialogue with the nineteenth-century liberator of South America, José de San Martin. Visiting San Martin's grave in Buenos Aires, Cuadra imagined him describing fascism as a form of realism. Fascist dictatorship meant terror and the dictatorial will to "exterminate" a part of the nation—the opposition—because "the enemies of authority are always the friends of foreigners." In this fascist fantasy, San Martin said that he had been a "victim of democracy" and stated, "I am a fascist, because I want the discipline of the homeland. I know that discipline will only be achieved by the vigorous arm of a dictator."[19]

Fascists dismissed liberal democracy, regarding it as a "mere transition" that had proved itself to be intermittent. The final fight would be between communist and nationalist dictatorships. In a sort of fascist negative dialectic, if liberal democracy engendered the communist dictatorship, the latter engendered the fascist one. As Argentine fascist Leopoldo Lugones put it in 1923, the contest between revolutionary dictators became the "ultimate clash" because "the dictatorship of the proletariat creates by reaction the dictatorship of patriotism; but both incarnate in a leader [jefe], that is to say in a superior type: Mussolini or Lenin."[20] Lugones, of course, sided with Mussolini.

The impact of Mussolini cannot be overstated. The Mussolini dictatorship was the first time a dictatorship was able to counteract liberalism and socialism by allegedly embodying the national will. Hitler agreed that Mussolini represented a new era of national revolution. The German dictator claimed that in fascist Italy "a single man has inscribed his name for all time through a civilizing and national revolution of secular dimensions."[21]

Fascists regarded the change from popular representation to permanent incarnation as epochal, indeed "civilizational." This new form of popular, endless personification made the fascist dictatorship different from the communist "dictatorship of the proletariat." Fascist dictatorship was regarded as truly revolutionary in the sense that it was permanent. And it was permanent in both theoretical and practical terms.

Fascists regarded themselves as constituting an anti-party, a movement that took over the state and radically transformed it from above into a one-party apparatus concentrated in the power of the Duce. Fascism created a new totalitarian order because it was a "revolutionary dictatorship." It did so because it was insurrectional. It wanted to change the system of government, and so it disregarded existing laws and constitutionality. It represented a legally unrestrained power. As Italian Catholic anti-fascist Luigi Sturzo noted as early as 1924, fascism first presented itself as a form of legality, but the dynamics of revolutionary dictatorship increasingly turned fascism away from legality and into something else. Sturzo noted that fascism had left the constitutional and parliamentary track and taken a completely different path. While fascism outwardly displayed elements of legalism and constitutionality, the substance of its rule was entirely new. This initial dualism between form and substance could not be sustained in "perpetual equilibrium"; the choices were legalism or "revolutionary dictatorship."[22] Fellow travelers of fascism, like Vilfredo Pareto, hoped that the "present dictatorship" of fascism would turn in a constitutional direction, but the opposite was true.[23]

The same naivety regarding the revolutionary dimension of fascist dictatorship applied to a wide collection of conservative enablers, as well as to the international press. They wrongly believed fascism was going to be tamed by state institutions and legal procedures.

The dictator qua dictator was self-appointed. His extralegal powers did not emanate from any form of legality. Fascism in fact created its own reign of extralegality, which made the established law a shadow of its former self. This was a seminal argument made by Kelsen in 1936: "Since the centre of political gravity lies now in the machinery of the party, the question as to the form of the constitution has a relatively secondary importance. Monarchy or republic are transformed into purely external forms stripped of any material significance, either form serve equally well as a façade to the inner development of the party-dictatorship." Although Kelsen conflated the Bolshevik search for a new legality with the fascist extermination of legality, his argument remains important.[24]

This was also destined to become a key argument in Ernst Fraenkel's influential analysis of the Nazi dictatorship as a dual state. As he argued in 1941, the totalitarian state in Germany was twofold: both a "normative state" and a "prerogative state." In practice this meant that political considerations were more important than the written law. The latter only functioned normally when the Nazis did not care about the legal matter at hand. In other words, the legal theory of dictatorship aimed to make a distinction between political and nonpolitical acts. The instruments of dictatorship took precedence over the traditional judicial bodies in the case of the former, while the old legal state still applied to the latter. In this totalitarian context, increasingly more dimensions of society became political, and the legal state was increasingly diminished. A combination of arbitrariness and efficiency in legal matters was successful in veiling the illegal "true face" of the Nazi dictatorship. Fraenkel stressed how a patina of legality promoted the legend that German fascists had accomplished a "legal revolution." However, in fact, their dictatorship was not founded on valid laws. As Fraenkel explained, "Endowed with all the powers required by a state of siege, the National-Socialists were able to transform the constitutional and temporary dictatorship (intended to restore public order) into an unconstitutional and permanent dictatorship and to provide the framework of the National-Socialist state with unlimited powers."[25]

Fascist dictators were not dictatorial heads of normal states. They unleashed illegal forms of extreme repression and terror that radically turned their political systems into unlimited permanent dictatorships. This change was made in the name of the one who incarnated the national revolution. This is why the Nazis claimed that the highest law in Germany was not the command of the dictator but his will. Legality was in total contradiction with the new legitimacy of the fascist revolution.[26]

The way Argentine clerico-fascist Franceschi told it, fascism created a theory of a permanent and absolute revolutionary dictatorship, which was considered the "normal form of government." Its totalitarianism was absolute and, in its own way, religious. Its regime did not lead to the "attenuation but the perpetuation of dictatorship."[27]

Fascist dictatorial rule was different because it was perpetual. This was the point made in the most systematic fascist attempt to think through the umbilical relation between fascism and dictatorship: the work of fascist scholar Sergio Panunzio. He first published his thesis in Mussolini's flagship journal *Gerarchia*, under the ambitious title of "General Theory of Dictatorship" (1936). He later included it in his work of 1937, *A General Theory of the Fascist State*. Based on his lectures at the faculty of political science of the University of Roma, and like Carl Schmitt (whose work he cited), Panunzio lent academic gravitas to the fascist understanding of its government as a revolutionary dictatorship that was made to last.[28]

Revolutionary parties were a new form of sovereignty ("the subject and moral and juridical personification of the revolution"), and when they triumphed they created a new legality in the form of a new state.[29] Like the Nazi Schmitt and the fascist sociologist Robert Michels, Panunzio put forward a notion of dictatorship as emanating from a collective will that, for him, had incarnated in a form of charismatic leadership.[30] But he also stressed how in fascism dictatorship was no longer the expression of a "constituent power" but the dialectical integration of force and violence. While juridical dictatorships like the Roman ones were based on the concept of force, true revolutionary dictatorships were based on violence. While force was generated from above, violence came from below. Force was rooted in the past, while violence was posed toward the future.[31] As a third form of dictatorship, fascism arose from the dialectical integration of the two previous forms. Panunzio said that fascist rule included both juridical and revolutionary moments of dictatorship, and that the integration of both led to a significant change. Emergencies were not occasional but became permanent. Revolution became "totalitarian," leading to the creation of something new. In short, fascism had changed the "value and meaning" of the "concept of the dictator." This happened because the fascist dictatorship was a "heroic dictatorship" that emanated from the people. It was a people's dictatorship incarnated in the Duce.[32]

A Dictatorship Embodied in One Man

The centrality of the dictator in defining the dictatorship was made clear in the entry for the word *dictatorship* in the "Dictionary of Politics of the National Fascist Party" published in 1940. The entry was written by fascist intellectual Carlo Curcio. Citing authors like Schmitt and Panunzio, Curcio's theory of fascist dictatorship combined permanent power with extreme personalization. He proposed the word *dominator* to better define the fascist dictatorship and its notion that fascism was a dictatorship "in the moral sense."[33]

In the 1920s and 1930s, fascists started to read the present backward, anachronistically imposing fascist forms on the classic past. For example, a fascist expert on dictatorship maintained that Caesar was far from being a reactionary, in the sense that his reforms of the state were "pretty definitely Fascist" and this explained "Mussolini's worship of the 'divine Julius.'"[34]

When asked by Ludwig, "Is dictatorship an Italian specific?," Mussolini replied, "Maybe. Italy has always been a country of outstanding individuals. Here in ancient Rome there have been more than seventy dictatorships." Interestingly, and wrongly, Mussolini conflated Republican and legal Roman dictatorship with the will of the outstanding individual, when in fact, he put forward a notion of dictatorship as embodied in one irreplaceable man, asserting that "there will not be a Duce number two."[35]

As Uruguayan fascist Adolfo Agorio put it in 1923, there are geniuses for many fields and dictatorship was not exempted. Some people "came to the planet" as natural-born dictators: "A dictator is born, in the same way that poets or musicians are born. Dictatorship is the science of thinking through acts. Hence it is the more objective instrument for the genius."[36]

If fascist dictatorship relies on a militaristic notion of power, it is also ingrained in a deep-seated personality cult of the leader.[37] Unlike the communist theory of dictatorship (often contradicted by its practice), fascist dictatorship is always about the top guy, the messianic leader represented as a "saint," the redeemer of the nation.

To be sure, many fascists rejected the word *dictatorship* because it traditionally had negative associations with tyranny and despotism, words they associated with egalitarianism and liberalism but also with Judaism and communism. However, they all agreed fascism was a form of one-person absolute and permanent rule. In a 1921 speech on the fascist program, Mussolini explained they accepted the word *dictatorship* because it was what the nation needed, while in 1919 he had opposed the possibility of a military dictatorship while reclaiming the need for a revolutionary "blood bath." In *Mein Kampf*, Hitler noted that dictatorship as a concept and a practice had a bad reputation even in cases of obvious need. Worse, it had been appropriated by the enemies: "Thereupon the analphabetic Russian became the slave of his Jewish dictators who, on their side, were shrewd enough to name their dictatorship 'The Dictatorship of the People.'"[38]

In 1933 Hitler said, "When our opponents say, 'It is easy for you, you are a dictator'—we answer them, 'No, gentlemen, you are wrong; there is no single dictator, but ten thousand, each in his own place.'" But the little dictators had to follow the supreme authority to the end: "We have in our movement developed this loyalty in following the leader, this blind obedience of which all the others know nothing, and which gave to us the power to surmount everything."[39] A state based on terror and the absolute, permanent rule of the *Führerprinzip* (the notion that Hitler's command was unlimited and all power derived from his authority) became "Hitler's state [*Führerstaat*]" and not a juridical state. It was an extreme form of dictatorship. But Hitler and other Nazi luminaries were deeply uninterested in theoretical questions. To be sure, Hitler supported a model in which the unification of "popularity, force and tradition" made authority "unshakable."[40] But the task of defining the dictatorial nature of Nazis was left to Carl Schmitt. Schmitt, the theorist and explainer of dictatorships, claimed that Hitler's leadership could not be easily explained or represented. The reality of Hitler's rule explained itself. In one of his most fascist books, Schmitt wrote that conducting the people could not be equated with a simple command because "being a dictator does not mean ruling a bureaucratic centralist way or other type of domination." And yet, he insisted that using categories such as dictatorship for Nazism ran the risk of losing the uniqueness of Hitler's rule (*Führung*). Schmitt asserted that Hitler's way of leading was unlike other dictatorships, even if they were necessary and healthy: "We have to guard against the danger that a specifically German and National Socialist concept is clouded and weakened by comparison with foreign categories."[41] Clearly, Schmitt thought Hitler and Mussolini were dictators and wanted to demonstrate that a fascist order is superior to any written law.[42] Most fascists shared this view of Hitler as the dictator of a new order. In 1925, Goebbels assured himself of the fact that Hitler was predestined to be a dictator:

"This man has all it takes to become a king. A born people's tribune. The coming dictator."[43]

After their power grab and the affirmation of dictatorial rule, many fascists, for strategic reasons, promised their dictatorship was not a dictatorship, or that it was going to be transitory, or that it was a dictatorship against enemies but not vis-à-vis the state.[44] Others also rejected the word *dictatorship* as inadequate because in its traditional sense it meant a temporary remedy, not the permanent form of power that fascism put forward.[45] And others lied about the fact that fascist dictatorship was permanent, without denying the essential role of the dictator and the fact that it was he alone who defined the new world of politics. For example, British fascist Strachey Barnes promised that "there will be no dictatorship when the revolutionary period is over. Fascism does not stand for a dictatorship, neither of a person nor of a class." This was an argument that resembled the communist idea of dictatorship, but in reality, fascists created a cult of the leader that affirmed his permanent power: "If there is a dictatorship in Italy now, it is because the revolutionary organisation has taken this form by an accident of history. The accident in question is the presence of a genius, a man of the people, with that medium-like gift of intuitioning and interpreting the vast subconscious ideals of historical Italy dormant in the heart of every true Italian. This, I believe, is the secret of his success, this and his passionate sincerity and disinterestedness. The Italian adores a saint who shows himself to be no fool either to boot."[46]

One problem that arises from extremely personalized fascist dictatorship is the problem of succession.[47] In justifying the legitimacy of the dictator as part of a political theology and its subsequent political religion, fascists can never easily transfer the charismatic nature of their unique transcendental leadership. Many mini-Hitlers or little Mussolinis tried to become the inheritors of something that in principle was not transferable. In a sense, fascist dictators were sterile: they could not procreate successors. The power of this kind of ruler could not be contained, much less passed on.[48]

It would be difficult to understand the history of fascism without considering the importance of the personalized cult of the dictator, whose power was believed to be sacred. This form of dictatorship defied the abstractions of authority, hierarchy, and obedience by making them tangible in the persona of the leader.[49] It was not only "strictly political" but "human" in the sense that one person held absolute power. The Capo (the Chief) emanated from the "heart of the people" and was conceived as the source of ethical authority and power.[50] This implied that the leader's individuality was restricted insofar as he represented the collective movement and nation. As French fascist Drieu La Rochelle explained, fascism "did not come out from Mussolini's brain like Minerva from the forehead of Jupiter." In Italy, fascism embodied a whole movement. It was "the whole effort of a generation that sought and found fascism" and who at the same time sought and found itself in Mussolini.[51] Dictatorship was the result of a national search for incarnation. As Panunzio put it, "The revolution is an idea; and the revolutionary dictatorship is, as we know, the dictatorship of the idea. But this idea must find its Man, its body, the Hero. Hence it can be said that the heroic dictatorship is subjectivity, the awareness of the idea of a people, in its march and its journey through history."[52] In fact, it was not history but myth that enabled the divinization of the heroic leader.

This is what fascists called an epochal "miracle," the wonder of a "dictatorship of one man."[53] Fascists wanted to believe that the extremely antidemocratic politics of one man's unlimited personal power represented a form of real democracy.

The Dictatorship of the People

In 1923, Anne O'Hare McCormick, a correspondent for the *New York Times*, explained that Mussolini really knew his own people. This was supposed to be something strange for Americans living in democracy: "No citizen of a strictly limited democracy like ours can imagine the relief of being ruled by a good, strong, forthright autocrat after the absolute, unbridled, impossibly logical form of self-government suffered in Italy. The people were already yearning for a dictatorship when Mussolini appointed himself a dictator. So far from a usurpation of authority against the popular will, his march on Rome was like an answer to prayer."[54] Mussolini fascinated the media and even those journalists who were supposed to provide critical information about his dictatorship rather than propping up its international and national legitimacy. Readers of the *New York Times* were informed that the lesser Italian people needed dictatorship. The way McCormick told it, the people wanted autocratic rule and spectacle: "The new Government cultivates the spectator. One of the reasons for its popularity among a people smarting under a sense of being undervalued in the world is that it gives them at last a leader who is a headliner, so to speak, able to command public attention and keep Italy on the front page. And Mussolini concentrates most of his efforts on healing the wounded amour propre and building up the morale of the nation. He makes politics a kind of noble show and keeps enlivened and interested the audience, so bored by his predecessors."[55]

These forms of misinformation cemented fascist rules and manufactured the persona of the dictator.[56] All over the world, fascists identified with the distorted examples of Hitler's and Mussolini's dictatorships, and this influenced their own transnational ideas of fascist dictatorship.

As an Argentine fascist put it in 1933, there were two types of dictatorships—those that relied on coercion, and those of Hitler and Mussolini, which reformed the "conscience" of the people. The former were "ephemeral" and the latter "permanent." Fascist dictatorships were "made by the people."[57]

In China, the fascist Blue Shirts argued that existing liberal democracies were the antithesis of the successful revolutionary movements that would "lay the foundation for a people's democracy." Similarly, Spanish fascists denounced "the old lies of democracy" and identified popular sovereignty with the "doctrines and the procedures of redemptive fascism."[58]

The Peruvian fascist poet Chocano put forward his idea of "an organized dictatorship" that could defeat the "democratic farse" in the name of what the people wanted. Chocano praised dictatorship as the best form of government for "tropical" Latin America. He wanted dictators to stand above the law and to suspend all individual guarantees. This dictatorship was anti-political. It was designed for the people "who live outside of politics" and wanted "the dictatorship of a single responsible man and not that of four hundred irresponsible ones even by their number."[59]

Similarly, the British fascist leader Sir Oswald Mosley explained the popular nature of fascism as an outcome of people's desires. For him, this was why fascism was not tyrannical but an expression of genuine popular leadership: "The Dictatorship is a Dictatorship of the will of the people expressed through a Leadership and

Government of their own choice." Mosley portrayed present-day democracies as the "dictatorship of vested interests." Fascism replaced them with "a Dictatorship of the people themselves." The people gave fascists the power to act and carry out their will: "Fascism restores to power the people. That power can only be expressed through Leadership voluntarily accepted and chosen, but armed by the people with power to do what they want done."[60]

Acclamation, and, if necessary, elections, reinforced the fascist understanding of why and how the dictator came to power—and just as importantly, why the dictatorship's revolutionary nature was the product of the militarization of politics.[61] Somehow, the idea of paramilitary formations fighting in the political arena led fascists to believe their groups represented the warring will of the nation. The fascist dictatorship was a form of natural salvation because the leader transformed popular ideology into practice— the practice of an "objective political truth" that derived from "a natural" reality."[62]

Words and concepts could not keep up with what was going on. Fascism supposedly "creates a dictatorship that is not dictatorship." This confusing argument was explained by the fact that the fascist suppression of freedoms was "willingly accepted by an entire people."[63]

This belief in the popular delegation of power led fascists to affirm the idea of the dictator as "speaking directly to the people." Mussolini claimed that fascism was the first "people's regime" in Italian history, and this is why it was "perfectly idiotic" to define his mandate as tyrannic.[64] With this dubious logic, fascists based the legitimacy of their rule in the claim that the dictator was the people incarnated.

Impossible to prove, this assertion that it was self-appointed provided the foundation for the fascist dictatorship. The old juridical ideas of dictatorship could not possibly be further away, and yet Mussolini circled back to Rome. He stressed the Roman roots of dictatorship and contrasted its long-standing power with present-day conditions, which he dismissed as "indirect" and "collective."[65] Inspired by Roman dictatorship, Mussolini's idea was nonetheless the opposite of a temporary commission; instead, it was a new form of authoritarian politics, "the rule of one." The dictator stood against the "extremist" ideal of democracy as the rule of the many for all. Mussolini augured the end of "democratic conquests." He regarded liberal democracy as a decrepit "old game."[66]

In 1920, Lenin insisted that the issue of the dictatorship of the proletariat was central to the working-class movement and that the key difference from previous dictatorships was that other dictatorships represented the power of minorities over the people.[67] Fascists contested this but agreed on the need for a dictatorship of the people based on force, unchecked by previous forms of legality. They saw only themselves, and especially the leader, as personifying the majority. They argued that neither democracy nor communist dictatorship represented the will of the whole nation. In his criticism of Bolshevik dictatorship, Mussolini questioned the notion of the party as a vanguard that could channel the will of the majority and argued, "There is a dictatorship of a few non-working intellectual men, belonging to a fraction of the socialist party, fought by all the other fractions. This dictatorship of a few men is called Bolshevism."[68]

Mussolini's critique was unoriginal and disingenuous.[69] Interestingly, Mussolini wondered how a few people (the communists) could actually represent more than themselves without noting that anti-fascists wondered the same thing about his justification for one-person rule. Fascists were not, of course, concerned with the loss of equality, but rather with the fact that, like Donoso, they thought revolutions were carried out by elites, rather than the real people that Mussolini claimed he exclusively represented.[70] Fascists believed that dictatorship was permanent precisely because it affirmed what the people desired without the need to constantly ask them what they wanted through the medium of electoral representation.

Positioned against democracy, fascists replaced indirect representation with the persona of the dictator. Their convoluted argument was that if the leader truly and permanently embodied the people and the nation, there was no need to put the one-man leadership into question. This, of course, relied on the need to have faith in a fantasy about the leadership's power literally emanating from the people. Dictatorship could "engender" a new nation. It was the source of a better, new country.[71] The fascist national revolution changed the world of politics. As the Portuguese dictator Oliveira Salazar put it, "Dictatorship has nothing to do with politics. Dictatorship is itself the solution to the political problem."[72]

Regarding his own rule, Hitler argued that it was not electoral legitimacy in a liberal democratic sense but natural selection that made him the leader of the people: "They talk of democracies and dictatorships; but they fail to grasp the fact that in this country a radical transformation has taken place." He described himself as a man of the people: "I myself, to whom the people have given their trust and who has been called to be their leader, come from the people."[73] And yet, it was unclear to many people that the leader's position only reflected popular sovereignty. In 1936, the German dictator maintained that no one placed him in his leadership role. Ironically, he made this remark in the context of rigged elections that he organized in order to provide a referendum in the form of a parliamentary election. Only the Nazi party and its friends were allowed to participate. In 1937, Mussolini explained that "the referendum is fine when it comes to choosing the most suitable place to place the village fountain, but when the supreme interests of a people are at stake, even ultra-democratic governments are careful not to leave them to the judgment of the people themselves."[74]

In fascism, elections were valid only if they confirmed the dictatorship, but they were not meaningful otherwise. Having decimated all opposition during the Spanish Civil War—half a million people were killed, and nearly as many went into exile—Franco called a referendum in 1947, confirming himself as head of state for life. Franco argued that this dubious election was extremely "free and welcoming." His ultimate lie was his argument that dictatorship and freedom were compatible.[75] In these dictatorial regimes, where repression reigned supreme and the free press had been eliminated, elections were not real or free—they were manipulated to show that the leader's role was somehow organic. Hitler stated, "Out of the people I have grown, in the people I have remained, to the people I return." This constant sense of emanating in and through the people made the Führer note "the fact that I know of no statesman in the world who can say with greater right than I that he is the representative of a people." But what gave him the right to claim exclusive representation of a people? Elections were not enough. Hitler asked the German people for their full devotion.[76] He demanded irrational submission. Goebbels explicitly combined divine sovereignty with popular sovereignty when he said, in reference to Hitler, "Who is this man? Half plebeian, half God! Is this really Christ or just John the Baptist?"[77] The Führer explicitly stated that full unconditional belief was the thing that made him the leader of his people: "I appeal to you to support me with your faith."[78]

Fascist leaders were presented as being from, by, and for the people, but they never truly did what a majority of the people wanted. On the contrary, they asserted that they were permanently ruling for transcendental reasons and causes.

Regarding the Second World War, Hitler maintained that "as long as Providence willed that the German people could not be spared this battle, I am grateful they entrusted me with the leadership of a struggle which shall decide not only our German history but that of Europe, and even that of the entire world for the next 500 or 1000 years." In short, the leader of the people was responsible for the salvation or destruction of the world. Hitler claimed, "I take as a particular obligation to carry out the historical mission with which the Creator has entrusted me."[79] The results of shifting common politics into the realm of the sacred and a denial of reality were catastrophic.

Populists and Dictators

Populism cannot be considered dictatorial since, especially after 1945, it explicitly stressed the political primacy of democratic representation. Modern populism is not a form of dictatorship for two reasons: First is the populist rejection of fascist dictatorial terror. Second is the use of electoral representation. These two reasons are eminently ideological, and not only a matter of style or strategy.

There is no populism with dictatorship. Populist leaders regarded dictatorship as anathema to their politics. Fascists like Hitler and Mussolini had destroyed democracy from within to create a dictatorship from above. Early populists did the opposite. Postwar populists in power had been dictators, former fascists, and fellow travelers to totalitarian leaders who had changed and created and enlarged democracies. For example, Juan Domingo Perón destroyed dictatorship from within to create a dictatorship from above. He had been the strongman in the 1943–1945 dictatorship, but he called for free elections, which he won in 1946. Getulio Vargas in Brazil had been a dictator from the 1930s until 1945 and became a democratically elected president in 1951. In Bolivia, Victor Paz Estenssoro and his National Revolutionary Movement (MNR) had participated in the protofascist dictatorship of Colonel Gualberto Villarroel (1943–1946), and then, after a coup, Estenssoro became democratically elected in 1954. In Venezuela, Romulo Betancourt had a history of supporting dictatorships and was the president of a junta in 1945; later, he created a new democracy and became democratically elected in 1950. Sooner or later, all these populist leaders realized that dictatorship was a toxic remnant of the past.

Overall, while fascism clearly rejected democratic procedures, populist versions of democracy after 1945, such as Peronism in Argentina or Varguismo in Brazil, embraced free elections and electoral representation. In this formal sense, and from its modern inception, populism cannot be considered a form of dictatorship. But populism proposed a rejection of "demo-liberalism" that often conflated legality with political legitimacy. It was based on majoritarian views but also on the cult of the leader. Populists ignored some political freedoms while stressing or even expanding social rights and/or voters' participation in the electoral process.

Populism is not fascism at all, which is to say that it is not dictatorial in the fascist, anti-institutional, revolutionary sense.

Historians of fascism and Nazism, like Paul Corner and Alan Steinweis, among many others, have stressed the repressive, dictatorial, and violent elements of fascism.[80] These elements mark a key boundary, an epistemic frontier, between populism and fascism.

For General Perón, fascism could not be replicated; this was a new epoch, and a new truth was needed. Perón proposed a new form of "organic" democracy.[81] The organic nature of the movement would lead to political supremacy in the long term: "Our aspiration is not to rule for six years but to secure sixty years of government."[82] It was clear to everyone that this supremacy would be achieved by winning plebiscitary elections that confirmed the dual nature of the leader, who was both an elected representative and a quasi-transcendental conductor of the people—like a fascist "natural born" dictator, but confirmed by legitimate votes. As Perón often said, "The people should know . . . that the conductor is born. He is not made, not by decree nor by elections." He added, "It is essential that the conductor finds his own molds, to later fill them with a content that will be in direct relation, according to his efficiency, with the sacred oil of Samuel that the conductor has received from God."[83]

Populism's anti-institutional attributes, its idea that legitimacy was derived not only from the people's sovereignty but also from sacred mandates, were both a result of the fascist past and a negation of it. Classic populism was connected to fascist dictatorial theory and practice but also explicitly proposed its demise to make way for the creation of an anti-liberal, anti-communist, "third way" democracy.

Modern populism is not theoretically rooted in violent foundations but rather in electoral decisions made by a majority of citizens. Even though leaders like Perón, Commander Hugo Chávez in Venezuela, and many others had attempted coups in their previous roles, as populist leaders they more or less rejected the violence that is typical of dictatorships. They eventually relied on elections and other democratic procedures to justify their rule, and this made an impact with respect to the use of state violence against the opposition. Most histories of populism show that, as a regime, it combined (and still combines) a high degree of anti-institutional politics with a low degree of anti-institutional violence. Populism embraced democratic elections, and at the same time it could also be radically disruptive to politics without fully spurning legality.[84]

Perón stated that after fascism was defeated, nothing changed. The postwar world was even more unjust and unfree than it had been before. The two main challenges to justice and freedom remained: liberalism and communism.[85] In this sense, Eva Perón explained that Peronism used the providential nature of its leader against communism and capitalism: "Our only advantage is that here we have not had the misfortune of suffering the horrors of two disastrous wars and, instead, we have had the privilege that God has given us a conductor of the carats of Perón."[86]

In the pages of the magazine *Peronist World* in 1952, early populists rejected "fascism, a foreign, alien word that has nothing to do with what is Argentine." They advised the Peronista youth to reject it and be offended if somebody used it to describe Peronism: "We give you permission to get angry and shout when you hear that General Perón is a dictator or a fascist. Perón is the Head of the extraordinary popular movement. Dictators have no account to the People but they enslave them."[87]

Populists advanced the idea that democracy could be blended with the leader's incarnation of the people. In theory, this meant reviving Mussolini's combination of revolution and reaction. As one of the most incisive theorists of Peronism, Ernesto Palacio, put it, "Revolution only is legitimate when it implies a restauration of order." This model allowed Palacio to imply that Peronists' dictatorial antecedents had worked in a classic juridical way. Citing authors like Carl Schmitt, Palacio argued that reality, the "primacy of the world," should overcome "the fiction of legality." Supreme power resided in the will of the strongest. For him, this meant that the best expression of democratic government was decisionism. History demonstrated that the caudillo was the emanation of the will of the people: "Personal power coincides historically with democracy, with the exaltation of the democratic spirit."[88] As a former fascist and racist who had exalted forms of fascism and popular dictatorship during the war, Palacio, who became an elected Peronist representative in Congress in 1946, argued in 1948 that "it is frequent, in our days, that the crudest phenomena of oligarchy and Caesarism are concealed under a liberal or democratic political legislation." Going back to the examples of the Roman Tribunes and Caesar, he maintained that "the democratic revolution, embodied in the leadership of a caudillo, establishes a new regime in which the elements of power subsist, naturally, with the same structure that they presented in the monarchy and in the aristocracy, but inspired by other principles." The leader of a democratic revolution preceded by dictatorship was a perfect embodiment of popular sovereignty, acting and governing "in the name of the people."[89] The idea of representation was more ambivalent in the populist model than it had been for fascism. As Palacio stated, "Representation cannot be given. Either one has it or not." Elections could only be the confirmation of the leader's incarnation of the people, or, as Palacio also put it, "The people do not choose their leaders. They consecrate them."⁹⁰ This idea had dangerous potential: a negative electoral result could be eventually construed as fake. But this didn't happen until the following century with the wannabe fascists.

Perón said he wanted to replace formal democracy with "real democracy." He admitted that "in this regard, I am indeed totalitarian."⁹¹ What he meant is that his politics did not involve liberal forms of deliberation with people who disagreed with him. And yet, Perón found the accusation of being a totalitarian dictator especially insulting. In accordance with the clerico-fascist theories of Father Franceschi, Perón saw fascism, "plutocracy," and communism as "totalitarian forms."⁹²

Perón considered his regime to be the opposite of dictatorship, because dictatorships "insectify men" and they cannot last longer than the man who rules them.⁹³ Perón also argued that the problem with dictatorship was that it misunderstood the role of violence: "A minority enthroned in government via fraud or violence constitutes an arbitrary dictatorship which is the antithesis of all democratic meaning." Reflecting upon his own transition from dictator to elected president, Perón argued, "A soldier can only be a ruler if he is capable of throwing his inner general out the window, renounce violence and submit to law."⁹⁴

This was the opposite of what many dictators like Hitler and Mussolini did. Perón believed he was called totalitarian because he was an enemy of communism and liberal democracy. As a dictatorial figure transitioning to democracy in 1944, Perón found it difficult to deny the charge. Even then, he asserted the transitionary nature of his dictatorship and claimed he was defending the constitution and popular sovereignty.⁹⁵ But once he had created a new democracy, he wanted to adapt the "revolutionary principles" to the preexisting legality. The dictatorship was over, changes had been integrated, and they did not entirely replace the previous system. He defined dictatorship in the traditional Roman juridical sense, but he still used the fascist language of revolution. And yet, unlike the fascists, his revolutionary dictatorship led to democracy, or as he put it, "The 1943 coup d'état was exalted to the highest quality of people's revolution." By electoral means, the "revolution was converted into government."[96]

After 1946, Perón asked how he could be a dictator when had been elected and reelected by a majority of the people. He said, "If a ruler elected by his people, does what his people want and in this concept fights for social justice, economic independence and the sovereignty of his country, he is declared a 'dictator' and his government 'totalitarian.'"[97]

In other countries, the concept of totalitarianism and the notion of similarities between fascist and communist dictatorships were at the center of the populist rejection of dictatorship. Ecuadorian populist leader Velasco Ibarra explicitly rejected the pro-dictatorial positions of fascists like Chocano and Lugones, saying it wasn't about the dilemma of "Rome or Moscow" but the need to reject both fascism and Bolshevism. Fascism was "the same" as "Leninism," sharing its dictatorial procedures but with a totally different ideological perspective. Rome and Moscow represented dictatorship, and he rejected both. Smart and energetic leaders needed to combine their prowess with democratic politics. For Velasco, the problem behind totalitarian dictatorships was that of "Caesarism."[98]

All in all, these early populists recognized that 1945 changed the political world, but they often failed to recognize their own previous participation in dictatorial governments. In Venezuela,

Betancourt, just before he was going to become the president of a revolutionary junta after a coup, said that the era of dictatorship announced by Lugones in 1924 was finished. He contrasted the interwar success of fascism with the postwar context: "There was a reason that can explain that retreat of the popular movement: it was time for the rise of fascism, it was the hour of the sword, as Leopoldo Lugones said; but in 1945 the situation is absolutely different: we are universally living the hour of free elections."[99]

Wannabe Fascists and the History of Coups

Regarding permanent dictatorial power, wannabe fascists fall somewhere between fascists and classic populists. Unlike the former, their attempts to interrupt democracy are not followed to their ultimate consequences. Unlike the latter, they do not flatly reject the possibility of a dictatorial coup.

In a weird moment of introspection, Trump stated that "people with no ego will have very little life force, and people with too much will tend toward dictatorial personalities."[100] And yet, a dictatorial personality does not make dictatorship. It is well known, for example, that Trump and Bolsonaro did not achieve their dictatorial aims in 2021 and 2023. Wannabe fascists tend to downgrade democracy, curtailing freedoms and rights, sometimes even through attempted insurrection—but they eventually cop out. In contrast, full-fledged fascists do not fear the consequences and will do anything in their power to destroy democracy. Despite this key distinction, fascists and wannabe fascists share a lack of concern over authoritarian trends, and sometimes enable them. The support for extremism by conservative business interests that act as enablers is no small matter. As Peruvian anti-fascist José Carlos

Mariátegui observed in 1925, it was the bourgeoisie that had "apostatized from its democratic faith, and has opposed the dictatorship of the proletariat with its own dictatorship."[101]

When fascists came to power and then destroyed democracy from within, almost nobody cared, or perhaps they did not care enough. At the international level, in democracies like the United States, the fantasy of American exceptionalism contrasted with the real Jim Crow America and its own fascist characteristics. The idea that "it cannot happen here," so well criticized in Sinclair Lewis's book in 1935, not only ignored fascism and fascist traditions such as the Ku Klux Klan at home, but also enabled fascism abroad until it was too late.

This first happened with Benito Mussolini, who received worldwide admiration and also drew worldwide condescension for Italians.[102] The mainstream media ascribed Mussolini's destruction of democracy to natural causes and justified his dictatorship as the outcome of his embodiment of the people, which allowed fascist dictators to continue their work of destruction.

In the case of Italian fascism, it took some years to solidify the dictatorship. But in 1924, after fascists close to Mussolini assassinated the most important figure of the opposition, it became clear that Mussolini was openly moving toward dictatorship. In the case of Nazism, the transition was accelerated by the same pattern of conservative enablement and an apathetic reaction to Nazi terror.[103]

Fascism destroyed democracy after using it to gain power. As Joseph Goebbels stated, "Democracy permitted us to use democratic methods in the time of our opposition, it was because this was necessary under a democratic system. We National Socialists have never maintained that we were representatives of a democratic viewpoint, but we have openly declared that we only made use of democratic means in order to gain power, and that after the seizure of power we would ruthlessly deny to our opponents all those means."[104]

Fascists have no qualms about questioning democracy within democracy. Mussolini, a few months before the March on Rome in 1922, stated that in light of the political experience of parliamentarism, "The eventuality of a dictatorship needs to be seriously considered."[105] On October 29, 1922, during the March on Rome, fascists claimed they had "a dictatorial mandate."[106]

Fascist strategies for winning power involved military insurrection and civil war (Spain) or becoming a puppet fascist regime after a fascist invasion and occupation (France, Norway, Romania, and Hungary). At other times, fascist groups have been part of a larger right-wing coalition, such as the Blue Shirts in China, the *nacionalistas* in Argentina in 1930–1932, or the Japanese fascists. And fascist fellow travelers can act as instruments or allies of fascist powers, as with the case of Subhas Chandra Bose in India.[107]

Coups are an exemplary form of fascism attacking democracy. What fascist Curzio Malaparte called the "technique of the coup d'état" was a key tactic in fascist strategies to gain power.[108] Coups in general do not lead to fascism in particular, but to dictatorship. Historically, when constitutionally elected leaders were denied their legitimate mandate, there was just one word for it: coup. Think of the emblematic cases of Salvador Allende in Chile (1973) and Jacobo Arbenz in Guatemala (1954)—both democratically elected leaders who were toppled by the military. In other cases, such as in Uruguay in 1973, Peru in 1992, and Venezuela in 2017, presidents decided to ignore the law and attempted to stay in power indefinitely through self-coup.

A coup against a democratic regime can be defined as any political action by state actors that aims to either maintain or seize power by unconstitutional means. There is a coup whenever military renegades or democratically elected leaders suspend the democratic process.[109]

This definition—and its global history—is why Donald Trump's long-standing refusal to accept his electoral defeat and his instigation of the attack on the Capitol have alarmed so many people, as they were clear warning signs of dictatorship and even fascism.

Trump's coup failed, but his actions—denying and attempting to overturn the results of the election and getting top Republicans to indulge these dangerous efforts—are still symptoms of the fragility of American democracy at this moment.

And this is exactly why we must know about the history of coups—how they happened and, most importantly, how they have been stopped. Trump's big lies about the election, the failed coup, and his statements about the dubious legitimacy of future elections constitute an attack on the state and democratic government. While his words and actions may be dismissed as merely tantrums,[110] the history of dictators in Latin America, and of fascist dictators in other parts of the world over the past century, suggests the need to take this dangerous moment seriously.

In Latin America, there have been several political leaders and civil servants who betrayed their countries' constitutions and democratic rule by launching coups. For example, conservative politicians in Argentina lost the 1928 presidential election and then supported Argentina's first coup in 1930, led by General José Felix Uriburu, who wanted to permanently change the nation from a democracy to a new corporatist and dictatorial fascistic republic.

The Supreme Court, days after the takeover by Uriburu, officially recognized the de facto situation and legitimized the coup on extraconstitutional grounds—the stability and survival of the republic. The justices prioritized social order and political security over democratic legitimacy, setting up a legal precedent for future dictators.

In other Latin American cases, courts were not enablers; instead, coups were legitimized by conservative and anti-communist parties that controlled the national legislatures. Following a defeat at the ballot boxes, these conservatives consolidated and seized power within governing institutions to then advance unpopular and unequal policies.

For example, in Brazil in 1964, conservative politicians, including the majority in Congress, supported a coup against elected president João Goulart. In Chile, Augusto Pinochet led a coup against the legitimately elected Allende, overtaking the government by force in 1973. The dictator immediately dissolved Congress, but conservative parties supported the coup. The United States supported both of these coups as part of its Cold War anti-leftist crusade.

There were also cases of Latin American elected presidents who executed *auto-golpes* (self-coups) through the implementation of emergency laws when they were facing democratic impediments to their power. For example, in Uruguay, President Juan María Bordaberry decreed a state of emergency to install a civic-military regime to face the *tupamaros* guerrilla insurgency in 1973. In Peru in 1992, right-wing populist Alberto Fujimori dissolved Congress to enact controversial security and economic changes by executive decree. In Venezuela in 2017, President Nicolás Maduro shut down Congress to rule without checks on his power. In these three cases, elected civilian governments morphed into dictatorships through the manipulation of legal procedures and technicalities.

In most cases, the press and certain sectors of the population either condoned, supported, or normalized these seizures of power, while others remained apathetic about the demise of democracy and/or fearful of the ongoing repression and terror.

An important moment in the 1980s provides us with a template for the present—a moment when a coup failed because citizens united to defend democracy.

After the bruising experience of the fascist-inspired "Dirty War" dictatorship from 1976 to 1983, democratic governance was restored in Argentina. When President Raúl Ricardo Alfonsín was elected in 1983, Argentines and their government decided to investigate crimes committed during the dictatorship, hear testimony of survivors, and create a truth commission to research these crimes and eventually provide evidence to prosecute the perpetrators.[111]

Antidemocratic forces did not want to recognize the legitimacy of the new democratically elected government. They worked to interrupt these trials and pursued a coup. In early 1987, renegade soldiers attempted to topple the Alfonsín government by mobilizing troops in open insurrection.

But massive peaceful protests denied these attempts to overthrow democracy. Spontaneously, hundreds of thousands of citizens took to the streets to support democracy. In Buenos Aires, more than two hundred thousand marched to the House of Government, the Pink House, to support the elected leaders.

The media also played an important role. The main newspapers and radio and television channels reported and criticized the illegal actions of the coup plotters and defended the democratic system. So did state institutions, including Congress and the majority of the armed forces and the police, who sided not with the rebel coup leader Colonel Aldo Rico, but with the constitution. The result was neither a violent overthrow of government nor a manipulation of the law to undermine the way democratic institutions functioned. Rather, it was democratic participation on display: citizens peacefully protested and defended democracy on the streets instead of being passive and apathetic when the military tried to take over. I was there with my family. I was twelve, and I still have vivid memories of the moment the would-be dictators were stopped.

This is why Trump's actions after his defeat in the 2020 election seemed like a return of the repressed memories of the past.

On January 6, 2021, Donald Trump attempted a coup. Had he succeeded, Trump would have become a dictator. But he failed. Once out of power, Trump stated in a famous speech in North Carolina in 2021, "I am not the one trying to undermine American Democracy, I'm the one trying to save it."[112] True to form, Trump also falsely intimated to several people that he could return as president before the next presidential election. Following Trump's example, Bolsonaro's followers also attempted a failed coup on January 8, 2023.

In the same way that Mussolini's dictatorship in the 1920s influenced Hitler's path in the following decade, including his failed coup of 1923, the Trumpist coup influenced Bolsonarism. In fact, the day after the seizure of the Capitol, Bolsonaro threatened that Brazil was "going to have a worse problem" if it did not change its electoral systems—that is, if he lost the elections.[113] After denying any participation in the seizure of the three branches of power, Bolsonaro reposted on his Facebook account a text saying that Luiz Inácio Lula da Silva was not elected by the people but by the courts of justice.[114] Since Bolsonaro and Trump were not immediately held accountable for their continued instigation of crimes against democracy, other similar actions will be seen again. These lies about democracy and dictatorship motivated Trump's and Bolsonaro's supporters to take over their respective Congresses, and both men continue to motivate the conspiratorial fantasies of global right-wing extremism. The similarities between the two factions are a product of mutual ideological influences. In both cases, fascism is just around the corner.

There is an old joke in Latin America that explains the absence of coups in American history. The reason behind this absence, the joke says, is that the United States is the only country in the world lacking an American embassy. To be sure, the United States has participated in the overthrow of dozens of Latin American governments since the late nineteenth century. These interventions have taken the form of direct military attacks, covert operations (often involving the CIA), and different forms of aid to rogue internal actors bidding for power. What we saw in the United States with Trump's failed coup was not an external matter but a result of overt antidemocratic tendencies within Trumpism and American history as a whole. The joke no longer works (if it ever did) because it misses two points. The first is that for a coup to succeed you need strong supporters and enablers within the press, the armed forces, Congress, and the judiciary. The second point is that the United States is like the rest of the world. American democracy is not as strong as it was assumed to be, and this is why it needs to be constantly defended like any other democracy.

History teaches us that whether a coup succeeds may depend on how democratic institutions, media, and citizens respond. Institutions play a significant role in taming fascism. If we ignore or normalize even timid coup attempts, authoritarian flirtations with coups could become more serious.

Without clear boundaries between democratic legality and authoritarian illegality, power grabs become easier. In his last years as dictator, Mussolini pondered whether his full power had been an "illusion." He wondered how, in a few hours in 1943, his dictatorial power had disappeared.[115] And yet, he soon would return to power with the help of his Nazi friends in the puppet republic of Salò between 1943 and 1945.

Hitler admired Mussolini so much that he never truly blamed him for his many war failures. Trump also admires dictators and autocrats, and although he has degraded American democracy, his power grabs have been prevented by its institutions, media, and citizens. Americans voted him out of office and in future presidential elections they will have more chances to stop his would-be fascist legacy. Trump's behavior—and the refusal of Republicans and their media allies to condemn it—is how antidemocratic movements and fascism begin. This is why it is critically important that citizens and institutions exercise vigilance over dictatorial behavior and refuse to take democracy for granted.

Epilogue

After failed coup attempts, fascists sometimes resorted to other means by a so-called "legal revolution." As historian Alan E. Steinweis explains, "It was crucial that Nazi rule be perceived as the consequence of a legal process rather than as some form of coup d'état. But neither Nazi propaganda, nor the self-deception or self-serving dishonesty of those Germans who were prepared to accept it, should be allowed to distract historians from the fundamentally anti-democratic and anti-constitutional process that gave birth to the Third Reich in 1933."[1]

Whether fascists admitted it or not, dictatorship was a natural outcome of fascism in power. Hans Frank, Nazi minister of justice and later governor of occupied Poland, told his interrogators at Nuremberg, "Hitler gave an oath before the Reich Supreme Court in Leipzig that he would come to power only legally and if he came to power he would govern legally. As long as the Fuehrer was in the position before he came to power to need lawyers and judges, he could need me, but once he had come to power, I felt more and more that he would drop these formalities and rule in an authoritarian way, as a dictator."[2] By then, Frank had joined other Nazis in trying to distance themselves from the Nazi dictatorship.

Franz's attitude was typical and extended to global allies. As recalled by Nazi leader Albert Speer in 1945, with Hitler's Nazi project foundering, "the rats deserted the sinking ship."[3]

Against expectations, none of this happened with Trumpism after its crushing electoral defeat in 2020.[4] Like the fanatical Goebbels, who stayed with the sinking ship of Nazism to the end, Donald Trump's ardent admirers and followers showed no signs of abandoning the destructive politics of their leader.

Major national and international allies did not desert Trump, either. Trumpism and the new politics of wannabe fascism that defined it are here to stay. This is very clear when we assess the state of global autocracy after Trump. Moreover, for many dictators the autocratic ship is not sinking at all, and many mainstream, center-right politicians in the US and abroad took the wrong lesson from the wreck.

It is difficult to say whether Trumpism's fall from power, or its imminent return in the form of impersonators or the man himself, can mobilize democratic forces worldwide. But after all the talk—around the time of Trump's election win in 2016 and Brexit in the United Kingdom—of a global populist insurgency from the right, it is important to wonder if, despite the clear failures of wannabe fascist politics, we are still on the cusp of a deeper shift toward that disastrous path. It might be too soon to tell whether this is the case. Authoritarianism is not mechanical, unstoppable, or unaffected by processes of resistance and the empowerment of democracy. This is why we should learn about those processes as part of the broader histories of fascism and populism.

This is a global phenomenon. While it is understandable that so much media, and pundit and academic, attention has focused on Trump and the aftermath of the US election, it is disappointing that there has been little discussion in Anglophone media of the pogroms and increasing repression in India, Bolsonaro's criminal mishandling of COVID-19 and the failed coup of 2023, and the success of mini-Trumpists like Nayib Bukele in El Salvador, the populist-neofascist alliance of Giorgia Meloni and Matteo Salvini in Italy, or the prospects for other autocratic leaders, including Juan Antonio Kast in Chile, Santiago Abascal in Spain, and Marine Le Pen in France. In short, there is not much discussion of the global potential for the destruction of democracy from within that Trumpism represented so well.

Although for many people in the United States, indeed, the majority of its voters, Trumpism had to go, the force of the former president's words still commanded attention after his defeat in 2020. World autocrats already missed Trumpism in power, and in many countries their attacks on democracy and their politics of hatred have persisted and even increased in recent years. While the pandemic has made clear the limits of authoritarian rule in democratic countries, in most autocratic contexts the pandemic and the ensuing political and economic instability gave leaders a rationale to engineer more crises and more suppression of the press and the opposition.

Exclusively focusing on the United States presents significant obstacles to understanding the world, and even to understanding the United States. We must assess the broader state of global autocracy in light of its past challenges to democracy in order to understand future ones. What are the prospects for global autocrats, especially the ones who want to abuse democracy, to downgrade and even destroy it from within? To be sure, autocrats thrived well before Trump's rise to power. But countries where democracy does not exist or is seriously limited will continue to develop, irrespective of the more recent global phenomenon of populist autocrats who want to return to the ways of fascism. Indeed, countries like Turkey, China, North Korea, Zimbabwe, Venezuela, Iran, Saudi Arabia, Cuba, Russia, and Belarus cannot be explained within the framework of the recent attempts to degrade or even destroy democracy. When there is only one party or no party at all, when popular demands are not channeled by elections, protests, and media criticism, democracy simply does not exist. The outcome of this suppression is more traditional forms of autocracy—namely, despotism, tyranny, and dictatorship. Where autocracy exists without democracy, Trump's defeat was less consequential. Countries like Russia and North Korea actively preferred Trump's more empathetic positions toward them, and in the case of the former, even tried their best to affect the results of the 2020 election (as they might also have done in 2016), but these autocrats were the least affected by Trump's demise. Other countries like Iran, a dictatorial theocracy where elections are curtailed by the power of religious authority, might have been happier with Trump being gone, but this in no way affected the stability of their authoritarian leaders. The same applies to dictatorships like Syria. In fact, Trump's confrontational, often erratic positions served to strengthen these types of autocrats by allowing them to use nationalism and anti-imperialism to hide their structural problems of repression, inequality, and poverty. China, the most powerful non-democratic country in the world, could find itself in the same situation.

China, North Korea, and Vietnam have been communist autocracies for decades, and their politics did not change significantly after 2020. Among other global autocrats not very affected by the fall of Trumpism or wannabe fascism as a whole, we should probably count those whom Trump ardently supported and even enabled, such as the leaders of Saudi Arabia and Egypt.[5]

The same is also true of countries where democratic life is minimal. For hybrid regimes such as Turkey, Ethiopia, Rwanda, and Venezuela, where certain freedoms exist in an otherwise extremely repressive environment, the fall of Trumpism meant geopolitical changes but not a big internal change. Autocratic leaders like Recep Tayyip Erdoğan, Nicolás Maduro, Daniel Ortega, and Vladimir Putin have fused repression, nationalism, and fear to keep themselves in power.

Trump had an ambivalent relationship with Erdoğan, driven by tricky geopolitics in the Middle East but never affected by Trump's repressive nature. In contrast, Trump often used Maduro as a foil, promising aggressive action against his dictatorship that never took place. This recalled the Bay of Pigs fiasco and Latin American memories of American imperialism in the region, and it had the dual outcome of generating support for Maduro inside and outside his country, as well as motivating American citizens of Venezuelan and Cuban origin to vote for Trump, especially in the 2020 election. The relationship between Trump and Putin remained a mystery to many. Why did the American president fear his Russian counterpart, almost never criticizing Putin for actions that ran contrary to American interests and lives? Future historians with access to more archival information might be able to answer these questions, but in any case, it is possible to argue that while Putin certainly missed Trump, his rule was not affected by Trump's departure. Autocrats in Africa like João Manuel Gonçalves Lourenço in Angola, Paul Kagame in Rwanda, and Emmerson Mnangagwa in Zimbabwe were not much affected by Trumpism either. This was also the case with autocratic leaders in Ethiopia, Congo, Cameroon, and Mali. Trumpism had a similar absence of relevance in Asian autocracies like Uzbekistan, Thailand, Kazakhstan, Malaysia, and, more recently, Myanmar. In short, autocratic governments with no or not much democracy were not very affected by the American caudillo's disgrace. The pervasive effects of Trumpism worldwide and the politics of wannabe fascism that they legitimized on a global scale are especially connected to places where democracy still exists. Trump's effects have been most pervasive on leaders of democracies, and perhaps democratic countries might find his absence from power to be a positive situation.

This is an important historical lesson: when democracy still exists and its essential features (free elections, pluralism, equality, anti-racism, the free press) are attacked from above, the legacy of fascism remains a threat. This was precisely the case with Trump, but it was not originally or essentially American.

In truth, Trumpism is part of a global attack on democracy from within democracy. This is what links Trumpism to a new trend of global autocratic movements. This autocratic destruction of democracy from the inside echoes past historical ideologies, such as fascism. Trump's populism is the latest chapter in a long history.

The paradox of populism is that it often identifies real problems but seeks to replace them with something worse. Wannabe fascism represents the latest attempt to create a third position between liberal democracy and more traditional forms of dictatorship.[6]

With his characteristic lack of humility, Donald Trump attempted to define the new state of the world as "the age of Trump." But in the run-up to the 2024 presidential election, it has been clear to anyone living outside the United States that even if it is true that Trumpism provided a global boost to the legitimacy of autocrats worldwide, autocrats of his kind had existed before Trump and will remain after Trumpism disappears or morphs into something else. The four pillars of fascism are built upon societal factors that provide support and legitimacy. Even without Trump in power, we will still have Trumpism by other means. Trumpism is part of a twenty-first-century global trend toward autocracy that has reformulated the history of populism, turning it into wannabe fascism.

Populism, especially after the defeat of fascism in 1945, moved beyond the four key elements of fascism: totalitarian lying, dictatorship, xenophobia, and the glorification of violence and the militarization of politics. But wannabe fascists have reengaged these four key elements and have, to different degrees, turned populism toward the ways of fascism.

To be sure, the rise of Trumpism and its ignominious retreat four years later through a lost election and a failed coup was highly influential for the fate of democracies on a global scale. But autocrats and fascists existed before Trump.

The political, social, and economic problems that supported the rise of these authoritarians still exist, and they need to be addressed. Especially in the United States, there are signs of hope that anti-fascist and anti-racist politics can be more egalitarian, safeguarding the environment and generating jobs. But even if that's prematurely optimistic, it is important to think that a more inclusive United States—or Europe, or Asia, or Africa, or Latin America—can be an example to others in the world, helping them confront their own antidemocratic actors. This is not only a US issue. But it is clear that a less confrontational American diplomacy might play a role in bringing about a reversal.

In the past, when anti-fascist forces put aside their differences and resisted together, democracy prevailed. Autocratic fascists acting within democracy only succeeded when independent media was attacked and not defended, when the separation of power and the rule of law were minimized or destroyed, when the radical left did not care about liberal democracy, when conservatives replicated the arguments of autocrats, and when the armed forces and the police sided with the authoritarian leader instead of the constitution. When this happened, democracy was lost and terrorist dictatorships began. In contrast, when fascism was fought and democracy defended, fascism did not rise or could not be sustained. It is difficult to know what will happen, but a lot depends on the actions of governments and citizens opposed to these autocrats.

Fascism lost legitimacy when people actively engaged in politics by giving the state an important role in addressing issues of inequality, such as reversing unequal taxation and fighting poverty. In the present, this could be a more democratic exit strategy for populism and fascism. But we have yet to see if this strategy would be successful—whether it could convince voters to turn against authoritarian options.

By returning to the histories of fascism and populism, this book has presented a historical explanation of a new development in history and the fascist-inspired danger that Trumpism and global autocrats represent.

Trump's main contribution to the legitimacy of global autocracy has been to make toxic, fascist politics viable again. But Trump is one among many. The politics he represents are far from over. Perhaps his long-standing influence will be the global normalization of wannabe fascists.

Acknowledgments

In November of 2021, I was invited to a panel organized by the Brazilian Supreme Court president, Luis Fux. This meaningful context provided me with an opportunity to exchange views with and learn from other members of the panel, including Judge Alexandre de Moraes, a member of Brazil's Supreme Court, who was a key figure in defending Brazilian democracy from Bolsonaro's attacks, including his failed coup. This panel, titled "Encontro virtual sobre liberdade de expressão: Desinformação como ameaça aos direitos humanos e à democracia," provided an opportunity to present my argument about the need to learn from history to gain an understanding of the fascist dangers of the present. In this context, I would like to thank the other participants, especially Jean Wyllys and Daniela Mercury.

In 2022, I was interviewed by a team of investigative counsels and experts from the Select Committee to Investigate the January 6th Attack on the United States Capitol. Their main concern was determining the root causes and long-term implications of that attack against American democracy, which is, to a great extent, the subject of this book.

I was then asked to submit a written statement for the Congressional Committee. I cowrote a report with my friend and colleague, and expert on fascism, Professor Jason Stanley. The title of the report was "The Fascist Danger to Democracy Represented by the Events of January 6, 2021." I have cowritten many op-eds with Jason over the past few years for many newspapers and websites, including Project Syndicate, the *Los Angeles Times*, and the *New Republic*. I have learned a lot from this collaboration, and I want to thank Jason for our conversations and his friendship.

I also want to thank my colleagues and friends for our conversations and collaborations: Melissa Amezcua, Carlos de la Torre, Luis Herrán Ávila, Antonio Costa Pinto, Emmanuel Guerisoli, Andrea Mammone, and Pablo Piccato, as well as Enzo Traverso, Angelo Ventrone, and Nadia Urbinati.

I have presented some of my main arguments in lectures and workshops at universities and academic institutes in many countries, including the United States, Mexico, India, Israel, Spain, Switzerland, the United Kingdom, Costa Rica, Portugal, Italy, Brazil, and Uruguay. I have also presented them in public contexts, including articles in newspapers such as the *Washington Post*, the *New York Times*, *Clarín* (Argentina), *Folha de S.Paulo* (Brazil), *Domani giornale* (Italy), *El faro* (El Salvador), and *El país* (Spain). I would especially like to mention my collaboration with the excellent Latin American media platform Latinoamérica21.

In the spring of 2023, I co-taught a graduate seminar on the history and theory of dictatorship with my dear friend and colleague at the New School for Social Research, Andreas Kalyvas. It was an ideal opportunity to learn from him and also to finish writing chapter 4 of this book while teaching and discussing these topics. Andreas knows more about the theories of dictatorship than anyone, and my thinking is deeply indebted to his.

My thanks also to Giulia Albanese, José Alves Neto, Andrew Arato, Luis Fernando Beneduzi, Ruth Ben-Ghiat, Mabel Berezin, Bruno Bimbi, Fabián Bosoer, Odilon Caldeira Neto, Renato Camurri, Claudia Costin, Carolyn Dean, Paula Diehl, Patrizia Dogliani, Oz Frankel, Maximiliano Fuentes Codera, Valeria Galimi, Fabio Gentile, Jerónimo Giorgi, Jacob Glick, Nicolas Goldbart, Susanne Hillman, Natalia Jacovkis, Dominick LaCapra, Simon Levis Sullam, George Lucas, Oscar Mazzoleni, Sandra McGee Deutsch, José Moya, Julia Ott, José Ragas, Raanan Rein, Sven Reichardt, Javier Rodrigo, Hector Raul Solis Gadea, Alberto Spektorowski, Alan Steinweis, Maria Bonaria Urban, Benjamin Zachariah, and Fulvia Zega.

My deep thanks to Kate Marshall, my excellent editor at UC Press. At UC Press, my appreciation also goes to Chad Attenborough, as well as to Brian Hurley for his editing work and Linda Gorman for the copyediting.

My thanks to my parents, Norma and Jaime, and my siblings, Diego and Inés. *Mi agradecimiento más profundo* to my wife, Laura, and my daughters, Gabriela and Lucia. This book is dedicated to them.

Notes

Introduction

1. Federico Finchelstein, "What the History of Coups Tells Us about Trump's Refusal to Concede," *Washington Post*, November 16, 2020, https://www.washingtonpost.com/outlook/2020/11/16/what-history-coups-tells-us-about-trumps-refusal-concede.

2. See Federico Finchelstein, "Biden Called Trumpism 'Semi-fascism': The Term Makes Sense, Historically," *Washington Post*, September 1, 2022, https://www.washingtonpost.com/made-by-history/2022/09/01/biden-called-trumpism-semi-fascism-term-makes-sense-historically; and "Jair Bolsonaro's Model Isn't Berlusconi: It's Goebbels," *Foreign Policy*, October 5, 2018, https://foreignpolicy.com/2018/10/05/bolsonaros-model-its-goebbels-fascism-nazism-brazil-latin-america-populism-argentina-venezuela.

3. Federico Finchelstein, "An Argentine Dictator's Legacy," *New York Times*, May 28, 2013, https://www.nytimes.com/2013/05/28/opinion/global/an-argentine-dictators-legacy.html.

4. Benito Mussolini, *La nuova politica dell'Italia: Discorsi e dichiarazioni* (Milan: Alpes, 1925), 222. On semi-fascism at the time of fascism, see Gustavo Barroso, *O integralismo e o mundo* (Rio de Janeiro: Civilização Brasileira, 1936), 112.

5. On aspirational fascism, see William E. Connolly, *Aspirational Fascism: The Struggle for Multifaceted Democracy under Trumpism* (Minneapolis: University of Minnesota Press, 2017).

6. Walter Benjamin, "On the Concept of History," in *Selected Writings, 1938–1940*, ed. Howard Eiland and Michael W. Jennings (Cambridge, MA: Harvard University, 2006), 4:392.

7. For an idiosyncratic example, see Corey Robin, "Triumph of the Shill: The Political Theory of Trumpism," *n+1*, no. 29 (2017), https://nplusonemag.com/issue-29/politics/triumph-of-the-shill.

8. For some key works on fascism, see Zeev Sternhell, *The Birth of Fascist Ideology: From Cultural Rebellion to Political Revolution*, with Mario Sznajder and Maia Asheri (Princeton, NJ: Princeton University Press, 1994); Ruth Ben-Ghiat, *Fascist Modernities* (Berkeley: University of California Press, 2001); Emilio Gentile, *Fascismo: Storia e interpretazione* (Rome-Bari: Laterza, 2002); Robert Paxton, *The Anatomy of Fascism* (New York: Knopf, 2004); Mabel Berezin, *Making the Fascist Self: The Political Culture of Interwar Italy* (Ithaca, NY: Cornell University Press, 1997); Geoff Eley, *Nazism as Fascism: Violence, Ideology, and the Ground of Consent in Germany, 1930–1945* (New York: Routledge, 2013); Antonio Costa Pinto, *The Nature of Fascism Revisited* (Boulder, CO: Social Science Monographs, 2012); and Sandra McGee Deutsch, *Las Derechas: The Extreme Right in Argentina, Brazil, and Chile, 1890–1939* (Stanford, CA: Stanford University Press, 1999).

9. For some key works on populism, see Nadia Urbinati, *Democracy Disfigured: Opinion, Truth, and the People* (Cambridge, MA: Harvard University Press, 2014); Carlos de la Torre, *Populist Seduction in Latin America* (Athens: Ohio University Press, 2010); Ernesto Laclau, *On Populist Reason* (London: Verso, 2005); Andrew Arato, *Post Sovereign Constitution Making: Learning and Legitimacy* (Oxford: Oxford University Press, 2016); and Andrew Arato and Jean L. Cohen, *Populism and Civil Society: The Challenge to Constitutional Democracy* (New York: Oxford University Press, 2022).

10. Franz L. Neumann, "Notes on the Theory of Dictatorship," in his *The Democratic and Authoritarian State* (New York: Free Press, 1964), 245.

11. Among the best critics, see Bruce Kuklick, *Fascism Comes to America: A Century of Obsession in Politics and Culture* (Chicago: Chicago University Press, 2022).

12. Several excellent books already exist about either the connections between Trumpism and fascism or Trumpism and populism. In some cases, these books are written by experts of either populism or fascism. While authors stressing the fascism hypothesis highlight the fascist or post-fascist qualities of

present autocrats, other writers omit fascism from the present picture entirely. For example, Jason Stanley's *How Fascism Works* (New York: Random House, 2018) and Tim Snyder's *On Tyranny* (New York: Tim Duggan Books, 2017) lucidly explain the fascist dimensions of populism. In contrast, experts on populism like Pippa Norris and Ronald Inglehart in *Cultural Backlash: Trump, Brexit, and Authoritarian Populism* (New York: Cambridge University Press, 2019), 239, minimize the fascist dimensions of Trumpism while stressing the populist ones. For an incisive analysis, see Mabel Berezin, "Fascism and Populism: Are They Useful Categories for Comparative Sociological Analysis?," *Annual Review of Sociology* 45 (2019): 345–61. In my own work on transnational fascism, I explored the bifurcations of fascism to neofascism, to dictatorship, and also to populism and back. Other key historians of fascism and neofascism, like Andrea Mammone, have similarly explained why one cannot stop analyzing fascism after the defeat of Hitler and Mussolini. Andrea Mammone, *Transnational Neofascism in France and Italy* (New York: Cambridge University Press, 2015). See also Ruth Ben-Ghiat, *Mussolini to the Present* (New York: Norton, 2020); Enzo Traverso, *The New Faces of Fascism: Populism and the Far Right* (New York: Verso, 2019); Javier Rodrigo and Maximiliano Fuentes Codera, *Ellos, los fascistas* (Barcelona: Deusto, 2022); Carlos de la Torre and Treethep Srisa-nga, *Global Populisms* (London: Routledge, 2021); John Foot, *Blood and Power: The Rise and Fall of Italian Fascism* (London: Bloomsbury, 2022). Other books by prominent pundits, law experts, or politicians often equate fascism with the present but without offering a historically nuanced view of fascism's global nature, its connections to populism, or its changes over time. In short, they present a fascism without history and, generally, without non-European examples. Among these works, I would mention Madeleine Albright's *Fascism: A Warning* (New York: Harper Perennial, 2018). As an expert on both fascism and populism in Europe and the Global South, I strive to bring these worlds together.

13. Cited in de la Torre and Srisa-nga, *Global Populisms*, 2–3.

14. Michael D. Shear, "Trump Asked Aide Why His Generals Couldn't Be Like Hitler's, Book Says," *New York Times*, August 8, 2022, https://www.nytimes.com/2022/08/08/us/politics/trump-book-mark-milley.html.

15. Analyzing this statement, Theodor Adorno said, on the same page after this quote by Hitler, "This is by its intrinsic logic tantamount to contempt for truth per se." See Hitler cited in Theodor W. Adorno, Else Frenkel-Brunswik,

Daniel J. Levinson, and R. Nevitt Sanford, *The Authoritarian Personality* (New York: Verso, 2019 [1950]), 733.

16. Philip Bump, "A New Peak in Trump's Efforts to Foster Misinformation," *Washington Post*, July 25, 2018, https://www.washingtonpost.com/news/politics/wp/2018/07/25/a-new-peak-in-trumps-efforts-to-foster-misinformation/.

Chapter 1. Violence and the Militarization of Politics

1. David Smith, "US Under Siege from 'Far-Left Fascism,' says Trump in Mount Rushmore Speech," *Guardian*, July 4, 2020, https://www.theguardian.com/us-news/2020/jul/04/us-under-siege-from-far-left-fascism-says-trump-in-mount-rushmore-speech.

2. The history of fascist violence belongs to a broader field that researches its practical and symbolical dimensions. As Pablo Piccato explains, violence is a serious matter of historical research and cannot be essentialized. By studying the causes and effects of violence, historians address not only the key dimensions of violence's material and communicative effects but also the history of its conceptualizations over time. See Pablo Piccato, *Historia mínima de la violencia en México* (Mexico: El Colegio de México, 2022), 16. See also Hannah Arendt, *On Violence* (New York: Harcourt, 1970). Benjamin Brower explains, à propos Arendt's approach to violence, that "violence reveals itself best in its local and contingent dimensions. Every assassination, riot, lynching, battle, mass killing, strike or famine carries within itself an overdetermined set of causes. The same holds true for occasions of violence occurring outside of the event, the violence of pollution, poverty, hunger and illness. The historian pulling a fine-toothed comb through the sources best grasps each instance's specific logic as well as how it is embedded in otherwise invisible economic systems and social structures." Benjamin Brower, "Genealogies of Modern Violence, Arendt and Imperialism in Africa, 1830–1914," in *The Cambridge History of Violence*, ed. Louise Edwards, Nigel Penn, and Jay Winter (Cambridge: Cambridge University Press, 2020), 4:246. On violence, see also Étienne Balibar, "Outlines of a Topography of Cruelty: Citizenship and Civility in the Era of Global Violence," *Constellations* 8, no. 1 (2001): 15–29; Étienne Balibar, *Violence and Civility* (New York: Columbia University Press, 2015); Gema Kloppe-Santamaría, *In the Vortex of Violence: Lynching, Extralegal Justice, and the State*

in *Post-Revolutionary Mexico* (Oakland: University of California Press, 2020); and Philip Dwyer, *Violence: A Very Short Introduction* (New York: Oxford University Press, 2022).

3. Yitzhak Arad, Yisrael Gutman, and Abraham Margaliot, eds., *Documents on the Holocaust* (Lincoln: University of Nebraska Press, 1999), 134.

4. Smith, "US Under Siege from 'Far-Left Fascism.'"

5. See Arad, Gutman, and Margaliot, *Documents on the Holocaust*, 134.

6. Adolf Hitler, *Mein Kampf* (New York: Mariner, 1999), 357–58, 172.

7. "Io ho fatto l'apologia della violenza per quasi tutta la mia vita." See Benito Mussolini, "Il discorso dell'Ascensione," in *Opera omnia*, ed. Edoardo Susmel and Duilio Susmel (Florence: La Fenice, 1951–1962), 22:381.

8. Federico Finchelstein, *From Fascism to Populism in History* (Oakland: University of California Press, 2017), 78.

9. Paul Corner, *The Fascist Party and Popular Opinion in Mussolini's Italy* (New York: Oxford University Press, 2012), 69.

10. Plínio Salgado, *Palavra nova dos tempos novos* (Rio de Janeiro: Olympio, 1936), 99.

11. See Phillips Talbot, "The Khaksar Movement," *Indian Journal of Social Work* 2, no.2 (1941): 187.

12. Pablo Antonio Cuadra, *Breviario imperial* (Madrid: Cultura Española, 1940), 73.

13. See Benito Mussolini, "Discorso di Udine," in *Opera omnia*, ed. Edoardo Susmel and Duilio Susmel (Florence: La Fenice, 1951–1962), 18:411–19.

14. Corner, *The Fascist Party*, 69.

15. The precedents for fascist ideas are to be found in the tradition of the anti-Enlightenment, namely, a total revision of the key principles of democracy, reason, and political liberalism. For the great historian of fascism Zeev Sternhell, fascism always had two essential components: (1) a brand of anti-liberal and anti-bourgeois tribal nationalism based on social Darwinism and, often, biological determinism; and (2) a radical, formerly leftist, anti-materialist revision of Marxism. Thus, fascism combined anti-rationalist thinkers like the French Catholic chauvinist Charles Maurras and Georges Sorel—a leftist anti-Marxist philosopher who proposed myth and violence as a road map for revolutionary politics—and reformulated nationalist and social themes in an extreme right-wing form. Fascism had an alternative vision of the world, which was politically and morally different from other ideologies. See Zeev Sternhell, *The*

Birth of Fascist Ideology: From Cultural Rebellion to Political Revolution, with Mario Sznajder and Maia Asheri (Princeton, NJ: Princeton University Press, 1994); and Zeev Sternhell, *Neither Right nor Left: Fascist Ideology in France* (Berkeley: University of California Press, 1986).

16. As historian Robert Paxton explained, the cycles of fascism had five stages: (1) the founding of movements, (2) their political expansion, (3) the fascist seizure of power, (4) fascism as a ruling power, and (5) "finally, the long duration, during which the fascist regime chooses either radicalization or entropy." As Paxton argued, "Though each stage is a prerequisite for the next, nothing requires a fascist movement to complete all of them, or even to move in only one direction. Most fascisms stopped short, some slipped back, and sometimes features of several stages remained operative at once. Whereas most modern societies spawned fascist movements in the twentieth century, only a few had fascist regimes. Only in Nazi Germany did a fascist regime approach the outer horizons of radicalization." Violence was at the center of this radicalization. As Paxton explains, "Fascist violence was neither random nor indiscriminate. It carried a well-calculated set of coded messages: that communist violence was rising, that the democratic state was responding to it ineptly, and that only the fascists were tough enough to save the nation from antinational terrorists. An essential step in the fascist march to acceptance and power was to persuade law-and-order conservatives and members of the middle class to tolerate fascist violence as a harsh necessity in the face of Left provocation. It helped, of course, that many ordinary citizens never feared fascist violence against themselves, because they were reassured that it was reserved for national enemies and 'terrorists' who deserved it." As Paxton put it, "The legitimation of violence against a demonized internal enemy brings us close to the heart of fascism." Robert Paxton, *The Anatomy of Fascism* (New York: Vintage, 2005), 23, 84.

17. Norberto Bobbio, *Dal fascismo alla democrazia* (Milan: Baldini Castoldi, 1997), 40.

18. See Hannah Arendt, *The Origins of Totalitarianism* (New York: Meridian, 1959), 468. On ideology, see Zeev Sternhell, "How to Think about Fascism and Its Ideology," *Constellations* 15, no. 3 (2008): 280-90; and Jason Stanley, *How Propaganda Works* (Princeton, NJ: Princeton University Press, 2015), 178-22.

19. Finchelstein, *From Fascism to Populism in History*, 17.

20. See Mussolini, "Discorso di Udine," 411-19.

21. M.S. Golwalkar, *We or Our Nationhood Defined* (Nagpur, India: Bharat, 1939), 53. Like Golwalkar, the Indo-Muslim fascist leader Mashriqi in Punjab admired the violent example of Nazism, but he also argued that his own fascism was more legitimate because it was both sacred and a source of inspiration for Nazism. See Markus Daechsel, "Scientism and Its Discontents: The Indo-Muslim 'Fascism' of Inayatullah Khan al-Mashriqi," *Modern Intellectual History* 3, no. 3 (2006): 452–53. See also Talbot, "The Khaksar Movement," 189–90. On Indian fascism, see the key works by Benjamin Zachariah: "At the Fuzzy Edges of Fascism: Framing the Volk in India," *South Asia: Journal of South Asian Studies*, 38, no. 4 (2015): 639–55; and "A Voluntary Gleichschaltung? Indian Perspectives towards a Non-Eurocentric Understanding of Fascism," *Transcultural Studies* 2 (2014): 63–100.

22. See the General Jewish Council, *Father Coughlin: His "Facts" and Arguments* (New York: General Jewish Council, 1939), 7, 49; and Albin Krebs, "Charles Coughlin, 30's 'Radio Priest,'" *New York Times*, October 28, 1979, https://www.nytimes.com/1979/10/28/archives/charles-coughlin-30s-radio-priest-dies-fiery-sermons-stirred-furor.html. On American fascism, see Sarah Churchwell, *Behold America: The Entangled History of "America First" and "the American Dream"* (New York: Basic Books, 2018), and her "The Return of American Fascism," *New Statesman*, September 2, 2020, https://www.newstatesman.com/long-reads/2020/09/return-american-fascism; and Richard Steigmann-Gall, "Star-Spangled Fascism: American Interwar Political Extremism in Comparative Perspective," *Social History* 42, no. 1 (2017): 94–119.

23. See Virgilio Filippo, "Quiénes tienen las manos limpias?," in *Estudios sociológicos* (Buenos Aires: Tor, 1939), 92–93, 136. These arguments regarding God and political enemies would later be presented in a shocking exchange between the wife of a Supreme Court justice of the United States and Trump's cabinet chief. Violence was needed in the battle between God and Evil during the coup attempt of January 6, 2021. Meadows texted, "Evil always looks like the victor until the King of Kings triumphs. . . . Do not grow weary." Greg Sargent, "'Morning Joe' Shock over Ginni Thomas Points to a Hidden Jan. 6 Truth," *Washington Post*, March 25, 2022, shttps://www.washingtonpost.com/opinions/2022/03/25/joe-scarborough-ginni-thomas-mark-meadows-texts.

24. Mussolini, "Il discorso dell'Ascensione," 381–82.

25. See Dominick LaCapra, *History and Memory after Auschwitz* (Ithaca, NY: Cornell University Press, 1998), 27-30, and *Writing History, Writing Trauma* (Baltimore: Johns Hopkins University Press, 2001),166-69.

26. See document 161 in Arad, Gutman, and Margaliot, *Documents on the Holocaust*, 344.

27. See document 161 in Arad, Gutman, and Margaliot, 344.

28. Document 161 in Arad, Gutman, and Margaliot, 344-45. For an analysis of Nazi "morality," see Claudia Koonz, *The Nazi Conscience* (Cambridge, MA: Harvard University Press, 2003).

29. Benito Mussolini, "La violenza è immorale quando è fredda e calcolata, non già quando è istintiva e impulsiva," in *Opera omnia*, ed. Edoardo Susmel and Duilio Susmel (Florence: La Fenice, 1951-1962), 12:7. See also Curzio Malaparte, *Kaputt* (New York: New York Review Books, 2005), 266.

30. The SS leader argued, "It's good that we were tough enough to exterminate the Jews in our area." Himmler, as cited in Peter Longerich, *Heinrich Himmler: A Life* (New York: Oxford University Press, 2012), 695.

31. See Benito Mussolini, "Popolo italiano! Corri alle armi," in *Opera omnia*, ed. Edoardo Susmel and Duilio Susmel (Florence: La Fenice, 1951-1962), 29:404.

32. Hitler, *Mein Kampf*, 454-55.

33. Hitler, *Mein Kampf*, 455. As Sternhell argued, "The brutality of a regime is certainly not a criterion for judging its fascist character: what is important is the ideology, the vision of man and society, the aims a movement sets itself and what is commonly known as its philosophy of history. Fascism, in Italy like in other countries, including France, had a vision of society: it fought the heritage of the Enlightenment, democracy and the intellectual (though not the economic) content of liberalism." Zeev Sternhell, "How to Think about Fascism," 283.

34. On Marx and violence, see Hannah Arendt, *Essays in Understanding, 1930-1954* (New York: Harcourt Brace, 1994), 375, and her *Origins of Totalitarianism*. Mao said, "Power grows out of the barrel of a gun," cited in Arendt, *On Violence*, 11.

35. Bobbio, *Dal fascismo alla democrazia*, 39-40, 50; and Norberto Bobbio, *De senectute e altri scritti autobiografici* (Turin, Italy: Einaudi, 1996), 157-58. Hannah Arendt similarly believed that real, legitimate power cannot be

achieved with radical violence and this is why democracy is the best option against violence. See Arendt, *On Violence*.

36. To be sure, historians like Paxton downplayed the centrality of ideas that trigger fascist action, but these actions, and especially violence, cannot be easily separated.

37. See Benito Mussolini, "La dottrina del fascismo," in *Opera omnia*, ed. Edoardo Susmel and Duilio Susmel (Florence: La Fenice, 1951–1962), 34:119–21.

38. Mussolini, as cited in Giulia Albanese, *The March on Rome: Violence and the Rise of Italian Fascism* (New York: Routledge, 2019), 41.

39. Enzo Traverso, *The Origins of Nazi Violence* (New York: New Press, 2003), 93.

40. See Isabel V. Hull, *Absolute Destruction: Military Culture and the Practices of War in Imperial Germany* (Ithaca, NY: Cornell University Press, 2005), 135.

41. Sven Reichardt, "Fascism's Stages: Imperial Violence, Entanglement, and Processualization," *Journal of the History of Ideas* 82, no. 1 (2021): 86; Mark Mazower, *Hitler's Empire: How the Nazis Ruled Europe* (Penguin: New York, 2009); and Shelley Baranowski, *Nazi Empire: German Colonialism and Imperialism from Bismarck to Hitler* (New York: Cambridge University Press, 2010).

42. Arendt, *Origins of Totalitarianism*, 137, 331.

43. Traverso, *Origins of Nazi Violence*, 93. This is what historian Angelo Ventrone called the "totalitarian seduction" of fascism. See Angelo Ventrone, *La seduzione totalitaria* (Rome: Donzelli, 2003).

44. Sven Reichardt, *Camicie nere, camicie brune* (Bologna: Il Mulino, 2009); and George L. Mosse, *Fallen Soldiers: Reshaping the Memory of the World Wars* (New York: Oxford University Press, 1990).

45. Walter Benjamin, "The Work of Art in the Age of Mechanical Reproduction," in *Illuminations*, ed. Hannah Arendt (New York: Schocken, 1969), 241. On Benjamin's notions of fascism, see also Walter Benjamin, "Theories of German Fascism," *New German Critique* 17 (1979): 120–28. On this topic, see also Simonetta Falasca-Zamponi, "Fascism and Aesthetics," *Constellations* 15, no. 3 (2008): 351–65; and Mabel Berezin, *Making the Fascist Self: The Political Culture of Interwar Italy* (Ithaca, NY: Cornell University Press, 1997).

46. "Militarization thus became, in fascism, a redefinition of the citizen's identity—a sharp antithesis to the bourgeois civilization, which had developed

on the basis of the differentiation between the civilian and military dimensions." See Emilio Gentile, "A Provisional Dwelling: The Origin and Development of the Concept of Fascism in Mosse's Historiography," in *What History Tells: George L. Mosse and the Culture of Modern Europe*, ed. Stanley G. Payne, David J. Sorkin, and John S. Tortorice (Madison: University of Wisconsin Press, 2004), 102-3.

47. As Arendt noted not without irony with respect to the Nazis, "Militaristic propaganda was more popular in postwar Germany than military training, and uniforms did not enhance the military value of paramilitary troops, though they were useful as a clear indication of the abolition of civilian standards and morals; somehow these uniforms eased considerably the consciences of the murderers and also made them even more receptive to unquestioning obedience and unquestioned authority." Arendt, *Origins of Totalitarianism*, 370.

48. Daechsel, "Scientism and Its Discontents," 451.

49. The supreme leader stated, "The Khaksar movement has again after 1350 years reiterated the truth that the true fitting example of the Prophet of the True Islam—the original religion of God—means one and only one thing, viz., a soldierly life!" See Talbot, "The Khaksar Movement," 190-92, 195.

50. Finchelstein, *From Fascism to Populism in History*, 77-78.

51. "He is a perfect military man. The Khaksar commander is not a nominal commander. He is a military commander. The line of Khaksars is not a row of toys glittering in gay attire; it is the line of undaunted fearless soldiers." See Talbot, "The Khaksar Movement," 197. Members of Romanian fascism were called legionaries, as the leader Codreanu stated their attitude was martial and their "eyes do not lie." Violence was presented as intuitive and yet fully codified in a changing set of precepts, rules, or manuals. Corneliu Zelea Codreanu, *Manual del jefe* (Munich: Europa, 2004), 73.

52. As one Ukrainian fascist put it, their nationalism "attempts to cultivate a high spiritual level of uncritical thinking by awakening instincts, passion, hatred toward enemies, the most advanced rapacity, and by activating a vigorous elite that by means of violence and unscrupulous terror, 'with knife and blood,' will impose its will upon the masses." See Grzegorz Rossoliński-Liebe, "The Fascist Kernel of Ukrainian Genocidal Nationalism," *Carl Beck Papers in Russian and East European Studies*, no. 2402 (2015): 33.

53. I want to thank Gema Kloppe-Santamaria for her comments on this gendered dimension of fascist practice.

54. José Antonio Primo de Rivera, "Una bandera que se alza," *Acción Española*, November 1, 1933, 368.

55. These tribulations were as follows: (1) Religious sectarianism that was corrected because "in Khaksars there are no debates, only action." (2) Wearing uniforms corrected the "lack of equality. In Khaksars everyone wears one uniform and stands in one line." (3) The loss of the sense of obedience was corrected by accepting that "obedience is the essence of the Khaksars." (4) The lack of leadership ability was corrected by giving neighborhood leaders "dictatorial power." (5) The absence of public support for reforms was somehow solved because the Khaksars "give this support." (6) The lack of physical fitness was corrected because the "Khaksars build fitness." (7) Finally, the lack of firmness was corrected because "the Khaksars are instilling this in a nation that after many unsuccessful movements now . . . is overtaxed and infirm like an old man after a copulation." Cited in Talbot, "The Khaksar Movement," 190-92.

56. See Ernesto Giménez Caballero, *La nueva catolicidad: Teoría general sobre el fascismo en Europa* (Madrid: La Gazeta Literaria, 1933), 178. See also "Puntos de partida," *El fascio* 1 (1933): 3.

57. José Ortega y Gasset, "Sobre el fascismo," in *Obras completas: El espectador (1916-34)* (Madrid: Revista de Occidente, 1963), 2:502.

58. José Pemartín, "España como pensamiento," *Acción Española*, March 1937, 370.

59. See Benito Mussolini, "Disciplina assoluta!," in *Opera omnia*, ed. Edoardo Susmel and Duilio Susmel (Florence: La Fenice, 1951-1962), 18:392.

60. Salgado, *Palavra nova dos tempos novos*, 104-5.

61. Jorge González von Marées, *El mal de Chile (sus causas y sus remedios)* (Santiago: Talleres gráficos "Portales," 1940), 17. As historian Giulia Albanese demonstrated, "Violence constituted the cornerstone of fascist action." It was the outcome of a clear political project to seize power and bring about radical antidemocratic transformation of state institutions: "The aim was to acquire a kind of power that would not be subject—as was typically the case in those years—to constant limitation from political opponents, and especially the law. Fascist political violence was driven by a plan that, far from having been made necessary by particular historical circumstances, could have been thwarted. At the same time, this plan—both as a whole and with regard to the individual incidents it led to—cannot be regarded as exclusively or chiefly reactive in nature. The Fascist strategy to seize power and its main objectives clearly prove that

the opposite is the case." Albanese, *March on Rome*, xiii, 44. See also John Foot, *Blood and Power: The Rise and Fall of Italian Fascism* (London: Bloomsbury, 2022), 4.

62. Daechsel, "Scientism and Its Discontents," 466–71.

63. See Partha Chakrabartty's interview with Benjamin Zachariah, "India Has the Longest Running Fascist Movement in the World—the RSS," *The Wire*, January 22, 2020, https://thewire.in/politics/benjamin-zachariah-fascism-sangh-parivar.

64. Parvis Ghassem-Fachandi, *Pogrom in Gujarat: Hindu Nationalism and Anti-Muslim Violence in India* (Princeton, NJ: Princeton University Press, 2012), 4.

65. Finchelstein, *From Fascism to Populism in History*, 171.

66. Juan Domingo Perón, *Obras completas* (Buenos Aires: Docencia, 1998), 18:208.

67. Juan Domingo Perón, *Obras completas* (Buenos Aires: Docencia, 1998), 14:168. In contrast, as anti-fascist historian Gaetano Salvemini explained, fascists adopted the conviction that blind obedience to Mussolini was "essential to the existence of fascism." As he further explained, "Each Fascist owes unquestioning obedience to his superior. The new recruit takes the following oath: 'I swear to obey without discussion the orders of my duce and to serve the cause of the Fascist Revolution with all my power, if need be, with my blood.'" See Gaetano Salvemini, *The Origins of Fascism in Italy* (New York: Harper Torchbooks, 1973), 408, 410.

68. Getúlio Vargas, *Discursos: Janeiro-junho 1951* (Rio de Janeiro: Agência Nacional, 1951), 35.

69. José María Velasco Ibarra, *Meditaciones y luchas* (Quito: Lexigrama, 1974), 2:196.

70. See *Discurso de Eva Perón en el acto inaugural de la primera asamblea nacional del Movimiento Peronista Femenino* (Subsecretaría de Informaciones de la Presidencia de la Nación, 1949), 20, 29.

71. "Que ha cesado el traqueteo de las ametralladoras y el estallido de las bombas en una contienda criminal que provocó el ímpetu de voracidad conquistadora del nazi-fascismo, pero que fue posible por la miope y alcahueta actitud frente a Berlín y Roma asumida por los dirigentes de las decadentes democracias capitalistas de Occidente." See Rómulo Betancourt, *Selección de escritos políticos* (1929-1981) (Caracas: Fundación Rómulo Betancourt, 2006), 162.

72. "El fascismo por esta realidad de vitalismo biológico que es su fondo primordial, no solo no repudia la guerra, sino que ama la guerra, ennoblece la guerra y la acepta como uno de los constitutivos esenciales de la sociedad. ¿Por que? Porque si la vida es lucha y en la lucha debe vencer el fuerte sobre el débil, para lograr la raza superior, para que el hombre superior eleve a la especie por su superioridad misma, entonces la guerra, que es el momento culminante de esa depuración sociológica y biológica, no solo no es repulsiva, no solo no es repudiable, sino al contrario aconsejable como uno de los elementos de culminación para realizar ese fin biologico y sociológico que persigue el fascismo." See Jorge Eliécer Gaitán, *Los mejores discursos: 1919-1948*, ed. Jorge Villaveces (Bogota: Editorial Jorvi, 1968), 366, 480-81. He also implored the Lord, in his famous oration of 1948, to "prevent violence"; "we want the defense of human life, which is the least a people can ask for" (507). See also Jorge Eliécer Gaitán, *Discurso-programa del Doctor Jorge Eliécer Gaitán en la proclamación de su candidatura a la presidencia de la República* (Bogota, 1945), 8.

73. See Enrique Pavón Pereyra, *Perón tal como fue/2* (Buenos Aires: CEAL, 1986), 201.

74. Getúlio Vargas, *A política trabalhista no Brasil* (Rio de Janeiro: Olympio, 1950), 30.

75. Finchelstein, *From Fascism to Populism in History*, 24.

76. See "Desde los balcones de la casa de gobierno despidiéndose de los trabajadores concentrados en la Plaza de Mayo: Octubre 17 de 1945," in Coronel Juan Perón, *El pueblo ya sabe de qué se trata: Discursos* (Buenos Aires, 1946), 186.

77. "No se vence con violencia: Se vence con inteligencia y organización." Perón, *Obras completas*, 18:208.

78. "Discurso pronunciado por el vicepresidente y Ministro de Guerra, Coronel Juan Perón en representación de las 'alas de la Patria,'" *Retaguardia*, July 8, 1945, 6.

79. "Florilegio del Sr. Presidente," *La vanguardia*, July 8, 1947.

80. "El último decálogo," *La vanguardia*, September 21, 1948, 2.

81. "El ultimo decálogo," 2.

82. Perón, *Obras completas*, 24:14. In fact, Perón accused the anti-populists of having adopted the "political tactic" of "terrorism and violence." Eugenio P. Rom, *Así hablaba Juan Perón* (Buenos Aires: A. Peña Lillo Editor, 1980), 127.

83. "Matar como a víboras," *La vanguardia*, July 8, 1947.

84. Finchelstein, *From Fascism to Populism in History*, 6, 24, 28.

85. As Arendt explained, "The artificial creation of civil-war conditions by which the Nazis blackmailed their way into power has more than the obvious advantage of stirring up trouble. For the movement, organized violence is the most efficient of the many protective walls which surround its fictitious world, whose 'reality' is proved when a member fears leaving the movement more than he fears the consequences of his complicity in illegal actions, and feels more secure as a member than as an opponent. This feeling of security, resulting from the organized violence with which the elite formations protect the party members from the outside world, is as important to the integrity of the fictitious world of the organization as the fear of its terror." See Arendt, *Origins of Totalitarianism*, 373.

86. See Paul Preston, *La Guerra Civil Española* (Madrid: Debate, 2017), 319, also 320-30. See also Francisco Espinosa Maestre, "La represión franquista: Un combate por la historia y la memoria," in *Violencia roja y azul: España, 1936-1950*, ed. Francisco Espinosa Maestre (Barcelona: Crítica, 2010); Francisco Sevillano Calero, *Exterminar: El terror con Franco* (Madrid: Oberon, 2004); Julián Casanova, ed., *Morir, matar, sobrevivir: La violencia en la dictadura de Franco* (Barcelona: Crítica, 2002); and Javier Muñoz Soro, José Luis Ledesma, and Javier Rodrigo, eds., *Culturas y políticas de la violencia España Siglo XX* (Madrid: Siete Mares, 2005). There is a debate among historians of the Spanish Civil War regarding the number of victims, but most agree that Franco's killings tripled those of the Republic. The justification of those killings in the name of the sacred and the leader put Franco in a fascist league of his own.

87. R. J. B. Bosworth explained that the fascist regime "at a minimal count, with its repressive policies at home and its aggressive wars in its empire and in Europe, must bear responsibility for the premature death of a million people." See R. J. B. Bosworth, *Mussolini's Italy: Life under the Fascist Dictatorship, 1915-1945* (New York: Penguin, 2007), 4.

88. See Raul Hilberg, *The Destruction of the European Jews* (New York: Holmes & Meier, 1985). See also Federico Finchelstein, "The Holocaust Canon: Rereading Raul Hilberg," *New German Critique*, no. 96 (Fall 2005): 3-48.

89. See Hilberg, *Destruction of the European Jews*.

90. On the notion of fascism as a "set of relations to politics," see Geoff Eley, *Nazism as Fascism: Violence, Ideology, and the Ground of Consent in Germany 1930-1945* (New York: Routledge, 2013), 214, and his "What Is Fascism

and Where Does It Come From?," *History Workshop Journal* 91, no. 1 (2021): 1–28.

91. Alex Ward, "US Park Police Denies Using Tear Gas on Peaceful Protesters: Evidence Suggests Otherwise," *Vox*, June 2, 2020, https://www.vox.com/2020/6/2/21278559/tear-gas-white-house-protest-park-police; and "Trump Campaign Statement on Media 'Tear Gas' Lie," American Presidency Project, June 2, 2020, https://www.presidency.ucsb.edu/documents/trump-campaign-statement-media-tear-gas-lie.

92. Lisa Lerer and Nicholas Fandos, "Already Distorting Jan. 6, G.O.P. Now Concocts Entire Counternarrative," *New York Times*, July 31, 2021, https://www.nytimes.com/2021/07/31/us/politics/jan-6-capitol-riot-pelosi.html.

93. "President Trump's Speech in AZ July 24, 2021," C-SPAN, July 26, 2021, video, 56:30, https://www.c-span.org/video/?c4971162/user-clip-president-trumps-speech-az-july-24-2021.

94. See the essays in João Roberto Martins Filho, ed., *Os militares e a crise brasileira, organizado* (São Paulo: Alameda, 2021), especially 9-10, 124, https://olavodecarvalho.org/sobre-a-violencia-e-as-armas.

95. "Bolsonaro lança programa para implementar escolas cívico-militares," *UOL*, September 5, 2019, https://educacao.uol.com.br/noticias/2019/09/05/bolsonaro-lanca-programa-para-implementar-escolas-civico-militares.htm.

96. Ciara Nugent and Billy Perrigo, "Facebook Owner Meta Is Failing to Prevent Repeat of Jan. 6 in Brazil, Report Warns," *Time*, September 5, 2022, https://time.com/6210985/brazil-facebook-whatsapp-election-disinformation.

97. Tom C. Avendaño, "Bolsonaro: Amenaza ultra en Brasil," *El país*, September 28, 2018, https://elpais.com/internacional/2018/09/28/actualidad/1538153452_095290.html.

98. Ghassem-Fachandi, *Pogrom in Gujarat*, 62, 64.

99. Ghassem-Fachandi, 32.

100. Ghassem-Fachandi, 64; and Martin Gilbert, *Kristallnacht: Prelude to Destruction* (London: Harper Perennial, 2007), 29.

101. Libby Cathey and Meghan Keneally, "A Look Back at Trump Comments Perceived by Some as Inciting Violence," *ABC News*, May 30, 2020, https://abcnews.go.com/Politics/back-trump-comments-perceived-encouraging-violence/story?id=48415766.

102. Christophe Jaffrelot, *Modi's India: Hindu Nationalism and the Rise of Ethnic Democracy* (Princeton, NJ: Princeton University Press, 2021), 446. As Jaffrelot explains, "The promotion of Hindu nationalism at the expense of secularism took the form of attacks against liberals (including NGOs, intellectuals, and universities like JNU) and the Saffronization of education. At the same time, minorities were subjected to both physical and symbolic violence by Hindu vigilante groups, which exerted a new form of cultural policing. These groups, usually under the umbrella of the Sangh Parivar, started to form a parallel state—with the tacit approval of the official state—as they launched one campaign after another, such as their fight against love jihad and land jihad, their attempts at reconverting those whose forefathers had embraced Islam or Christianity, and their attacks against people accused of slaughtering cows—a very emotional issue that was the root cause of a series of lynchings. Vigilantes were active not only in the street but also online, as evident from the psychological violence exerted by trolls—again with the blessings of the country's rulers."

103. Jaffrelot explains that Modi's Indian populism rose to hitherto unknown levels. See Jaffrelot, *Modi's India*, 148.

104. See Jaffrelot, 314.

105. See Jaffrelot, 451.

106. See Jaffrelot, 85.

107. Duterte buried the former dictator, Ferdinand Marcos, in the National Heroes Cemetery. See Walden Bello, "Rodrigo Duterte: A Fascist Original," in *A Duterte Reader: Critical Essays on Rodrigo Duterte's Early Presidency*, ed. Nicole Curato (Ithaca, NY: Cornell University Press, 2017), 80.

108. As de la Torre and Srisa-nga explain, "Duterte never ceased to flaunt his manhood which he believed was far superior to anyone else's. He talked favorably of rapes, harassment, his sex life, or even the size of his penis at public rallies. Recounting the story of his teenage years when he was living in Manila YMCA, he said his childhood friends frequently admired him for being extraordinarily 'highly-equipped' with his turgid penis 'that points all the way up' to his bellybutton. . . . At one time he revealed he had been gay but 'cured' himself and 'became a man again' after marrying his ex-wife. . . . He also boasted that his first sexual experience took place when he, as a teenager, violated his maid several times during her sleep." See Carlos de la Torre and Treethep Srisa-nga, *Global Populisms* (New York: Routledge, 2022), 82. On macho populism, see also Finchelstein, *From Fascism to Populism in History*, 240–45.

Duterte said, "When I become president, I'll order the police and the military to find (criminals and drug pushers) and kill them. . . . The funeral parlors will be packed. . . . I'll supply the dead bodies." Cited in Richard Javad Heydarian, *The Rise of Duterte: A Populist Revolt against Elite Democracy* (Singapore: Palgrave Macmillan, 2018), 94.

    109. Cited in de la Torre and Srisa-nga, *Global Populisms*, 82, 83. See also Javad Heydarian, *Rise of Duterte*, 32–33; and Bello, "Rodrigo Duterte: A Fascist Original," 78.

    110. Karen Lema and Manuel Mogato, "Philippines' Duterte Likens Himself to Hitler, Wants to Kill Millions of Drug Users," Reuters, October 1, 2016, http://www.reuters.com/article/us-philippines-duterte-hitler-idUSKCN1200B9.

    111. Conrado Hübner Mendes, "21 técnicas de matar em silencio," *Folha*, February 2, 2022, https://www1.folha.uol.com.br/colunas/conrado-hubner-mendes/2022/02/21-tecnicas-de-matar-em-silencio.shtml.

    112. See Federico Finchelstein and Jason Stanley, "A Covid Genocide in the Americas?," *Project Syndicate*, January 18, 2021, https://www.project-syndicate.org/commentary/trump-bolsonaro-covid-genocide-politically-motivated-neglect-by-federico-finchelstein-and-jason-stanley-2021-01?barrier=accesspaylog. Stanley sees underlying fascist elements in American history and stresses how they were strengthened under Trumpism: "There have been years of media attention to the disaster of the policies emerging from the 'tough on crime' movements of the 1970s, 1980s, and 1990s, resulting in large bipartisan support for shifting from punitive crime policies to social programs. However, what has not accompanied this shift is an awareness that the underlying motivations for the hard-on-crime rhetoric and policies were fascist, set up to establish an us-versus-them dichotomy and reinforce preexisting hierarchal stereotypes." Jason Stanley, *How Fascism Works* (New York: Random House, 2018), 179. On deportation, see Adam Goodman, *The Deportation Machine* (Princeton, NJ: Princeton University Press, 2020). See also the essays in Kathleen Belew and Ramon Gutiérrez, eds., *A Field Guide to White Supremacy* (Oakland: University of California Press, 2021).

Chapter 2. Fascist Lies and Propaganda

    1. Victor Klemperer, *I Shall Bear Witness: The Diaries of Victor Klemperer, 1933–41* (London: Weidenfeld & Nicolson, 1998), 13.

2. Klemperer, *I Shall Bear Witness*, 13-14. With respect to the intrinsic connection between violence and propaganda, Arendt noted, "Only when terror is intended to coerce not merely from without but, as it were, from within, when the political regime wants more than power, is terror in need of propaganda. In this sense the Nazi theorist, Eugen Hadamovsky, could say in *Propaganda und nationale Macht, 1933*: 'Propaganda and violence are never contradictions. Use of violence can be part of the propaganda.'" Hannah Arendt, *The Origins of Totalitarianism* (New York: Meridian, 1959), 341.

3. Victor Klemperer, *The Language of the Third Reich* (New York: Bloomsbury Academic, 2020), 92-93.

4. Wendell Husebø, "Trump: Democrats Spreading 'Disinformation' That GOP Defunded Police," *Breitbart*, July 3, 2021, https://www.breitbart.com/politics/2021/07/03/trump-democrats-spreading-disinformation-that-gop-defunded-police.

5. "Donald Trump: 'What You're Seeing and What You're Reading Is Not What's Happening,'" BBC News, July 25, 2018, https://www.bbc.com/news/av/world-us-canada-44959340.

6. Peter Longerich, *Goebbels: A Biography* (New York: Random House, 2015), 71.

7. Longerich, *Goebbels: A Biography*, 70-71, 145, 696.

8. Jason Stanley, *How Propaganda Works* (Princeton, NJ: Princeton University Press, 2015), 43, 57, 178.

9. Benito Mussolini, "Il dovere dell'Italia," in *Opera omnia*, ed. Edoardo Susmel and Duilio Susmel (Florence: La Fenice, 1951-1962), 7:98.

10. Longerich, *Goebbels: A Biography*, 510.

11. Klemperer, *Language of the Third Reich*, 15. "Was it the individual speeches of Hitler and Goebbels, their pronouncements on this or that theme, their rabble-rousing against the Jews, against Bolshevism? Certainly not, because a lot of this was not even understood by the masses, or it bored them in its endless repetitions. On many occasions in public houses, while I was still allowed to enter a public house without wearing a star, and later on many occasions in the factory during air raid protection duty—when the Aryans had their own room and the Jews theirs, and the radio was located in the Aryan room (along with the heating and the food)—on many occasions I heard the cards being slapped down noisily on the table, and loud discussions about the rationing of meat and tobacco and about the cinema, whilst the Führer or one of his

henchmen was carrying on interminably. And the next day the papers claimed that the entire population had been hanging on their every word." Klemperer, *Language of the Third Reich*, 15. On this topic, see also Mabel Berezin, "Cultural Form and Political Meaning: State-Subsidized Theater, Ideology, and the Language of Style in Fascist Italy," *American Journal of Sociology* 99, no. 5 (March 1994): 1237–86.

12. Stephen Collinson, "Trump Seeks a 'Miracle' as Virus Fears Mount," *CNN*, February 28, 2020, https://www.cnn.com/2020/02/28/politics/donald-trump-coronavirus-miracle-stock-markets/index.html; and Philip Bump, "Most Americans Agree with Measures to Fight the Pandemic That Trump Claims 'Real People' Want to See End," *Washington Post*, March 25, 2020, https://www.washingtonpost.com/politics/2020/03/25/most-americans-agree-with-measures-fight-pandemic-that-trump-claims-real-people-want-see-end.

13. Greg Walters, "Trump's Judge Is Getting Threats, While Trump Calls NY Officials 'Perverts,'" *Vice News*, April 6, 2023, https://www.vice.com/en/article/qjvp9v/trump-calls-ny-officials-perverts-judge-merchan-gag-order.

14. Bess Levin, "Donald Trump Celebrates Mother's Day in the Most Donald Trump Way Possible," *Vanity Fair*, May 15, 2023, https://www.vanityfair.com/news/2023/05/donald-trump-melania-trump-mothers-day.

15. David Klepper, "Trump Arrest Prompts Jesus Comparisons: 'Spiritual Warfare,'" *AP News*, April 5, 2023, https://apnews.com/article/donald-trump-arraignment-jesus-christ-conspiracy-theory-670c45bd71b3466dcd6e8e-188badcd1d.

16. Arendt, *Origins of Totalitarianism*, 471.

17. Goebbels, as cited in Louis Lochner's "Introduction" to *The Goebbels Diaries*, ed. Louis P. Lochner (London: Hamish Hamilton, 1948), xxii.

18. Klemperer, *Language of the Third Reich*, 223–24.

19. Klemperer, 229.

20. Finchelstein, *Brief History of Fascist Lies*, 13.

21. Adolf Hitler, *Mein Kampf* (New York: Mariner, 1999), 232.

22. Stephen Collinson, "'Sore Loser' Trump Reaps Fruits of Election Lies in Arizona," CNN, July 25, 2021, https://www.cnn.com/2021/07/25/politics/donald-trump-arizona-audit-fraud-lies-election/index.html.

23. "Brazil's Bolsonaro Reaffirms Trump Ties, Cites Baseless Vote Fraud Claims," Reuters, January 6, 2021, https://www.reuters.com/article/us-usa

-election-brazil/brazils-bolsonaro-reaffirms-trump-ties-cites-baseless-vote-fraud-claims-idUSKBN29C01X. He reiterated these lies before meeting Biden in June of 2022: "The American people are the ones who talk about it (election fraud). . . . But Trump was doing really well." "Brazil's Bolsonaro Casts Doubt on Biden's 2020 Election Win Ahead of Meeting Him," Reuters, June 7, 2022, https://www.reuters.com/world/americas/brazils-bolsonaro-casts-doubt-bidens-2020-election-win-ahead-meeting-him-2022-06-07. I want to thank Javier Rodrigo for his suggestion of the idea of fascism as vocation.

24. Jack Nicas, Flávia Milhorance, and Ana Ionova, "How Bolsonaro Built the Myth of Stolen Elections in Brazil," *New York Times*, October 25, 2022, https://www.nytimes.com/interactive/2022/10/25/world/americas/brazil-bolsonaro-misinformation.html.

25. "Bolsonaro Says He Will Be Arrested, Killed or Declared Winner," Reuters, August 28, 2021, https://www.reuters.com/world/americas/bolsonaro-says-he-will-be-arrested-killed-or-declared-winner-2021-08-28.

26. "'Fake news faz parte da nossa vida,' diz Bolsonaro em defesa da alteração do Marco Civil," *Diario do nordeste*, September 15, 2021, https://diariodonordeste.verdesmares.com.br/pontopoder/fake-news-faz-parte-da-nossa-vida-diz-bolsonaro-em-defesa-da-alteracao-do-marco-civil-video-1.3136209.

27. Pablo Antonio Cuadra, *Breviario imperial* (Madrid: Cultura Española, 1940), 150.

28. Hitler, *Mein Kampf*, 242.

29. Richard J. Evans, "Whiter Washing," *London Review of Books*, June 6, 2019, https://www.lrb.co.uk/the-paper/v41/n11/richard-j.-evans/whiter-washing.

30. Hans V. Kaltenborn and Adolf Hitler, "An Interview with Hitler, August 17, 1932," in "Unpublished Documents on Nazi Germany from the Mass Communications History Center," *Wisconsin Magazine of History* 50, no. 4 (Summer 1967): 283–90.

31. Kaltenborn and Hitler, "An Interview with Hitler," 283–90.

32. J. M. Espigares Moreno, *Lo que me dijo el Gral. Uriburu* (Buenos Aires: Durruty y Kaplan, 1933), 54.

33. Emil Ludwig, *Colloqui con Mussolini* (Verona: Mondadori, 1932), 73–75.

34. Simon Levis Sullam, *I carnefici Italiani: Scene dal genocidio degli ebrei, 1943-1945* (Milan: Feltrinelli, 2015).

35. John Wagner, "Trump Abruptly Ends NPR Interview after He Is Pressed on Baseless Election Fraud Claims," *Washington Post*, January 12, 2022, https://www.washingtonpost.com/politics/trump-npr-interview/2022/01/12/a2d0a26e-7397-11ec-bc13-18891499c514_story.html.

36. M. S. Golwalkar, *We or Our Nationhood Defined* (Nagpur, India: Bharat, 1939), 120–21.

37. Ruth Ben-Ghiat, "Response to Matteo Millan: Mapping Squadrist Violence," *Contemporary European History* 22, no. 4 (November 2013): 579–83.

38. See Jason Stanley, *How Fascism Works* (New York: Random House, 2018), 3–6.

39. On Burmese fascism, see Matthew J. Bowser, "'Buddhism Has Been Insulted. Take Immediate Steps': Burmese Fascism and the Origins of Burmese Islamophobia, 1936–38," *Modern Asian Studies* 55, no. 4 (2021): 1112–50.

40. Dan Mangan, "'MAGA Bomber' Cesar Sayoc Sentenced to 20 Years in Prison for Trying to Kill Trump Critics, Including Obama, Clinton, Biden, Booker, Harris," CNBC, August 5, 2019, https://www.cnbc.com/2019/08/05/cesar-sayoc-sentenced-to-20-years-for-sending-bombs-to-trump-critics.html.

41. Federico Finchelstein, *From Fascism to Populism in History* (Oakland: University of California Press, 2017), 17. On fascism as political religion, see Mabel Berezin, *Making the Fascist Self: The Political Culture of Interwar Italy* (Ithaca, NY: Cornell University Press, 1997), 50; George L. Mosse, *The Nationalization of the Masses: Political Symbolism and Mass Movements in Germany from the Napoleonic Wars through the Third Reich* (Ithaca, NY: Cornell University Press, 1991); Emilio Gentile, *The Sacralization of Politics in Fascist Italy* (Cambridge, MA: Harvard University Press, 1996); and Richard Steigman-Gall, *The Holy Reich: Nazi Conceptions of Christianity, 1919–1945* (Cambridge: Cambridge University Press, 2003).

42. Hans Frank, cited in Hannah Arendt, *Eichmann in Jerusalem* (New York: Viking Press, 1965), 136.

43. "Abascal amenaza con 'animar' a sus simpatizantes a defenderse de las agresiones," *La vanguardia*, April 22, 2021, https://www.lavanguardia.com/politica/20210422/6990811/abascal-simpatizantes-agresiones-campana.html.

44. Juan Domingo Perón, *Conferencia pronunciada en el acto de clausura del Primer Congreso Nacional de Filosofía, Mendoza, 9 de abril de 1949* (Buenos Aires: Subsecretaria de Informaciones de la Presidencia de la Nación, 1949).

45. Siegfried Kracauer, *Selected Writings on Media, Propaganda, and Political Communication*, ed. Jaeho Kang, Graeme Gilloch, and John Abromeit (New York: Columbia University Press, 2022), 52. See also John Foot, *Blood and Power: The Rise and Fall of Italian Fascism* (London: Bloomsbury, 2022), 4.

46. Thus, despite the growing allegations about his misconduct as president and as a coup instigator, former president Trump remains idolized by many of his supporters and continues to be enabled by most members of the GOP. His rallies featured fans whose devotion is unwavering. A participant of those rallies, Ashli Babbit, wrote in her last tweet, "Nothing will stop us . . . they can try and try and try but the storm is here and it is descending upon DC in less than 24 hours . . . dark to light!" As her mother explained, her daughter "felt strongly enough about him to lay down her life for him and, in death, I believe she loves him still. I know she loves him still." In turn, Trump presented Babbit as "an innocent, wonderful, incredible woman, a military woman" and said her shooting was "a terrible thing." Trump reduced her demise to a ritual question he regularly asked, "Who shot Ashli Babbitt? We all saw the hand. We saw the gun. . . . You know, if that were on the other side, the person that did the shooting would be strung up and hung. Okay? Now, they don't want to give the name. . . . It's a terrible thing, right? Shot. Boom. And it's a terrible thing." But this was not a real question but a part of a new catechism with only faith-based answers. Thus, for leaders and followers, the answer is not empirical but mythical. Babbitt's death is the result of the actions of dark, evil forces that don't want to be named. Trump's propaganda version of "Who Framed Who" has clear fascist undertones precisely because in fascism violence and repression, and their fake memories, are presented as the way to create transcendental changes in the history of humanity. Wajahat Ali, "Why Trump Is Anointing Ashli Babbitt as MAGA's First Martyr," *Daily Beast*, July 8, 2021, https://www.thedailybeast.com/why-trump-is-anointing-ashli-babbitt-as-magas-first-martyr; Daniel Trotta, Gabriella Borter, and Jonathan Allen, "Woman Killed in Siege of U.S. Capitol Was Veteran Who Embraced Conspiracy Theories," Reuters, January 7, 2021, https://www.reuters.com/article/uk-usa-election-death-idUKKBN29C2NX; and Paul Schwartzman and Josh Dawsey, "How Ashli Babbitt Went from Capitol Rioter to Trump-Embraced Martyr," *Washington Post*, July 30, 2021, https://www.washingtonpost.com/dc-md-va/2021/07/30/ashli-babbitt-trump-capitol-martyr.

47. Melissa Fares and Gina Cherelus, "Trump Loves 'the Poorly Educated' . . . and Social Media Clamors," Reuters, February 24, 2016, https://www

.reuters.com/article/us-usa-election-trump-socialmedia/trump-loves-the-poorly-educated-and-social-media-clamors-idUSKCN0VX26B; and Maggie Haberman and Eileen Sullivan, "After Trump Body Shames Him, Supporter Says 'I Love the Guy,'" *New York Times*, August 16, 2019, https://www.nytimes.com/2019/08/16/us/politics/trump-fat-shames-frank-dawson.html. Trump counts among his fans not only voters but also fellow world leaders. Jair Bolsonaro, the Brazilian president, also explicitly told Trump "I love you" when they met at the United Nations. Lauro Jardim, "Bolsonaro para Trump: 'I Love You,'" https://blogs.oglobo.globo.com/lauro-jardim/post/bolsonaro-para-trump-i-love-you.html.

48. See Longerich, *Goebbels: A Biography*, 68.

49. On Nazism and its use of Christian symbols and language, see Ian Kershaw, *The "Hitler Myth": Image and Reality in the Third Reich* (Oxford: Oxford University Press, 1987). See also Steigmann-Gall, *The Holy Reich*.

50. Benito Mussolini, *Scritti e discorsi di Benito Mussolini* (Milan: Hoepli, 1934), 5:322; and Claudia Koonz, *Mothers in the Fatherland: Women, the Family, and Nazi Politics* (New York: St. Martin's Press, 1987), 268.

51. Hitler, *Mein Kampf*, 65.

52. In the face of controversial actions, such as Bolsonaro accusing Afro-Brazilians of being fat and lazy and defending the physical punishment of children to prevent them from being gay, Bolsonaro's most fanatic supporters believe that, as the Brazilian leader said, he is fulfilling "God's mission." He is casting himself as an epic hero, a Christian warrior of patriotism and family values who must never be questioned. Javier Lafuente and Felipe Betim, "Bolsonaro: 'Esta misión de Dios no se escoge, se cumple,'" *El país*, October 29, 2018, https://elpais.com/internacional/2018/10/29/america/1540772967_083447.html. Sociologist Mabel Berezin stresses the fascist celebration of feelings and emotions as a celebration of the nonrational. See Berezin, *Making the Fascist Self*, 29.

53. Maggie Haberman and Shane Goldmacher, "Trump, Vowing 'Retribution,' Foretells a Second Term of Spite," *New York Times*, March 7, 2023, https://www.nytimes.com/2023/03/07/us/politics/trump-2024-president.html.

54. Carl Hoffman, *Liar's Circus: A Strange and Terrifying Journey into the Upside Down World of Trump's MAGA Rallies* (New York: Custom House, 2020), 45.

55. Hoffman, *Liar's Circus*, 45.

56. Hitler, *Mein Kampf*, 351.

57. Gustavo Barroso, *Integralismo e catolicismo* (Rio de Janeiro: ABC, 1937), 5, and his *O integralismo em marcha* (Rio de Janeiro: Schmidt, 1933), 112.

58. Hitler, *Mein Kampf*, 349–51.

59. Hitler, 680.

60. Benito Mussolini, *Diuturna* (Milan: Imperia, 1924), 253.

61. Benito Mussolini, *Opera omnia*, ed. Edoardo Susmel and Duilio Susmel (Florence: La Fenice, 1951–1962), 18:84.

62. Golwalkar, *We or Our Nationhood Defined*, 53.

63. Leopoldo Lugones, *Acción: Las cuatro conferencias patrióticas del Coliseo* (Buenos Aires: Círculo Tradición Argentina, 1923), 25. Already in 1916, Lugones had talked about three key wars that created the country: "La guerra de la independencia que nos emancipó; la guerra civil que nos constituyó; la guerra con los indios que suprimió la barbarie en la totalidad del territorio." Leopoldo Lugones, *El payador* (Buenos Aires: Otero, 1916), 71.

64. "Los propios marxistas no quieren, por lo demás, abolir la guerra internacional, sino transformarla en guerra civil. Este es el objeto mismo de su propaganda. Y si se recuerda todavía que, para ellos, 'el pacifismo es un prejuicio.'" See Leopoldo Lugones, *La patria fuerte* (Buenos Aires: Circulo Militar-Biblioteca del Oficial, 1930), 88. Lugones also warned that the "extranjerismo es la peor debilidad, no sólo porque constituye un estado de alma indiferente, cuando no hostil a la Nación—el estado de guerra civil que preconiza el comunismo—sino porque alberga al enemigo mas pernicioso en la persona del huesped disconforme o agitador." Leopoldo Lugones, *Política revolucionaria* (Buenos Aires: Anaconda, 1931), 57.

65. See Plínio Salgado, *O doutrina do sigma* (Rio de Janeiro: Schmidt, 1937), 118, 120. Barroso similarly argued that liberalism and socialism produced civil wars. Barroso, *O integralismo em marcha*, 75, 76.

66. Christophe Jaffrelot, *Modi's India: Hindu Nationalism and the Rise of Ethnic Democracy* (Princeton, NJ: Princeton University Press, 2021), 111, 393.

67. All quotations are from Ken Bensinger and Sheera Frenkel, "After Mar-a-Lago Search, Talk of 'Civil War' Is Flaring Online," *New York Times*, October 5, 2022, https://www.nytimes.com/2022/10/05/us/politics/civil-war-social-media-trump.html.

68. Kiko Nogueira, "Sou a favor da tortura. Através do voto, você não muda nada no país. Tem que matar 30 mil," *Diario do centro do mundo*, October 5, 2017, https://www.diariodocentrodomundo.com.br/video-sou-favor-da-tortura-atraves-do-voto-voce-nao-muda-nada-no-pais-tem-que-matar-30-mil-diz-bolsonaro/.

69. Juan Domingo Perón, "Aspiramos a una sociedad sin divisiones de clase: En el Cine Park, 12 de agosto de 1944," in Juan Perón, *El pueblo quiere saber de qué se trata* (Buenos Aires, 1944), 149.

70. "Transcript: Donald Trump's Speech Responding to Assault Accusations," NPR, October 13, 2016, https://www.npr.org/2016/10/13/497857068/transcript-donald-trumps-speech-responding-to-assault-accusations.

71. "President Donald J. Trump Is Protecting America's Founding Ideals by Promoting Patriotic Education," White House, November 2, 2020, https://trumpwhitehouse.archives.gov/briefings-statements/president-donald-j-trump-protecting-americas-founding-ideals-promoting-patriotic-education/.

72. "Proclamation on Columbus Day, 2020," White House, October 9, 2020, https://trumpwhitehouse.archives.gov/presidential-actions/proclamation-columbus-day-2020/.

73. Maximiliano Fuentes Codera and Federico Finchelstein, "Defensores de un pasado fantástico," *El país*, November 18, 2021, https://elpais.com/opinion/2021-11-19/defensores-de-un-pasado-fantastico.html. Similarly, Argentine "mini-Trump" Javier Milei claimed that state violence during the 1970s, although excessive, was justified and its effects saved the country from a communist dictatorship. He repeated the arguments of the dictators and the ideology of fascism in Argentina. To minimize the systematic murder, torture, and rape of thousands; the kidnapping, retention, and commercialization of babies and children of the disappeared; and the construction of a clandestine network of concentration camps and call it "excessive action" is at best ignorant, and at worst a cover-up. It is the same logic of Trump in the United States and Bolsonaro in Brazil. See my article with sociologist Emmanuel Guerisoli, "A propaganda golpista volta à campanha eleitoral na Argentina," *Folha d. Sao Paulo*, September 26, 2023, https://www1.folha.uol.com.br/colunas/latinoamerica21/2023/09/a-propaganda-golpista-volta-a-campanha-eleitoral-na-argentina.shtml. On Milei as mini-Trump, see my interview with the *New York Times*: Jack Nicas, "Javier Milei, a 'Mini-Trump,' Could Be

Argentina's Next President," *New York Times*, October 20, 2023, https://www.nytimes.com/2023/10/20/world/americas/javier-milei-argentina-election.html. See also my article, "Javier Milei Is the World's Latest Wannabe Fascist," *Foreign Policy*, December 9, 2022, https://foreignpolicy.com/2023/12/09/javier-milei-is-the-worlds-latest-wannabe-fascist/.

74. Benito Mussolini, "Dal malinconico tramonto liberale all'aurora fascista della nuova Italia," in *Opera omnia*, ed. Edoardo Susmel and Duilio Susmel (Florence: La Fenice, 1951–1962), 18:432–33.

75. Constantin Iordachi, "God's Chosen Warriors," in *Comparative Fascist Studies*, ed. Constantin Iordachi (London: Routledge, 2010), 345–47.

76. See Augusto Pinochet, *Chile enciende la llama de la libertad* (Santiago: Editora Nacional Gabriela Mistral, 1975), 65, 67.

77. See Carlos de la Torre and Treethep Srisa-nga, *Global Populisms* (London: Routledge, 2021), 35–36, 158–71. As de la Torre and Srisa-nga note, "The web and social media have, on the one hand, democratized communication. However, at the same time, they opened the door for the circulation of communication that does not pretend to be informed by facts or by the truth. Conspiracy theories and commentaries based on strong opinions that reinforce people's already held opinions circulate freely as information. The opening of communication channels away from the control of professionals favors populism that thrives in contexts where the voices of experts are devalued as the opinion of the establishment. Populists politicize communication as an antagonistic space where the elites and the people struggle to impose their version and narrative of the truth" (158). See also Paolo Gerbaudo, *The Digital Party* (London: Pluto Press, 2019); and Silvio Waisbord, "Why Populism Is Troubling for Democratic Communication," *Communication, Culture and Critique* 11, no. 1 (2018): 21–34.

78. Ruth Ben-Ghiat, *Strongmen: Mussolini to the Present* (New York: Norton, 2020), 117. Like the fascist leaders of the past, wannabe fascists infamously accuse others of the violence they create. For example, Trump argued in 2018 that "the Fake News is doing everything in their power to blame Republicans, Conservatives and me for the division and hatred that has been going on for so long in our Country." In his view, he wasn't the one who created unrest—journalists did. He wrote, "Actually, it is their Fake & Dishonest reporting which is causing problems far greater than they understand!" "Trump on

Twitter (October 28)—FBI, Democrats, Fake News," Reuters, October 28, 2018, https://www.reuters.com/article/us-usa-trump-tweet-factbox/trump-on-twitter-fbi-democrats-fake-news-idUSKCN1N306G.

79. Michael D. Shear, "Trump Asked Aide Why His Generals Couldn't Be Like Hitler's, Book Says," *New York Times*, August 8, 2022, https://www.nytimes.com/2022/08/08/us/politics/trump-book-mark-milley.html.

80. Rosie Gray, "Trump Defends White-Nationalist Protesters: 'Some Very Fine People on Both Sides,'" *The Atlantic*, August 15, 2017, https://www.theatlantic.com/politics/archive/2017/08/trump-defends-white-nationalist-protesters-some-very-fine-people-on-both-sides/537012.

81. Alex Solnik, "Bolsonaro preferia ser comparado a Hitler que a gay," (blog) September 5, 2018, https://www.brasil247.com/blog/bolsonaro-preferia-ser-comparado-a-hitler-que-a-gay.

82. Norman Tebbit, "A History Lesson for Those Who Would Smear the Moderate Right: The Nazis Were Socialists," *Telegraph*, September 24, 2018, https://www.telegraph.co.uk/politics/2018/09/24/history-lesson-would-smear-moderate-right-nazis-socialists.

83. As Ben-Ghiat argues, these distortions of the history of fascist violence aim to whitewash right-wing history. "We Need to Talk about Alex Jones," *CNN*, updated May 2, 2019, https://www.cnn.com/2018/08/06/opinions/infowars-opinion-roundup/index.html.

84. Infamously, Brazil's culture secretary, Roberto Alvim, made a Nazi speech when he announced the prize as music from a Wagner opera played in the background: "Brazilian art in the next decade will be heroic and national. . . . It will be endowed with a great capacity for emotional involvement and will be equally imperative, since it is deeply linked to the urgent aspirations of our people, or else it will be nothing." Goebbels, Hitler's notorious ideologue, told theater directors during the Nazi regime that "German art in the next decade will be heroic, steely but romantic, factual without sentimentality; it will be nationalistic with a great depth of feeling; it will be binding and it will unite, or it will cease to exist." Sam Cowie, "Brazil Culture Secretary Fired after Echoing Words of Nazi Goebbels," *Guardian*, January 17, 2020, https://www.theguardian.com/world/2020/jan/17/brazil-culture-minister-goebbels-roberto-alvim-nazi.

85. Kracauer, *Selected Writings on Media*, 52, 53.

86. Klemperer, *I Shall Bear Witness*, 136.

Chapter 3. The Politics of Xenophobia

1. "In ogni società—rispose serenamente Mussolini—c'è bisogno di una parte dei cittadini che deve essere odiata." Emil Ludwig, *Colloqui con Mussolini* (Verona: Mondadori, 1932), 129.

2. Adolf Hitler, *Mein Kampf* (New York: Mariner, 1999), 351.

3. Aimé Césaire, *Discourse on Colonialism* (New York: Monthly Review Press, 2000), 37.

4. See Federico Finchelstein, *Fascismo, liturgia e imaginario: El mito del general Uriburu y la Argentina nacionalista* (Buenos Aires: Fondo de Cultura Económica, 2002), 144.

5. Hitler, *Mein Kampf*, 351.

6. Victor Klemperer, *The Language of the Third Reich* (New York: Bloomsbury Academic, 2020), 185.

7. Leopoldo Lugones, *Acción: Las cuatro conferencias patrióticas del Coliseo* (Buenos Aires: Círculo Tradición Argentina, 1923), 26.

8. Jason Stanley, *How Fascism Works: The Politics of Us and Them* (New York: Random House, 2018), 24, 106.

9. Enrique Osés, *Cuando la patria grite: ¡Ahora yo!* (Buenos Aires: La Mazorca, 1940), 8.

10. "Proclamen que, ante esta criminal confabulación cipaya que nos quiere arrastrar a la guerra para servir a la demoplutocracia yanqui—judía de Wall Street, de Roosevelt y de Churchill, los argentinos decimos que no. Y mil veces no!" Enrique Osés, *Medios y fines del nacionalismo* (Buenos Aires: La Mazorca, 1941), 43. See also the anti-Semitic argument of Ernesto Palacio, "Enemigos del país," *Nuevo orden*, July 25, 1940, 1.

11. José Vasconcelos, "En defensa propia: Los protocolos de los sabios de Sión," *Timón*, May 25, 1940. Reprinted in Itzhak M. Bar-Lewaw, ed., *La revista "Timón" y José Vasconcelos* (Mexico City: Edimex, 1971), 146.

12. Hannah Arendt, *The Origins of Totalitarianism* (New York: Meridian, 1959), 469.

13. *Nurnberg Military Tribunals: Indictments* (Nuremberg: Office of Military Government for Germany [US], 1946–1948), 12:362, https://www.loc.gov/item/2011525463.

14. "Father Coughlin's Answer to Critics," *Social Justice*, April 20, 1942, 8.

15. Gustavo Franceschi, "El problema judío VI," *Criterio*, July 13, 1939, 245–50.

16. On this topic, see David S. Wyman, *The Abandonment of the Jews: America and the Holocaust, 1941-1945* (New York: Pantheon, 1984); and Daniel Lvovich and Federico Finchelstein, "L'Holocauste et l'Eglise Argentine: Perceptions et réactions," *Bulletin trimestriel de la Fondation Auschwitz*, no. 76-77 (2002): 9-30.

17. Gustavo Franceschi, "Como se prepara una revolución," *Criterio*, September 14, 1933, 30. See also his article "Antisemitismo," *Criterio*, December 7, 1933, 321.

18. Julio Meinvielle, *Los tres pueblos bíblicos en su lucha por la dominación del mundo* (Buenos Aires: Adsum, 1937), 7, 27, 49, 55, 62.

19. Gustavo Barroso, *O integralismo e o mundo* (Rio de Janeiro: Civilização Brasileira, 1936), 13-18.

20. "Razzismo italiano," *Difesa della razza*, August 5, 1938, 1, 2; and "I 10 punti del Razzismo Fascista," *Difesa della razza*, March 1942, 3.

21. James Q. Whitman, *Hitler's American Model: The United States and the Making of Nazi Race Law* (Princeton, NJ: Princeton University Press, 2017), 75, 110. As Whitman notes, the story is complicated by the fact that State Secretary Freisler replied to Möbius, "But the Americans put in their own laws even more explicitly!"

22. Matthew F. Delmont, *Half American: The Epic Story of African Americans Fighting World War II at Home and Abroad* (New York: Viking, 2022), xii.

23. Langston Hughes, as cited in Delmont, *Half American*, 4.

24. On global anti-fascism, see Joseph Fronczak, *Everything Is Possible: Antifascism and the Left in the Age of Fascism* (New Haven, CT: Yale University Press, 2023). See also Sandra Mcgee Deutsch, *Gendering Anti-fascism: Women Activism in Argentina and the World, 1918-1947* (Pittsburgh: University of Pittsburgh Press, 2023); and Kasper Braskén, Nigel Copsey, and David J. Featherstone, eds., *Anti-fascism in a Global Perspective: Transnational Networks, Exile Communities, and Radical Internationalism* (London: Routledge, 2020).

25. Alfredo L. Palacios, *El ideal de las democracias iberoamericanas* (La Plata, Argentina: Talleres Gráficos Olivieri y Domínguez, 1923), 30.

26. Despite few anti-Semitic moments, and unlike the majority of Argentine fascists, Lugones was actually against anti-Semitism, which he saw as an importation. His racial enemies were not the Jews but Indians, Blacks, and *mestizos*. See, for example, Leopoldo Lugones, *El imperio jesuítico* (Buenos Aires:

Compañía Sudamericana de billetes de Banco, 1904), 316. See also Leopoldo Lugones, *El estado equitativo (Ensayo sobre la realidad Argentina)* (Buenos Aires: La Editora Argentina, 1932), 31, 83. Like Lugones, Argentine fascist Ernesto Palacio insisted that modern Argentina did not include indigenous elements but was fully white. The idea that indigenous peoples had contributed to Argentine culture was, for Palacio, "an invention" of "scholars" in the cities. He said, "I repeat, this polemic invention was never truly felt by the Argentine people of the countryside, who knew the Indians before their extermination." Ernesto Palacio, *La historia falsificada* (Buenos Aires: Difusión, 1939), 63.

27. See Jorge González von Marées, *Pueblo y estado* (Santiago: Antares, 1936), 4. See also MNS, *El Movimiento Nacional Socialista de Chile—Declaraciones fundamentales: Plan de acción—organización—programa* (Santiago: Imprenta la Tracción, 1932), 21.

28. Maggie Clinton, *Revolutionary Nativism: Fascism and Culture in China, 1925-1937* (Durham, NC: Duke University Press, 2017), 111.

29. Israel Gershoni and James Jankowski, *Confronting Fascism in Egypt: Dictatorship versus Democracy in the 1930s* (Stanford, CA: Stanford University Press, 2009), 149. On Musa, and more generally on the issue of fascism in the Middle East, see also Peter Wien, *Arab Nationalism: The Politics of History and Culture in the Modern Middle East* (London: Routledge, 2017), 176-77.

30. Gershoni and Jankowski, *Confronting Fascism in Egypt*, 255.

31. "Not only that she complements her army to an ever increasing degree from her enormous empire's reservoir of colored humanity, but racially as well, she is making such great progress in negrification that we can actually speak of an African state arising on European soil. The colonial policy of present day France cannot be compared with that of Germany in the past. If the development of France in the present style were to be continued for three hundred years, the last remnants of Frankish blood would be submerged in the developing European African mulatto state. An immense self contained area of settlement from the Rhine to the Congo, filled with a lower race gradually produced from continuous bastardization." Hitler, *Mein Kampf*, 644.

32. Hitler, *Mein Kampf*, 624.

33. See Yosef Hayim Yerushalmi, *Assimilation and Racial Anti-Semitism: The Iberian and the German Models* (New York: Leo Baeck Institute, 1982).

34. Streicher, as cited in Hans Habe, "The Nazi Plan for Negroes," *The Nation*, March 1, 1941, 232.

35. Whitman, *Hitler's American Model*, 135.

36. Giacomo Lumbroso, "I monarchici francesi ed il fascismo," *Gerarchia* (October 1923): 1271–80.

37. Silvio Villegas, *No hay enemigos a la derecha* (Manizales, Colombia: Arturo Zapata, 1937), 80.

38. See Norman A. Stillman, "Anti-Judaism and Antisemitism in the Arab and Islamic World Prior to 1948," in *Antisemitism: A History*, ed. Albert S. Lindemann and Richard S. Levy (Oxford: Oxford University Press, 2010), 219. See also Israel Gershoni, "Introduction: An Analysis of Arab Responses to Fascism and Nazism in Middle Eastern Studies," in *Arab Responses to Fascism and Nazism: Attraction and Repulsion*, ed. Israel Gershoni (Austin: University of Texas Press, 2014), 21, 23.

39. Barroso, *O integralismo e o mundo*, 102.

40. For example, Spanish fascist Giménez Caballero, who argued that Nazism was "too racist and *excluyente*." See Ernesto Giménez Caballero, *La nueva catolicidad: Teoría general sobre el fascismo en Europa* (Madrid: La Gaceta Literaria, 1933), 174.

41. See Gustavo Barroso, *Reflexões de um bode* (Rio de Janeiro: Gráf. Educadora, 1939), 80.

42. Terri E. Givens, *The Roots of Racism* (Bristol, England: Bristol University Press, 2022), 1.

43. See Leonard Dinnerstein, *Anti-Semitism in America* (New York: Oxford University Press, 1994), 83.

44. Benito Mussolini, "Anche nella questione della razza noi tireremo diritto," in *Opera omnia*, ed. Edoardo Susmel and Duilio Susmel (Florence: La Fenice, 1951–1962), 29:126.

45. Benito Mussolini, "Fascismo e 'pus,'" in *Opera omnia*, ed. Edoardo Susmel and Duilio Susmel (Florence: La Fenice, 1951–1962), 16:131.

46. Benito Mussolini, "Il programma fascista," in *Opera omnia*, ed. Edoardo Susmel and Duilio Susmel (Florence: La Fenice, 1951–1962), 17:219.

47. On this topic, see Michele Sarfatti, *Gli ebrei nell'Italia fascista: Vicende, identità, persecuzione* (Turin: Einaudi, 2000); Renzo De Felice, *Storia degli ebrei italiani sotto il fascismo* (Turin: Einaudi, 1993); Marie-Anne Matard-Bonucci, *L'Italie fasciste et la persécution des Juifs* (Paris: Perrin, 2007); Valeria Galimi, "Politica della razza, antisemitismo, Shoah," *Studi Storici* 1 (2014): 169–82; Valeria Gallimi, *Sotto gli occhi di tutti: La società italiana di fronte alle*

persecuzioni antiebraiche (Florence: Le Monnier, 2018); and Simon Levis Sullam, *I carnefici italiani: Scene dal genocidio degli Ebrei, 1943-1945* (Milan: Feltrinelli, 2015).

48. "Il problema razziale non è scoppiato all'improvviso come pensano coloro i quali sono abituati ai bruschi risvegli perché sono abituati ai lunghi sonni poltroni. È in relazione con la conquista dell'Impero, poiché la storia ci insegna che gli Imperi si conquistano con le armi, ma si tengono col prestigio. E per il prestigio occorre una chiara, severa, coscienza razziale, che stabilisca non soltanto delle differenze, ma delle superiorità nettissime. Il problema ebraico non è dunque che un aspetto di questo fenomeno. La nostra posizione è stata determinata da questi incontestabili dati di fatto. L'ebraismo mondiale è stato, durante sedici anni, malgrado la nostra politica, un nemico irreconciliabile del Fascismo." Benito Mussolini, "Discorso di Trieste," in *Opera omnia*, ed. Edoardo Susmel and Duilio Susmel (Florence: La Fenice, 1951-1962), 29:146.

49. On anti-Semitism as a cultural code, see Shulamit Volkov, "Anti-Semitism as a Cultural Code: Reflections on the History and Historiography of Anti-Semitism in Imperial Germany," *Leo Baeck Institute Year Book* 23 (1978): 25-46.

50. Angelo Ventrone, *Il nemico interno: Immagini, parole e simboli della lotta politica nell'Italia del novecento* (Rome: Donzelli, 2005), 3.

51. M.S. Golwalkar, *We or Our Nationhood Defined* (Nagpur, India: Bharat, 1939), 54-55.

52. Goebbels, as cited in State Department, European Affairs Division, *National Socialism: Basic Principles, Their Application by the Nazi Party's Foreign Organization, and the Use of Germans Abroad for Nazi Aims*, prepared by Raymond E. Murphy, Francis B. Stevens, Howard Trivers, and Joseph M. Roland (Washington, DC: US Government Printing Office, 1943), 63.

53. Robert Paxton, *The Anatomy of Fascism* (New York: Knopf, 2004), 196, 259.

54. Paxton, *Anatomy of Fascism*, 36-37.

55. George Mosse, *The Fascist Revolution: Toward a General Theory of Fascism* (New York: Howard Fertig, 1999), 65.

56. George L. Mosse, *The Image of Man: The Creation of Modern Masculinity* (New York: Oxford University Press, 1996), 178. "The idea of struggle was basic. After all, these regimes came to power, however legally, by first creating conditions of civil war and then, once in power, continuing the battle against real or imagined domestic and foreign enemies. Italian fascism and the movements

that followed its model had some difficulty designating the enemy once communism and socialism had been vanquished, and the attack continued mainly as rhetoric against all of those still holding oppositional beliefs rather than against a clearly defined and distinct group of people." As Mosse argues, this changed with the war in Ethiopia, "when blacks were often singled out for ridicule, and the mixing of races was strictly forbidden in order to preserve the so-called dignity of the white Italian race. Indeed, the declaration of the Fascist Grand Council, which in October 1938 sanctioned the exclusion of Jews from Italian life, starts by stating that the empire with its black population had made acquisition of racial consciousness a priority. The black enemy, however, was far away. The Jews, by contrast, were a clearly defined community inside the nation and they could serve to pinpoint enemies otherwise not so easy to detect. Once again, racism simplified recognition of the enemy. Thus the Nazis as well as Italian fascists, after their own racial laws of 1938, equated Jew and communist, and the Nazis themselves also identified the Jews with the Weimar Republic (*Judenrepublic*). The racial enemy was the cause of all of Germany's tribulation, the obstacle to Utopia. The Jew could not be completely divorced from the Aryan, for Aryan and Jew were tied to each other by the struggle that the Aryan had to wage in order to justify his own existence. To be sure, if Hitler had won the war, Europe would be without Jews, but another enemy and countertype would undoubtedly have taken their place." Mosse, *Image of Man*, 178.

57. See Phillips Talbot, "The Khaksar Movement," *Indian Journal of Social Work* 2, no. 2 (1941): 193.

58. "Caliban é o espirito materialista do Seculo. Caliban é a negação de Deus. Caliban é a violencia de Sorel e a oppressão dos plutocratas, a lei do odio dos communistas, a grosseria de uma sociedade governada pelo sexo e pelo estomago. Caliban é o imperialismo financeiro. Caliban são os golpes de Estado dos ambiciosos do Poder. Caliban é a bandeira dos instinctos desfraldada." Plínio Salgado, *Palavra nova dos tempos novos* (Rio de Janeiro: José Olympio, 1936), 157.

59. Giovanni Schiavi, "Ritorno alle origini del razzismo fascista," *Difesa della razza*, June 1943, 17.

60. *Clarinada*, December 31, 1941, 1.

61. See *Clarinada*, April 1941, 23, cited in Fulvia Zega, *Il mondo sotto la svastica: Migrazioni e politica in Argentina e in Brasile (1930–1960)* (Canterano, Italy: Aracne Editrice, 2018), 50.

62. Alberto D. Faleroni, "Los grandes enemigos del pueblo," *Clarinada*, April 30, 1941, 6.

63. Daniel Lvovich, "Un vocero antisemita en Buenos Aires: La revista Clarinada (1937–1945)," *Nuestra memoria* 7, no. 16 (2000): 24–25; and Zega, *Il mondo sotto la svastica*, 38–50. See also Norman Cohn, *El mito de la conspiración judía mundial* (Buenos Aires: Milá, 1988), 266.

64. "Judas, siempre es Judas!," *Clarinada*, July 31, 1941.

65. See *Clarinada*, September 30, 1941. For a converging motif, see "El rapto de America Latina," *Clarinada*, October–November 1941, front page. See also Sandra McGee Deutsch, "Contra 'el gran desorden sexual': Los nacionalistas y la sexualidad, 1919–1940," *Cuadernos del Cish*, no. 17–18 (2005): 127–50; Archivo General de la Nación, "Archivo Agustín P. Justo," Caja 49, Doc. 29; Sandra McGee Deutsch, *Las Derechas: The Extreme Right in Argentina, Brazil, and Chile, 1890–1939* (Redwood City, CA: Stanford University Press, 1999), 234–38; and Finchelstein, *Fascismo, liturgia e imaginario*, 113–30. On Argentine anti-Semitism, see also Daniel Lvovich, *Nacionalismo y antisemitismo en la Argentina* (Buenos Aires: Ed. Vergara, 2003).

66. See Santiago Diaz Vieyra, "La mujer y el nacionalismo," *Bandera Argentina*, September 6, 1933. See also Juan Carulla, "El voto femenino," *La nueva república*, April 28, 1928; "Encuesta de los principios: Sra ¿Quiere ud. votar?," *Los principios*, September 6, 1932, 3; Tomas D. Casares, *Catolicismo y acción Católica* (Buenos Aires: Junta Parroquial del Santísimo Redentor, 1932), 44. Una mujer Argentina, "La palabra de una mujer Argentina," *Abrojos*, November 1933, 12; "El mitin feminista," *Bandera Argentina*, September 25, 1932, 1; "Ha muerto una marimacho famosa," *Bandera Argentina*, June 22, 1932, 1; "Oscarwildeanos de 'amigos del arte,'" *Crisol*, October 8, 1936; "Regreso de la U.R.S.S por Andre Gide," *Bandera Argentina*, December 22, 1936; and Enrique Osés, "La patria ante todo," *El federal*, February 8, 1944, 1.

67. Ruth Ben-Ghiat, *Strongmen: Mussolini to the Present* (New York: Norton, 2020), 119, 120, 129.

68. See Maria Pia Casalena, "Le donne: Le nuove italiane," in *Il fascismo nella storia italiana*, ed. Salvatore Lupo and Angelo Ventrone (Rome: Donzelli, 2022), 334, 337. See also Victoria De Grazia, *How Fascism Ruled Women: Italy, 1922–1945* (Berkeley: University of California Press, 1992); Claudia Koonz, *Mothers in the Fatherland: Women, the Family, and Nazi Politics* (New York: St. Martin's Press, 1987); Lorenzo Benadusi, *The Enemy of the New Man: Homosex-*

uality in Fascist Italy (Madison: University of Wisconsin Press, 2012); and Jorge Dagnino, Matthew Feldman, and Paul Stocker, eds., *The "New Man" in Radical Right Ideology and Practice, 1919-45* (London: Bloomsbury Academic, 2018).

69. See Patrizia Dogliani, *Il fascismo degli italiani: Una storia sociale* (Turin: UTET, 2008), 118; and Casalena, "Le donne," 337.

70. José Santos Chocano, *Idearium tropical: Apuntes sobre las dictaduras organizadas y la farsa democrática* (Lima: Casa Editora la Opinión Nacional, 1922), 79.

71. Clinton, *Revolutionary Nativism*, 152, 149.

72. FSB, *La Falange Socialista Boliviana y las elecciones del 17 de junio* (Santiago: Publicación del Departamento de Informaciones de FSB, 1956), 8.

73. Leopoldo Lugones, *Prometeo (Un proscripto del sol)* (Buenos Aires: Otero, 1910), 334.

74. Leopoldo Lugones, *El problema feminista* (San José, Costa Rica: Imprenta Greñas, 1916), 9.

75. See "Proclamas del Partido Fascista Argentino," *Bandera Argentina*, August 20, 1932, 3.

76. I want to thank journalist Jean Guerrero of the *Los Angeles Times* for sharing a copy of the manifesto with me.

77. Mussolini warned of the impending "death of the white race." Il Duce stated that there was "a fatale declino" and this was why "i gridi d'allarme sorgere in tutte le parti del mondo. Nell'Ungheria si deplora dall'alto il costume oramai invalso della famiglia a figlio unico; nella Repubblica Argentina, grande dieci volte l'Italia e dove potrebbero comodamente vivere da 80 a 100 milioni di uomini, la denatalità fa strage." See Benito Mussolini, "La razza bianca muore?," *Il messaggero*, September 5, 1934. See also *Opera omnia di Benito Mussolini* (Florence: La Fenice, 1960), 26:312-15.

78. Kyle Burke, *Revolutionaries for the Right: Anticommunist Internationalism and Paramilitary Warfare in the Cold War* (Chapel Hill: University of North Carolina Press, 2018), 71-77; and Federico Finchelstein and Emmanuel Guerisoli, "La storia globale del fascismo che precede la strage di Buffalo," *Domani giornale*, May 24, 2022, https://www.editorialedomani.it/idee/fascismo-bianco-strage-buffalo-jwq35ojt. See also Luis Herrán-Ávila, "The Reinvention of the Latin American Right," NACLA, April 11, 2023, https://nacla.org/reinvention-latin-american-right; and Patrice McSherry, *Predatory States: Operation Condor and Covert War in Latin America* (Lanham, MD: Rowman and Littlefield, 2005).

79. See Federico Finchelstein, *The Ideological Origins of the Dirty War* (New York: Oxford University Press, 2014), 135.

80. Hitler, *Mein Kampf*, 562. As I have argued with philosopher Jason Stanley, "WRT [white replacement theory] and its ideological predecessors have been central to fascist movements in Europe, Asia, the United States and elsewhere. . . . WRT, for instance, is central to Orbán's explicit governing ideologies and also to the messages of powerful public figures such as Fox's Tucker Carlson. Just days before addressing the Conservative Political Action Committee (CPAC), which chose to convene in Budapest, Hungary's capital, Orbán placed WRT at the center of state ideology, declaring: 'I see the great European population exchange as a suicidal attempt to replace the lack of European, Christian children with adults from other civilizations—migrants.' To normalize something is to legitimate it, to make it a topic of legitimate public disagreement. These major figures have normalized WRT." See Jason Stanley and Federico Finchelstein, "White Replacement Theory Is Fascism's New Name," *Los Angeles Times*, May 24, 2022, https://www.latimes.com/opinion/story/2022-05-24/white-replacement-theory-fascism-europe-history.

81. Frederic J. Frommer, "MLK Gave His Last Sermon 55 Years Ago—and Warned of a Fascist Takeover," *Washington Post*, March 31, 2023, https://www.washingtonpost.com/history/2023/03/31/mlk-final-sermon-cathedral-fascism.

82. See Cynthia Miller-Idris, "Formulating Policy Responses to the Right-Wing Threat," in *Fascism in America: Past and Present*, ed. Gavriel D. Rosenfeld and Janet Ward (New York: Cambridge University Press, 2023), 518.

83. See Javier Rodrigo and Maximiliano Fuentes Codera, *Ellos, los fascistas* (Barcelona: Deusto, 2022), 174.

84. See Stanley and Finchelstein, "White Replacement Theory."

85. See Linda Gordon, "The American Fascists," in *Fascism in America: Past and Present*, ed. Gavriel D. Rosenfeld and Janet Ward (New York: Cambridge University Press, 2023), 217. On American fascism, see also Sarah Churchwell, "American Fascism: It Has Happened Here," *New York Review of Books*, June 22, 2020, https://www.nybooks.com/daily/2020/06/22/american-fascism-it-has-happened-here; and Richard Steigmann-Gall, "Star-Spangled Fascism: American Interwar Political Extremism in Comparative Perspective," *Social History* 42, no. 1 (2017): 94–119.

86. See Stanley and Finchelstein, "White Replacement Theory."

87. Coronel Juan Perón, *El pueblo ya sabe de qué se trata: Discursos* (Buenos Aires, 1946), 186.

88. Juan Perón, *El pueblo a través del pensamiento de Perón* (Buenos Aires: Presidencia de la Nación, Secretaria de Prensa y Difusión, 1955), 196. See also Juan Domingo Perón, *La fuerza es el derecho de las bestias* (Montevideo, Uruguay: Cicerón, 1958), 23.

89. On the friend-foe distinction, see the classic text by Carl Schmitt, *The Concept of the Political* (New Brunswick, NJ: Rutgers University Press, 1976), and more specifically, on his distinction between enemy and foe, see his *Theory of the Partisan: Intermediate Commentary on the Concept of the Political* (New York: Telos Press, 2007).

90. Juan Domingo Perón, *Los vendepatria: Las pruebas de una traición* (Buenos Aires: Liberación, 1958), 127, 228.

91. Juan Domingo Perón, *Obras completas* (Buenos Aires: Docencia, 1998), 2:536. See also Perón, *La fuerza es el derecho de las bestias*, 47–48.

92. Juan Domingo Perón, *Discurso del excelentísimo señor Presidente de la Nación Argentina, general Juan Perón, pronunciado en la comida anual de camaradería de las Fuerzas Armadas de la Nación* (Buenos Aires: Subsecretaria de Informaciones, 1950), 7.

93. Jorge Eliécer Gaitán, *Obras selectas* (Bogota: Imprenta Nacional, 1979), 1:234. Similarly, Ecuadorian populist leader Velasco Ibarra stated, "For fascism and Nazism the person is, above all, something mechanical and biological." José María Velasco Ibarra, *Estudios de derecho constitucional* (Quito: Editorial Santo Domingo, 1974), 2:220.

94. Getúlio Vargas, *O governo trabalhista no Brasil* (Rio de Janeiro: José Olympio, 1952), 457.

95. Rodrigo and Fuentes Codera, *Ellos, los fascistas*, 18.

96. Kim Lane Scheppele, "How Viktor Orbán Wins," *Journal of Democracy* 33, no. 3 (2022): 49; and Shaun Walker, "George Soros: Orbán Turns to Familiar Scapegoat as Hungary Rows with EU," *Guardian*, December 5, 2020, https://www.theguardian.com/world/2020/dec/05/george-soros-orban-turns-to-familiar-scapegoat-as-hungary-rows-with-eu.

97. Jonathan Weisman and Andrew Higgins, "Behind Trump Indictment, the Right Wing Finds a Familiar Villain in Soros," *New York Times*, April 4, 2023, https://www.nytimes.com/2023/04/04/us/politics/george-soros-bragg-trump.html; and "Statement by Donald J. Trump, 45th President of the United

States of America," on Donald Trump's official website, March 30, 2023, https://www.donaldjtrump.com/news/33268000-32c9-4f5b-87f8-fb0d1583e44b. See also George Conway's analysis, "Trump Is Out for Vengeance," *Washington Post*, November 15, 2022, https://www.washingtonpost.com/opinions/2022/11/15/george-conway-trump-2024-prosecution/.

98. Golwalkar, *We or Our Nationhood Defined*, 100.

99. Paxton, *Anatomy of Fascism*, 174.

100. Catie Edmondson, Jonathan Martin, and Nicholas Fandos, "Top House Republican Condemns Marjorie Taylor Greene's Comments, but Stands by Her," *New York Times*, February 3, 2021, https://www.nytimes.com/2021/02/03/us/politics/kevin-mccarthy-marjorie-taylor-greene.html.

101. Sinclair Lewis, *It Can't Happen Here* (New York: Signet Classics, 2014), 358. As Sarah Churchwell explains regarding the idea that fascism would appear in the United States wrapped in the American flag, "Because Lewis's novel is the best remembered of the many warnings against American fascism in the interwar years, he has latterly been credited with the admonition, but they are not Lewis's words. The adage probably originated instead with James Waterman Wise, son of the eminent American rabbi Stephen Wise. . . . 'The America of power and wealth,' Wise cautioned, is 'an America which needs fascism.' American fascism might emerge from 'patriotic orders, such as the American Legion and the Daughters of the American Revolution . . . and it may come to us wrapped in the American flag or a Hearst newspaper.' In another talk that year, he put it slightly differently: American fascism would likely come 'wrapped up in the American flag and heralded as a plea for liberty and preservation of the constitution.'" See Churchwell, "American Fascism."

102. John Hayward, "Exclusive—Donald Trump: 'I Am the Messenger,'" *Breitbart*, October 28, 2016, https://www.breitbart.com/radio/2016/10/28/exclusive-donald-trump-messenger; Annie Karni, "5 Takeaways from Trump's Inaugural Address," *Politico*, January 20, 2017, https://www.politico.com/story/2017/01/2017-trump-inauguration-5-takeaways-233925; and Nick Wing, "Donald Trump Says 'Police Are the Most Mistreated People' in America," *HuffPost*, January 14, 2016, https://www.huffpost.com/entry/donald-trump-police_n_569869d1e4b0b4eb759df9b8.

103. Linda Qiu, "Trump's False Claim That 'Nobody Has Ever Done' More for the Black Community than He Has," *New York Times*, June 5, 2020, https://

www.nytimes.com/2020/06/05/us/politics/trump-black-african-americans-fact-check.html; and Dan Mangan, "Trump Suggests Lincoln's Legacy Is 'Questionable,' Brags about His Own Work for Black Americans," CNBC, June 12, 2020, https://www.cnbc.com/2020/06/12/trump-criticizes-lincoln-brags-he-has-done-a-lot-to-help-black-americans.html.

104. Hitler, *Mein Kampf*, 326; and Rosalind Hedelind, "Trump Attacks American Jews, Posting They Must 'Get Their Act Together' on Israel," *Washington Post*, October 16, 2022, https://www.washingtonpost.com/politics/2022/10/16/trump-jews-israel.

105. See Federico Finchelstein, *The Origins of the Dirty War* (New York: Oxford University Press, 2014), 86.

106. Twitter post, January 27, 2021, https://mobile.twitter.com/bbimbi/status/1354575410848260097. The idea of "fake news" (a term that Trump once declared was one his greatest inventions) goes back to the Nazi term *lying press*, also currently being recuperated by German neo-Nazis. Alexander Griffing, "A Brief History of 'Lügenpresse,' the Nazi-Era Predecessor to Trump's 'Fake News,'" *Haaretz*, October 8, 2017, https://www.haaretz.com/us-news/2017-10-08/ty-article/the-ominous-nazi-era-precedent-to-trumps-fake-news-attacks/0000017f-e83e-d62c-a1ff-fc7ff8d50000; and Rick Noack, "The Ugly History of 'Lügenpresse,' a Nazi Slur Shouted at a Trump Rally," *Washington Post*, October 24, 2016, https://www.washingtonpost.com/news/worldviews/wp/2016/10/24/the-ugly-history-of-luegenpresse-a-nazi-slur-shouted-at-a-trump-rally.

107. Mira Kamdar, "What Happened in Delhi Was a Pogrom," *The Atlantic*, February 28, 2020, https://www.theatlantic.com/ideas/archive/2020/02/what-happened-delhi-was-pogrom/607198; and Patrick Cockburn, "While Muslims Are Being Murdered in India, the Rest of the World Is Too Slow to Condemn," *The Independent*, February 28, 2020, https://www.independent.co.uk/voices/delhi-riots-news-narendra-modi-muslims-hindus-jammu-kashmir-trump-a9365376.html.

108. "Philippines' Teodoro Locsin's 'Nazi' Tweets Spark Outrage," *BBC News*, October 7, 2016, https://www.bbc.com/news/world-asia-37582498; and Martin Pengelly, "Trump Told Chief of Staff Hitler 'Did a Lot of Good Things,' Book Says," *Guardian*, July 7, 2021, https://www.theguardian.com/us-news/2021/jul/06/donald-trump-hitler-michael-bender-book.

109. Hitler, *Mein Kampf*, 660–61.
110. Clinton, *Revolutionary Nativism*, 117.
111. Lugones, *Acción: Las cuatro conferencias patrióticas del Coliseo*, 58.
112. Hitler, *Mein Kampf*, 661.
113. Golwalkar, *We or Our Nationhood Defined*, 64–65.
114. Christophe Jaffrelot, *Modi's India: Hindu Nationalism and the Rise of Ethnic Democracy* (Princeton, NJ: Princeton University Press, 2021), 447.
115. Josh Dawsey, "Trump Derides Protections for Immigrants from 'Shithole' Countries," *Washington Post*, January 11, 2018, https://www.washingtonpost.com/politics/trump-attacks-protections-for-immigrants-from-shithole-countries-in-oval-office-meeting/2018/01/11/bfc0725c-f711-11e7-91af-31ac729add94_story.html.
116. See Trip Gabriel, "Trump Escalates Anti-Immigrant Rhetoric with 'Poisoning the Blood' Comment," *New York Times*, October 5, 2023, https://www.nytimes.com/2023/10/05/us/politics/trump-immigration-rhetoric.html; and Hitler, *Mein Kampf*, 296, 289.
117. Gustavo Segré, "10 frases que hicieron famoso al candidato presidencial brasileño Jair Bolsonaro," *Infobae*, September 10, 2018, https://www.infobae.com/america/america-latina/2018/09/10/10-frases-que-hicieron-famoso-al-candidato-presidencial-brasileno-jair-bolsonaro/; Pedro Henrique Leal, "Bolsonaro and the Brazilian Far Right," *Open Democracy*, April 24, 2017, https://www.opendemocracy.net/en/democraciaabierta/bolsonaro-and-brazilian-far-right/; and Federico Finchelstein, "Jair Bolsonaro's Model Isn't Berlusconi. It's Goebbels," *Foreign Policy*, October 5, 2018, https://foreignpolicy.com/2018/10/05/bolsonaros-model-its-goebbels-fascism-nazism-brazil-latin-america-populism-argentina-venezuela/.
118. "Don't Take the President Literally, Aide Says, after Women Deride 'Macho-Fascist' Duterte," Reuters, February 13, 2018, https://www.reuters.com/article/us-philippines-duterte/dont-take-the-president-literally-aide-says-after-women-deride-macho-fascist-duterte-idUSKBN1FX1FQ; and Walden Bello, "Rodrigo Duterte: A Fascist Original," in *A Duterte Reader: Critical Essays on Rodrigo Duterte's Early Presidency*, ed. Nicole Curato (Ithaca, NY: Cornell University Press, 2017), 80.
119. For Bolsonaro and other would-be fascist populist leaders around the world, Trump is an icon of success, a projection of their most extreme, destruc-

tive, violent desires. In 2017, Bolsonaro identified with Trump's self-portrayal as a victim. He said, "Trump faced the same attacks I am facing—that he was a homophobe, a fascist, a racist, a Nazi—but the people believed in his platform, and I was rooting for him." Brad Brooks, "A Trump-Bolsonaro Bromance Could Be Brewing after Brazilian's Big Win," Reuters, October 29, 2018, https://www.reuters.com/article/brazil-election-trump-idINKCN1N31BR.

120. Gustavo Segré, "10 frases que hicieron famoso al candidato presidencial Brasileño Jair Bolsonaro," *Infobae*, September 10, 2018, https://www.infobae.com/america/america-latina/2018/09/10/10-frases-que-hicieron-famoso-al-candidato-presidencial-brasileno-jair-bolsonaro; Da Redação, "Bolsonaro diz que eleição de 2022 para a presidência será uma 'luta do bem contra o mal,'" *Universo Online*, March 27, 2022, https://cultura.uol.com.br/noticias/47527_bolsonaro-diz-que-eleicao-de-2022-para-a-presidencia-sera-uma-luta-do-bem-contra-o-mal.html; and Jon Lee Anderson, "Jair Bolsonaro's Southern Strategy," *New Yorker*, March 25, 2019, https://www.newyorker.com/magazine/2019/04/01/jair-bolsonaros-southern-strategy.

121. Twitter post, April 11, 2023, https://twitter.com/atrupar/status/1645943664626003969.

122. "'Mussolini fue un buen político' y otros 4 episodios polémicos de Giorgia Meloni," *CNN Español*, September 26, 2022, https://cnnespanol.cnn.com/2022/09/26/giorgia-meloni-polemicas-orix.

123. Twitter posts, both September 30, 2022, https://twitter.com/carlosbolsonaro/status/1575947880178733056?lang=en, and https://twitter.com/BolsonaroSP/status/1575996865166082048. In 2019, Eduardo Bolsonaro mocked Estanislao Fernández, the son of Argentine president Alberto Fernández (2019–2023). He posted two photos: in one, Fernández, who is a drag performer and cosplayer, is dressed as Pikachu from Pokémon; in the other, Bolsonaro Jr. is holding an assault weapon and wearing a T-shirt with a picture of a dog doing its business on the symbol of the hammer and sickle. Sylvia Colombo, "Filho de Alberto Fernández responde a provocação de Eduardo Bolsonaro," *Universo Online*, October 30, 2019, https://www1.folha.uol.com.br/mundo/2019/10/filho-de-alberto-fernandez-responde-a-provocacao-de-eduardo-bolsonaro.shtml.

124. Hitler, *Mein Kampf*, 327.

125. Klemperer, *Language of the Third Reich*, 136.

Chapter 4. Dictatorship

1. Pierre Drieu La Rochelle, *Socialisme fasciste* (Paris: Gallimard, 1934), 129.

2. For Andreas Kalyvas, dictatorship is "a special modality of political power, temporarily released from various limits, for the purpose of securing preservation and survival during an apparent (real or supposed) urgent and exceptional situation of an existential threat, usually understood in terms of (external) war and (internal) sedition." Kalyvas notes that the original ancient Roman form became "the prototype" for all modern forms of emergency institutions. See Andreas Kalyvas, "Dictatorship," *Political Concepts: A Critical Lexicon* 6 (2022), https://www.politicalconcepts.org/dictatorship-andreas-kalyvas/. See also Andreas Kalyvas, "The Sublime Dignity of the Dictator: Republicanism and the Return of Dictatorship in Political Modernity," *Annual of European and Global Studies* 2 (2015), and his "The Logic of Dictatorship: Republicanism, Democracy, and the Enemy Within" (manuscript in preparation). On dictatorship, see also Andrew Arato, "Conceptual History of Dictatorship (and Its Rivals)," in *Critical Theory and Democracy: Civil Society, Dictatorship, and Constitutionalism in Andrew Arato's Democratic Theory*, ed. Enrique Peruzzoti and Martín Plot (New York: Routledge, 2013), 208–80; and Norberto Bobbio, *Democracy and Dictatorship* (Cambridge: Polity, 2006), 133–66.

3. Dionysius of Halicarnassus, *The Roman Antiquities* (Cambridge, MA: Harvard University Press, 1940), V–VI:48, 211; and Marcus Tullius Cicero, *Laws* (Cambridge, MA: Harvard University Press, 1994), III:469. See also Polybius, *The Rise of the Roman Empire* (London: Penguin, 1979), 254; Livy, *The Early History of Rome* (London: Penguin, 2002), 128–29; and Andreas Kalyvas, "The Tyranny of Dictatorship: When the Greek Tyrant Met the Roman Dictator," *Political Theory* 35, no. 4 (2007), 412–42.

4. V. I. Lenin, "The Dictatorship of the Proletariat," in *The Lenin Anthology*, ed. Robert C. Tucker (New York: Norton, 1975), 450–56, 489.

5. See Kalyvas, "Dictatorship"; and Hannah Arendt, *Thinking without a Banister* (New York: Schocken, 2018), 4.

6. See Carl Schmitt, *Dictatorship: From the Origin of the Modern Concept of Sovereignty to Proletarian Class Struggle* (1921; Cambridge: Polity, 2014), chapter 4; and Carl Schmitt, *The Crisis of Parliamentary Democracy* (Cambridge, MA: MIT Press, 1988), 51.

7. Juan Donoso Cortés, "Discurso pronunciado en el Congreso el 4 de enero de 1849," in *Obras de Don Juan Donoso Cortés* (Madrid: Tejado, 1854), 3:263-74.

8. Benito Mussolini, "Non esiste una dottrina sulla dittatura: Quando la dittatura è necessaria, bisogna attuarla," in *Opera omnia*, ed. Edoardo Susmel and Duilio Susmel (Florence: La Fenice, 1951-1962), 20:79.

9. Subhas Chandra Bose, *Netaji's Life and Writings, Part Two: The Indian Struggle* (Calcutta: Thacker, Spink, 1948), 2:431. Bose hoped for an ideological synthesis between fascism and communism, and wrote to a friend, "Nothing less than a dictator is needed to put our social customs right." See Roman Hayes, *Subhas Chandra Bose in Nazi Germany: Politics, Intelligence, and Propaganda, 1941-43* (New York: Columbia University Press, 2011), 14.

10. Hans Kelsen, "The Party-Dictatorship," *Politica* 2 (1936): 20-21, 32.

11. Kelsen, "The Party-Dictatorship," 28.

12. Schmitt states in this respect, "In practice that is an educational dictatorship. But if world history is to go forward, if the unreal must be continually defeated, then by necessity the dictatorship will become permanent." Carl Schmitt, *Crisis of Parliamentary Democracy*, 57.

13. Franz Neumann, "Notes on the Theory of Dictatorship," in *The Democratic and the Authoritarian State* (New York: Free Press, 1957), 248.

14. See Clinton Rossiter, *Constitutional Dictatorship: Crisis Government in the Modern Democracies* (New Brunswick, NJ: Transaction, 2004), 8.

15. Benito Mussolini, "Al popolo: Di Roma per il 28 ottobre," in *Opera omnia*, ed. Edoardo Susmel and Duilio Susmel (Florence: La Fenice, 1951-1962), 22:242.

16. See Benito Mussolini, *Discorsi politici* (Milan: Tipografia del Popolo d'Italia, 1921), 75.

17. José Santos Chocano, *Idearium tropical: Apuntes sobre las dictaduras organizadas y la farsa democrática* (Lima: Casa Editora La Opinión Nacional, 1922), 38. See also José Santos Chocano, *El libro de mi proceso* (Lima: Imprenta Americana, 1927), 1:109, 157, 326.

18. See review of Bainville by Jesús Marañón in "Lecturas," *Acción Española*, April 1936, 190, and *Les dictateurs* by Jacques Bainville (Paris, 1935), or in English, *Dictators* (London: Jonathan Cape, 1940). Although he did not cite him by name, Bainville was most probably influenced by the Venezuelan writer Vallenilla's concept of democratic Caesarism. See Laureano Vallenilla

Lanz, *Cesarismo democrático: Estudios sobre las bases sociológicas de la constitución efectiva de Venezuela* (Caracas: Empresa El Cojo, 1919).

19. Pablo Antonio Cuadra, "Hacia la cruz del sur," *Acción Española*, February 1936, 277-79.

20. Leopoldo Lugones, *Acción: Las cuatro conferencias patrióticas del Coliseo* (Buenos Aires: Círculo Tradición Argentina, 1923), 46. See also Silvio Villegas, *No hay enemigos a la derecha* (Manizales, Colombia: Arturo Zapata, 1937), 91, 94, 103.

21. Office of War Information, *Hitler's War Time Speeches* (Washington, DC: Bureau of Overseas, 1943), 79. On the relationship between Hitler and Mussolini, see the excellent book by Christian Goeschel, *Mussolini and Hitler: The Forging of the Fascist Alliance* (New Haven, CT: Yale University Press, 2018).

22. Luigi Sturzo, *Popolarismo e fascismo* (Torino: P. Gobetti, 1924), 254.

23. "La presente dittatura, tosto o tardi, metterà capo ad una riforma costituzionale. Meglio tosto che tardi. Conviene che la riforma rispettiquanto è possibile le forme esistenti, rinnovando la sostanza. Esempi: Roma antica; Inghilterra." Vilfredo Pareto, "Pochi punti di un futuro ordinamento costituzionale," *La vita italiana*, September-October, 1923, 165, 166.

24. Kelsen, "The Party-Dictatorship," 22.

25. Fraenkel said, "By the Prerogative State we mean that governmental system which exercises unlimited arbitrariness and violence unchecked by any legal guarantees, and by the Normative State an administrative body endowed with elaborate powers for safeguarding the legal order as expressed in statutes, decisions of the courts, and activities of the administrative agencies." Ernst Fraenkel, *The Dual State: A Contribution to the Theory of Dictatorship* (New York: Oxford University Press, 1941), xiii, xvi, 5, 37, 39.

26. See Arendt, *Thinking without a Banister*, 106.

27. Gustavo J. Franceschi, *Totalitarismos: Nacionalismo y fascismo* (Buenos Aires: Difusión, 1945), 151, 160, 161-73, 178, 180-81, 187, 191, 209, 248, 364. See also by Franceschi, "Estado totalitario, estado cristiano," *Criterio*, June 29, 1933, 296-99.

28. Sergio Panunzio, *Teoria generale dello stato fascista: Appunti di lezioni* (Padua, Italy: CEDAM, 1937), 104, 243, 246, 247.

29. Sergio Panunzio, "Teoria generale della dittatura (prima parte)," *Gerarchia*, April 1936, 229; and Panunzio, *Teoria generale dello stato fascista*, 243.

30. See Robert Michels, *Corso di sociologia politica* (Milan: Istituto Editoriale Scientifico, 1927), 93; and Schmitt, *Dictatorship*.

31. Panunzio, *Teoria generale dello stato fascista*, 248.
32. Panunzio, *Teoria generale dello stato fascista*, 243, 250.
33. "Dittatura" in Partito Nazionale Fascista, *Dizionario di politica* (Rome: Istituto della Enciclopedia Italiana, 1940), 1:808-9.
34. Bainville, *Dictators*, 50.
35. Emil Ludwig, *Colloqui con Mussolini* (Verona: Mondadori, 1932), 130-31.
36. Adolfo Agorio, *Ataraxia* (Madrid, 1923), 112. See also Adolfo Agorio, "La resurrección de los muertos," *La mañana*, September 8, 1935, 1.
37. On this point, see Neumann, "Notes on the Theory of Dictatorship," 253.
38. See Benito Mussolini, "Il progamma fascista," in *Opera omnia*, ed. Edoardo Susmel and Duilio Susmel (Florence: La Fenice, 1951-1962), 17:217; Benito Mussolini, "Il 'babau' della dittatura militare," in *Discorsi politici* (Milan: Esercizio Tipografico del Popolo D'italia, 1921), 84; and Adolf Hitler, *Mein Kampf* (New York: Mariner, 1999), 11. Typically, Hitler lied about parliament, which he destroyed, and dictatorship, which he created: "As a freedom loving man I could not even conceive of any other possibility of government, for the idea of any sort of dictatorship would . . . have seemed to me a crime against freedom and all reason" (524). For another example of the negative use of dictatorship by fascists, see Camillo Pellizzi, *Fascismo—Aristocrazia* (Milan: Alpes, 1925), 178.
39. State Department, European Affairs Division, *National Socialism: Basic Principles, Their Application by the Nazi Party's Foreign Organization, and the Use of Germans Abroad for Nazi Aims*, prepared by Raymond E. Murphy, Francis B. Stevens, Howard Trivers, and Joseph M. Roland (Washington, DC: US Government Printing Office, 1943), 40.
40. Eberhard Jäckel, *Hitler's World View: A Blueprint for Power* (Cambridge, MA: Harvard University Press, 1981), 79, 80-82.
41. In Carl Schmitt, *Principii politici del nazionalsocialismo* (Florence: Sansoni, 1935); and Carl Schmitt, *Un giurista davanti a se stesso: Saggi e interviste*, a cura di G. Agamben (Vicenza, Italy: Neri Pozza, 2005).
42. See Carl Schmitt, "El fuhrer defiende el derecho" [1934], in *Teólogo de la política*, ed. Héctor Orestes Aguilar (Mexico City: Fondo de Cultura Económica, 2001), 114-18, and his *Glossarium* (Seville, Spain: El Paseo, 2021), 125, 342, 560.
43. Goebbels, as cited in Peter Longerich, *Goebbels: A Biography* (New York: Random House, 2015), 63.

44. "Movimiento Español JON (Juntas de Ofensiva Nacional-sindicalista) que son las JONS," *El Fascio* (Madrid), March 16, 1933, 14; Avolio, "I limiti del fascismo," *Gerarchia* I (1922): 501.

45. This is how a Spanish fascist saw the discussion between fascism and the dictatorship of Primo de Rivera they had previously supported. See "El fascio no es un régimen esporádico," *El Fascio* (Madrid), March 16, 1933, 4.

46. James Strachey Barnes, *The Universal Aspect of Fascism* (London: Williams and Norgate, 1928), 25.

47. This was one of the concerns of French fascist intellectual Drieu La Rochelle. Without crisis, the dictatorship became moderate and a "burden" to the regime. Drieu La Rochelle, *Socialisme fasciste*, 124. See also José Pemartín, *Qué es lo nuevo* (Madrid: Espasa-Calpe, 1940), 71.

48. Arendt, *Thinking without a Banister*, 110.

49. Antonio Renda, "La dittatura per la libertà," *Critica Fascista*, November 1, 1923, 192.

50. Roberto Forges Davanzati, "Lo stato militante," *Costruire: Rivista mensile fascista* (July 1927): 35-36.

51. Drieu La Rochelle, *Socialisme fasciste*, 129.

52. Panunzio, *Teoria generale dello stato fascista*, 258.

53. Aurelio Palmieri, "La stampa anglosassone e Benito Mussolini," *La vita italiana*, August 15, 1923, 82.

54. Anne O'Hare McCormick, "The Swashbuckling Mussolini," *New York Times*, July 22, 1923, 1, 19.

55. McCormick, "The Swashbuckling Mussolini," 1, 19.

56. See Arendt, *Thinking without a Banister*, 491; and Finchelstein, *A Brief History of Fascist Lies*.

57. "Dictaduras efímeras y dictaduras permanentes," *Bandera Argentina*, April 5, 1933, 1. See also "El pueblo contra la libertad," *Aduna*, January 31, 1935, 1.

58. Maria Hsia Chang, *The Chinese Blue Shirts Society* (Berkeley, CA: Institute of East Asian Studies, 1985), 27, 19-20; and "El fascismo y la democracia," *El Fascio* (Madrid), March 16, 1933, 5.

59. Chocano, *Idearium tropical*, 61, 30.

60. Sir Oswald Mosley, *Fascism: 100 Questions Asked and Answered* (London: B.U.F., 1936), question 15.

61. See Onésimo Redondo, *El estado nacional* (Valladolid, Spain: Libertad, 1938), 118; and Onésimo Redondo, *Caudillo de Castilla* (Valladolid, Spain: Libertad, 1937), 101.

62. "Doctrina y acción" *Acción Española*, May 16, 1933, 454.

63. Libero Merlino, "Il fascismo come dottrina," *Gerarchia*, July 1927, 537.

64. Benito Mussolini, "Al popolo di Roma per il XXVIII," in *Opera omnia*, ed. Edoardo Susmel and Duilio Susmel (Florence: La Fenice, 1951–1962), 22:242.

65. Benito Mussolini, "I 'pensieri,'" in *Opera omnia*, ed. Edoardo Susmel and Duilio Susmel (Florence: La Fenice, 1951–1962), 34:280.

66. Benito Mussolini, *Diuturna* (Milan: Imperia, 1924), 376.

67. Lenin, "A Contribution to the History of the Question of Dictatorship," in *Collected Works* (Moscow: Progress, 1974), 31:346–47. See also V.I. Lenin, "Theses on Bourgeois Democracy and Proletarian Dictatorship," in *Against Revisionism* (Moscow: Foreign Languages, 1959), 494–95. As Kalyvas notes, Lenin situated his theory and practice of dictatorship within the framework of ultimate survival. Lenin conceived of it as existing within a "normless, violent zone of absolute combat, of the revolution as 'a war of extermination,' where life itself becomes the only finality of politics, the central task of the proletarian dictatorship, as Lenin defined it in highly dramatic terms, its 'main and fundamental task, is to save the life of the workers, to save the workers, for the workers are dying.'" See Kalyvas, "Dictatorship."

68. Benito Mussolini, "Discorso di trieste," in *Opera omnia*, ed. Edoardo Susmel and Duilio Susmel (Florence: La Fenice, 1951–1962), 15:214–23.

69. In fact, leftist thinker and activist Rosa Luxemburg had privately stated a similar critique of the Russian Revolution in 1918: "The few dozen party leaders of inexhaustible energy and boundless experience direct and rule. Among them only a dozen outstanding heads do the ruling, and an elite of the working class is invited from time to time to meetings where its members are to applaud the speeches of the leaders, and to approve proposed resolutions unanimously. . . . A dictatorship, to be sure; not the dictatorship of the proletariat, however, but of a handful of politicians." Cited in Arendt, *Thinking without a Banister*, 381.

70. Donoso Cortés, "Discurso pronunciado en el Congreso el 4 de enero de 1849," 3:263–74.

71. José Pemartín, *Los valores históricos en la dictadura Española* (Madrid: Publicaciones de la Junta Patriótica y Ciudadana, 1929), 19.

72. Oliveira Salazar, *El pensamiento de la revolución nacional* (Buenos Aires and Lisbon, 1938), 81. Salazar also presented his dictatorship as "the dictatorship of reason." Henri Massis, *Jefes* (Buenos Aires: Sol y Luna, 1939), 82. Lugones also described authoritarian rule as essentially anti-political. See Leopoldo Lugones, *El estado equitativo (Ensayo sobre la realidad Argentina)* (Buenos Aires: La Editora Argentina, 1932), 11.

73. Adolf Hitler, *Hitler's Words: Two Decades of National Socialism, 1923–1944*, ed. Gordon W. Prange (Washington, DC: American Council on Public Affairs, 1944), 47, 76.

74. Edgardo Sulis, ed., *Mussolini contro il mito di demos* (Milan: Hoepli, 1942), 107.

75. Francisco Franco, *Palabras del caudillo: 19 abril 1937-31 de diciembre 1938* (Barcelona: Ediciones Fe, 1939), 149, 161, 276, 278; and Finchelstein, *A Brief History of Fascist Lies*, 83.

76. Hitler, *Hitler's Words*, 111.

77. Cited in Longerich, *Goebbels: A Biography*, 63.

78. Hitler, *Hitler's Words*, 118.

79. Office of War Information, *Hitler's War Time Speeches*, 73.

80. See Paul Corner, *The Fascist Party and Popular Opinion in Mussolini's Italy* (Oxford: Oxford University Press, 2012). See also Paul Corner, "Italian Fascism: Whatever Happened to Dictatorship?," *Journal of Modern History* 74 (2002): 325–51; and Alan E. Steinweis, *The People's Dictatorship: A History of Nazi Germany* (Cambridge: Cambridge University Press, 2023).

81. Juan Perón, "En la ciudad de Santa Fe: 1 de enero de 1946," in *Obras completas* (Buenos Aires: Docencia, 1998), 8:18.

82. *Archivo Cedinci*, Folleto "Dijo el Coronel Perón."

83. Juan Domingo Perón, "Aspiramos a una sociedad sin divisiones de clase: En el cine park, 12 de agosto de 1944," in *El pueblo quiere saber de qué se trata* (Buenos Aires, 1944), 149.

84. Andrew Arato, "Dictatorship before and after Totalitarianism," *Social Research* 69, no. 2 (Summer 2002): 473–503. On the notion of dictatorship, see his "Good-Bye to Dictatorship?," *Social Research* 67, no. 4 (2000): 926, 937.

85. Juan Perón, "Política peronista," *Mundo Peronista*, August 15, 1951, 1. See also Descartes (Perón), "Las quintas columnas imperialistas," *Mundo Peronista*, October 10, 1951; and Descartes (Perón), "La guerra popular," *Mundo Peronista*, September 1, 1951.

86. Eva Perón, *La razón de mi vida* (Buenos Aires: Peuser, 1951), 121–22, 225.

87. "Los dictadores," *Mundo Peronista*, May 15, 1952, 50.

88. Ernesto Palacio, *Teoría del estado* (Buenos Aires: Editorial Política, 1949), 7–8, 25, 72, 74–75. In 1939, Palacio stressed the connections between myth, fascism, and popular support. He stated that to "adopt from fascism only its authoritarian shell when its essence is mystical, and when only this constitutes the architecture of the State, is insanity. . . . Popular support is what makes fascism strong, and it will lose it when it is lacking." One year later, Palacio denied that representative democracy could represent the "authentic" will of the people. See Ernesto Palacio, *La historia falsificada* (Buenos Aires: Difusión, 1939), 151, and his article "El régimen y el fraude," *Nuevo orden*, December 18, 1940, 1. See also his articles "Enemigos del país," *Nuevo orden*, July 25, 1940, 1, and "El sentido oculto del parlamento," *Nuevo orden*, October 4, 1940, 1.

89. Palacio, *Teoría del estado*, 84–85.

90. Palacio, 111.

91. Juan Domingo Perón, "Discurso de J.D. Perón en el acto de proclamación de su candidatura (12 de febrero de 1946)," in *Obras completas* (Buenos Aires: Docencia, 1998), 8:32.

92. See Descartes (Perón), "El imperialismo y la guerra," in *50 artículos de Descartes* (Buenos Aires, 1951), 98. For a similar argument by Argentine fascists regarding "totalitarian democracy," see "Hacia adelante," *Aduna*, January 31, 1935, 1.

93. Descartes (Perón), "La libertad," in *50 artículos de Descartes* (Buenos Aires, 1951), 20.

94. Juan Domingo Perón, *La fuerza es el derecho de las bestias* (Montevideo, Uruguay: Cicerón, 1958), 7.

95. Juan Domingo Perón, "¿Por qué el gobierno argentino no es fascista?," in *Obras completas* (Buenos Aires: Docencia, 1998), 6:571.

96. "El 24 de febrero de 1946, la Revolución fue convertida en gobierno por la avalancha silenciosa de la ciudadanía en pleno ejercicio de su derecho electoral." Juan Domingo Perón, *Mensaje del presidente la nación: Conceptos doctrinarios* (Buenos Aires: Presidencia de la Nación, 1955), 9.

97. Perón, *La fuerza es el derecho de las bestias*, 44. See also Descartes (Perón), "Así paga el Diablo," *Mundo Peronista*, November 1, 1951, 8; and Descartes (Perón), "La guerra popular."

98. José María Velasco Ibarra, *Conciencia o barbarie* (Buenos Aires: Claridad, 1938), 15, 16; and his *Obras completas: Democracia y constitcionalismo* (Quito: Lexigrama, 1973), 1:20-23, 122-23, 125, 131. In Bolivia in the 1950s, Paz Estenssoro still defended this "attempt at effective liberation" of the fascist dictatorship of Villarroel but was incensed by the accusation of being "totalitarian." Against "pseudo-democracy" he proposed "popular democracy." Víctor Paz Estenssoro, *Discursos y mensajes* (Buenos Aires: Meridiano, 1953), 364. In Venezuela, Betancourt opposed both fascist dictatorships and the communist ones. Another populist leader, the Colombian Jorge Eliecer Gaitán, rejected the common dictatorial foundation of fascism and communism but also noted their distinctions. See Jorge Eliecer Gaitán, "La UNIR no es fascista," in *Los mejores discursos de Gaitán: 1919-1948*, ed. Jorge Villaveces (Bogota: Editorial Jorvi, 1968), 117, 366, 374, 380.

99. Rómulo Betancourt, *Selección de escritos políticos (1929-1981)* (Caracas: Fundación Rómulo Betancourt, 2006), 179.

100. Donald Trump, *Think Like a Champion: An Informal Education in Business and Life* (New York: Vanguard Press, 2009), 78.

101. "Biología del fascismo" in José Carlos Mariátegui, *La escena contemporánea* (Lima: Minerva, 1925), 45, 76. For a key book on Mariátegui, see Juan De Castro, *Bread and Beauty: The Cultural Politics of José Carlos Mariátegui* (Chicago: Haymarket, 2021).

102. See McCormick, "The Swashbuckling Mussolini," 1, 19; and Palmieri, "La stampa anglosassone e Benito Mussolini," 86.

103. See Steinweis, *People's Dictatorship*, 55.

104. Goebbels, as cited in State Department, European Affairs Division, *National Socialism*, 63.

105. Mussolini, *Diuturna*, 404.

106. Mussolini, *Diuturna*, 474. See also Georges Valois, *Il fascismo Francese* (Rome: G. Marino, 1926), 34.

107. On this topic, see Maggie Clinton, *Revolutionary Nativism: Fascism and Culture in China, 1925-1937* (Durham, NC: Duke University Press, 2017); Reto Hofmann, *The Fascist Effect: Japan and Italy, 1915-1952* (Ithaca, NY:

Cornell University Press, 2015); and Hayes, *Subhas Chandra Bose in Nazi Germany*.

108. Curzio Malaparte, *Technique du coup d'état* (Paris: Glasset, 1931). English edition: *Coup d'État: The Technique of Revolution* (London: E.P. Dutton, 1932).

109. See Ko Maeda, "Two Modes of Democratic Breakdown: A Competing Risks Analysis of Democratic Durability," *Journal of Politics* 72, no. 4 (October 2010): 1129–43.

110. Paul McLeod, "Democratic Senators See Trump's Fight to Overturn the Election as a Tantrum, Not a Viable Threat," *BuzzFeed.News*, November 12, 2020, https://www.buzzfeednews.com/article/paulmcleod/democrat-senators-trump-election-tantrum.

111. The case of Argentina's Dirty War dictatorship (1976–1983) perfectly illustrates this point. The Dirty War was not a real war but an illegal militarization of state repression. This extreme violence was not exclusive of Cold War Argentina but also appeared in Chile, Guatemala, Indonesia, and many other dictatorial formations. They all shared a rejection of democratic procedures and they all engaged in widespread repression and killings. In the Argentine dictatorship of the 1970s, ideology drove bureaucratic processes of elimination. Technocratic mediations did not limit the radicalization of ideological imperatives. As was the case with other concentration camps in history, the administrative power of the state actually organized them as sites of ritualized violence. In the clandestine Argentine detention centers there was no limit to dictatorial violence. Within these camps, the dictatorship was fully hidden from public view and it imposed "total domination." The camps had a fascist ethos. They were a politically created universe where violence reigned supreme. They represented a world beyond the law, created to achieve, and reconfigure, the ideological postulates of fascist theory and its full anti-institutional victimizing drive. See Federico Finchelstein, *The Ideological Origins of the Dirty War: Fascism, Populism, and Dictatorship in Twentieth Century Argentina* (New York: Oxford University Press, 2014), 1–12.

112. Annie Karni and Maggie Haberman, "At Once Diminished and Dominating, Trump Begins His Next Act," *New York Times*, June 5, 2021, https://www.nytimes.com/2021/06/05/us/politics/donald-trump-republican-convention-speech.html.

113. Jack Nicas, "The Bolsonaro-Trump Connection Threatening Brazil's Elections," *New York Times*, November 11, 2021, https://www.nytimes.com/2021/11/11/world/americas/bolsonaro-trump-brazil-election.html.

114. Laís Martins, "Brazil's Bolsonaro Gives Testimony to Police on Jan. 8 Riot," *AP News*, April 26, 2023, https://apnews.com/article/brazil-bolsonaro-police-testimony-riot-deposition-uprising-62604db69fa774c-14fa3d9a6ac043d0f. In 2023, Bolsonaro's former secretary, Lieutenant Colonel Mauro Cid, reportedly told federal police investigators that Bolsonaro "met the heads of Brazil's army, navy and air force late last year to discuss a 'putschist plan' for a military coup." As the *Guardian* reported regarding this allegation by Mauro Cid, "The head of the army high command rejected the idea" but the navy commander had advised Bolsonaro that "his troops were ready to act [and were] only awaiting his order." See Tom Phillips, "Bolsonaro Met with Army, Navy and Air Force Heads to Discuss Coup – Reports," *Guardian*, September 21, 2023, https://www.theguardian.com/world/2023/sep/21/bolsonaro-military-coup-plans-former-secretary-reports.

115. Mussolini, "I 'pensieri,'" 278.

Epilogue

1. See Alan E. Steinweis, *The People's Dictatorship: A History of Nazi Germany* (Cambridge: Cambridge University Press, 2023), 55.

2. Excerpt from testimony of Hans Frank, taken at Nuremberg, Germany, September 1, 1945. Cited in Office of United States Chief Counsel for Prosecution of Axis Criminality, *Nazi Conspiracy and Aggression, Supplement B* (Washington, DC: US Government Printing Office, 1948), 1359.

3. John Kenneth Galbraith and George W. Ball, "The Interrogation of Albert Speer," *Life*, December 17, 1945, 66.

4. Eugene Robinson, "It's Time for the Rats to Leave Trump's Sinking Ship," *Washington Post*, November 19, 2018, https://www.washingtonpost.com/opinions/its-time-for-the-rats-to-leave-trumps-sinking-ship/2018/11/19/1720f592-ec3c-11e8-96d4-0d23f2aaad09_story.html; and Mary Papenfuss, "Dan Rather Explains How Actual Rats Are Better Than Trump-Supporting Republicans," *HuffPost*, October 17, 2020, https://www.huffpost.com/entry/republican-rats-sinking-ship-dan-rather_n_5f8b6272c5b67da85d1ec208.

5. Still, we also witnessed the Biden administration accommodating realpolitik needs and giving autocrats in these countries a pass for their infringements of basic freedoms.

6. David Smith, "'I Am Your Retribution': Trump Rules Supreme at CPAC as He Relaunches Bid for White House," *Guardian*, March 4, 2023, https://www.theguardian.com/us-news/2023/mar/05/i-am-your-retribution-trump-rules-supreme-at-cpac-as-he-relaunches-bid-for-white-house.

Index

Abascal, Santiago, 73, 87, 181
Adorno, Theodor W., 75, 191n15
Afghanistan, 120
Agorio, Adolfo, 152
Albanese, Giulia, 199n61
Alfonsin, Raul Ricardo, 174
al-Jundi, Sami, 106
Allende, Salvador, 171, 173
al-Mashriqi, Inayatullah Khan, 25, 34, 35, 36, 38, 53, 112, 195n21
Alvim, Roberto, 215n84
Angola, 120, 183
antifa, 48
antiliberal, 7, 34
anti-Semitism, 40, 59, 64, 68, 69, 97, 114, 127, 129, 139, 216n10, 217n26, 220n49, 222n65; anti-Jewish racism, 100, 102, 106, 107; Jewish conspiracy, 118; Pittsburgh attack, 120, 121
Arato, Andrew, 236n84
Arbenz, Jacobo, 171
Arendt, Hannah, 98, 192n2, 196nn34–35, 198n47, 202n85, 206n2; and ideology, 27, 98; and propaganda, 62, 63; and violence, 33
Argentina, 29, 35, 42, 44, 55, 68, 80, 85, 97, 99, 111, 114, 124, 131, 163; and clerico-fascism, 72, 75, 100, 102, 103, 106, 149; dictatorship, 1; Dirty War in, 2, 5, 50, 87, 88, 118, 119, 171, 172, 174; and *nacionalismo*, 7, 10
attack on the US Capitol, 1, 18, 19, 65, 71, 82, 90, 172, 175

Babbitt, Ashli, 71, 72, 210n46
Bainville, Jacques, 146, 231n18
Bannon, Steve, 19, 20, 49
Barroso, Gustavo, 79, 100, 106, 212n65
Bavarian National Socialist Party, 105
Belarus, 182
Ben-Ghiat, Ruth, 89, 90, 115, 215n83
Benjamin, Walter, 4, 34
Berlusconi, Silvio, 12, 50, 83, 89
Betancourt, Romulo, 10, 41, 163, 169, 238n98

Bharatiya Janata Party (BJP), 38, 39, 52, 53, 122, 133, 136
Biden, Joe, 75, 82, 208n23, 241n5
Black Lives Matter, 48
Bobbio, Norberto, 27, 32
Bolivia, 10, 11, 118, 163, 238n98
Bolshevism, 144, 159, 168, 206n11
Bolsonaro, Carlos "Carluxo", 139
Bolsonaro, Eduardo, 87, 139, 229n119
Bolsonaro, Jair, 1, 13, 19, 49, 65, 69, 72, 82, 87, 91, 132, 136, 169, 176, 181, 228n119; Carluxo and Eduardo Bolsonaro, 139, 229n123
Bordaberry, Juan Maria, 173
Bose, Subhas Chandra, 144, 171, 231n9
Bossi, Ugo, 117
Bosworth, R. J. B., 202n87
Braden, Spruille, 124
Bragg, Alvin, 127
Brazil, 1, 5, 10, 13, 15, 22, 25, 34, 37, 113, 118, 136, 163, 173, 175; dictatorship, 48, 50, 53, 55; and *integralismo*, 7, 75, 77, 79, 80, 81, 87, 90, 96, 100, 106
Brexit, 180
Brower, Benjamin, 192n2
Bucaram, Abdala, 89
Bukele, Nayib, 3, 181

Caesar, Julius, 142, 151, 166; Caesarism, 146, 166, 168, 231n18
Caliban, as mythical image, 113, 221
Cameroon, 183
Camus, Renaud, 121
Cardoso, Fernando Henrique, 50
Carlson, Tucker, 224n80
Carvalho, Olavo de, 49, 87

Cassirer, Ernst, 59
Cesaire, Aime, 95
Chavez, Hugo, 12, 50, 165
Chile, 44, 50, 55, 88, 89, 118, 119, 171, 173, 181, 239n111
Chilean *Nacis*, 37, 103
China, 5, 33, 75, 106, 157, 171, 182
Chinese Blue Shirts, 25, 75, 134, 157, 171
Chocano Santos, Jose, 116, 145, 146, 157, 168
Churchwell, Sarah, 226n101
Cicero, Marcus Tullius, 146
Cid, Mauro, 240n114
Clarinada, 114
clerico-fascism, 72, 75, 100, 102, 103, 106, 149, 167
Clinton, Maggie, 116
Codreanu, Corneliu, 75, 198n51
Collor de Mello, Fernando, 50
Colombia, 73
communism, 11, 15, 29, 39, 41, 81, 113, 116, 120, 127, 134, 143, 152, 165, 167
Congo, 183
Corner, Paul, 26, 164
Correa, Rafael, 50
Coughlin, Charles, Fr., 29, 99, 107
coup d'états, 10, 11, 12, 44, 45, 68, 88, 142, 163, 168, 169, 172, 176, 177; autocoups (*auto-golpes*, self-coups), 18, 171, 173; coup attempts, 1, 4, 48, 57, 64, 65, 72, 85, 165, 174–75, 179, 181, 185, 195n23
COVID-19, 48, 49, 55, 57, 60–61, 181
Criterio Revista, 99
Croatia, 120
Cruz, Ted, 87
Cuadra, Pablo, 26, 66, 146

Cuba, 182
Curcio, Carlo, 151

de La Torre, Carlos, 204n108, 214n77
Delmont, Matthew F., 102
democracy: attack on, 1, 9, 13, 14, 15, 18, 24, 46, 49, 177, 180, 184, 196n33, 238n98; authoritarian, 7, 10, 12, 39, 40, 131; communism as, 144, 145; constitutional, 8, 45; corporatism as, 172; defense of, 86, 93, 174, 175; fascist ideas of, 37, 50, 96, 106, 110, 122, 134, 146, 156, 159, 162, 166, 169; ideology, 26, 126, 193n15; liberal, 41, 81; populist, 44, 164, 165, 167–68; regime as, 54, 56, 132, 141, 143, 176, 185, 186; representative, 237n88
Der Stürmer, 114
DeSantis, Ron, 127
Difesa della razza, 113, 128
Dionysius of Halicarnassus, 143
Dirty Wars in Latin America, 44, 87; and Operation Condor, 118
Dogliani, Patrizia, 115
Donoso Cortes, Juan, 143, 146, 160
Duterte, Rodrigo, 53, 54, 55, 133, 136, 138, 204nn107–8

Ecuador, 11, 50
Egypt, 5, 15, 25, 183
Egyptian Blue Shirts, 25
Egyptian Green Shirts, 103
El Paso, Texas, fascist terrorist attack, 120
El Salvador, 5, 181
Erdogan, Tayyip, 183

Ethiopia, 46, 102, 118, 183
Ethiopian War, 221
ethnocracy, 127
eugenics, 103, 122
Evans, Hiram Wesley, 122
Evans, Richard, 67

fascism: American, 29, 99, 107, 129, 145, 226n101; as antidemocratic, 4, 6, 24, 32, 50, 60, 68, 70, 78, 156, 174, 176, 185, 199n61; anti-fascism, 48, 73, 74, 102, 159, 169, 185, 217n24; in Argentina, 35, 72, 80, 96, 97, 100, 114, 119, 135, 146, 149, 157, 213n73, 217n26, 237nn88,92; in Bolivia, 116; in Brazil, 25, 37, 79, 81, 100, 106, 113; in Britain, 157; Burmese, 209n39; in Chile, 103; in China, 103, 116, 157; in Colombia, 105, 238n98; dictatorship, 4, 6, 8, 17, 19, 22, 68, 86, 96, 115, 142, 144, 151, 154, 157; in Egypt, 103; in France, 142, 146, 155, 234n47; and gender and sexuality, 116, German, 56, 57, 149; Hungarian, 46; in India, 28, 38, 39, 51, 53, 80, 110, 112, 128, 135–36, 195n21; Italian, 46, 74, 101, 113, 128, 147, 155, 170, 220nn48,56; Japanese, 88, 171; and masculinity, 35, 111; messianic conception, 6, 17, 72, 79, 152; in Mexico, 97; and myth, 6, 17, 21, 27, 32, 34, 58, 64, 68, 70, 83, 86, 132, 155, 193n14; neofascism, 8, 11, 44, 46, 48, 119, 120, 138, 181, 191n12; in Nicaragua, 26, 66; in Peru, 106, 116, 145, 146, 157; and racism, 9, 15, 20, 27, 32, 39, 48,

Index [245]

fascism *(continiued)*
    68, 81, 86, 92, 101, 114, 120;
    revolution, 7, 31, 68, 88, 145, 152,
    154, 158, 160, 163, 166, 168, 179;
    Romanian, 46, 88, 198n51;
    semi-fascism, 3, 9; in Spain, 35–36,
    45, 73, 157, 219n40, 234n45; and
    terror, 10, 45, 56, 75, 86, 120, 146,
    149, 153, 162, 198n52, 202n85; and
    terrorism, 24, 53, 71, 73, 90, 118,
    186, 194n16, 201n72; transna-
    tional, 7, 16, 102, 119, 120, 121, 157,
    191n12; Ukrainian, 46, 198n52;
    Uruguayan, 152; violence and
    militarization of politics, 3, 4, 11,
    16, 18, 23, 31, 34, 35, 41–42, 44, 45,
    47, 49, 50, 53, 55, 64, 71, 144, 158,
    185, 197nn35,46, 239n111;
    wannabe fascists, 2, 9, 10, 22, 39,
    47, 65, 75, 83, 122, 130, 167, 180
Fernández, Alberto, 229n123
Fernández, Cristina de Kirchner, 50
Fernández, Estanislao, 229n123
Filippo, Virgilio, Fr., 29, 195n23
Final Solution, the, 133; as Holo-
    caust, 23, 30, 31, 46, 47, 54, 55, 69,
    77, 90, 99, 122, 127
First World War, 32, 109, 111
Floyd, George, 48, 51, 52, 131
Ford, Henry, 107
Foreign Policy, 1
Fraenkel, Ernst, 148, 149, 232n25
France, 7, 15, 55, 104, 121, 171, 181,
    196n33, 218n31
Franceschi, Gustavo, Fr., 99, 100,
    149, 167
Franco, Francisco, 45–46, 75, 161,
    202n86

Frank, Hans, 72, 179, 240n2
Fuentes, Codera, Maximiliano, 127
Fujimori, Alberto, 173
Fujimori, Keiko, 13, 55, 87

Gaitan, Jorge Eliecer, 41, 43, 126,
    201n72, 238n98
Gandhi, Mahatma, 39
Gentile, Giovanni, 74
Gerarchia, 105, 150
Germany, 7, 11, 18, 33, 51, 54, 88, 91,
    104, 106, 111, 117, 122, 135, 148
Gershoni, Israel, 103
Gimenez Caballero, Ernesto, 36,
    219n40
Givens, Terri, 106
Goebbels, Joseph, 4, 51, 58, 62, 66,
    75, 110, 153, 161, 170, 180
Golden Dawn (Greece), 8
Golwalkar, M. S., 28, 38, 53, 122,
    195n21; Hinduvta ideology, 38
Gordon, Linda, 122
Goulart, João, 173
"great replacement theory," 118, 121
Greece, 8
Greene, Marjorie Taylor, 62, 82, 127,
    129
Guardian, 240n114
Guerisoli, Emmanuel, 213n73

Haiti, 137
Harguindeguy, Albano, 119
Hegelian dialectic, 25
Hilberg, Raul, 46, 47
Himmler, Heinrich, 29, 30, 31,
    196n30
Hitler, Adolf, 3, 11, 20, 31, 45, 51, 67,
    72, 102, 115, 133, 147, 153, 160, 177;

Hitlerism, 87, 91, 120; and *Mein Kampf*, 24, 67, 79, 97, 107, 120, 131, 134, 137, 152, 157
Hoffman, Carl, 78
Holocaust, 23, 30, 31, 46, 47, 54, 55, 69, 77, 90, 99, 122, 127
Hubner Mendes, Conrado, 55
Hughes, Langston, 102
Hungary, 5, 106, 127, 171
Husayn, Ahmad, 15, 103, 104

India, 5, 7, 28, 34, 39, 51, 77, 80, 106, 110, 122, 133, 136, 171, 181
Italy, 7, 11, 24, 33, 50, 69, 80, 88, 106, 120, 128, 139, 145, 155, 181, 196n33
Iran, 182
Israel, 13

Jaffrelot, Christophe, 82, 136, 204nn102-3
Jankowski, James, 103
Japan, 5, 7, 32, 88, 106

Kaiser Wilhelm II, 33
Kai-shek, Chiang, 75, 134
Kaltenborn, Hans, 67, 68
Kalyvas, Andreas, 230n2, 235n67
Kast, Jose Antonio, 55, 181
Kazakhstan, 184
Kelsen, Hans, 144, 148
Kershaw, Ian, 76
Khaksar movement, 25, 34, 38, 53, 112, 198nn49,51, 199n55
King, Dr. Martin Luther, Jr., 121
Kirchner, Nestor, 50
Klemperer, Victor, 56, 60, 63, 93, 96, 139, 206n11

Kloppe-Santamaria, Gema, 198n53
Kracauer, Siegfried, 74, 93
Ku Klux Klan (KKK), 102, 105, 107, 122, 170

La Rochelle, Pierre Drieu, 142, 155, 234n47
Latin American Anticommunist Federation, 118
Lega Nord, 117, 120
Lenin, Vladimir, 142, 143, 147, 159, 235n67; Leninism, 168
Leopards, the, 105
Le Pen, Marine, 55, 121, 181
Levis Sullam, Simon, 69
Lewis, Sinclair, 129, 170, 226n101
liberalism, 6, 11, 15, 26, 32, 39, 41, 44, 92, 104, 113, 145, 147, 152, 165
Locsin, Teddy, Jr., 133, 136
Loggia P2, 119
Longerich, Peter, 58
Lourenço Gonçalves, João Manuel, 183
Ludwig, Emil, 69, 151
Lugones, Leopoldo, 80, 81, 102, 116, 119, 134, 146-47, 168, 169, 212nn63-64, 217n26, 236n72
Luxemburg, Rosa, 235n67

Machiavelli, Niccolò, 142, 143
Maduro, Nicolás, 173, 183
Malaparte, Curzio, 30, 171; *Kaputt* (novel), 30
Malaysia, 184
Mali, 184
Mammone, Andrea, 191n12
Marañón, Jesús, 231n18
Marcos, Ferdinand, 204n107

Mariatégui, José Carlos, 169, 170
Marx, Karl, 32, 142, 196n34
Marxism, 25, 26, 32, 61, 81, 193n15, 212n64; anti-Marxism, 9, 193n15
Mashriqi, Khan Inayatullah, al-, 25, 34–35, 36, 38, 53, 112, 195n21
Maurras, Charles, 193n15
McCormick O'Hare, Anne, 156
Meinvielle, Julio, Fr., 100
Meloni, Georgia, 138, 181
Mendel, Gregor, 111
Menem, Carlos Saul, 50, 89
Michels, Robert, 150
Milei, Javier, 55, 69, 87, 213n73
Miller, Stephen, 20
Miller-Idris, Cynthia, 121
Mnangagwa, Emmerson, 183
Modi, Narendra, 3, 38, 39, 51, 52–53, 55, 81, 83, 89, 122, 133, 136, 204nn102–3
Mosse, George, 111, 221
Musa, Salama, 103, 218n29
Mosley, Oswald Sir, 157, 158
Mussolini, Benito, 2, 15, 24, 37, 45, 59, 68, 88, 102, 115, 126, 134, 144, 155, 177
Myanmar, 184

Namibia, extermination of Herero, 33
National Socialism, 24, 92
Nazis and Nazism, 1, 11, 18, 29, 40, 51, 95, 101, 110, 138, 150, 164, 177, 180, 194n16; dictatorship, 148, 149, 179; *Führerprinzip*, 68, 72, 153; *Führerstaat*, 153; *Führung*, 153; morality, 196n28; neo-, 52, 53, 91, 121; party, 92, 122, 161; propaganda, 67, 75, 76, 91, 92, 93, 104, 179; racism, 69, 106, 122; terror, 24, 31, 34, 153, 170, 206n11
Netanyahu, Benjamin, 13
Neumann, Franz, 145
New York Times, 29, 48, 65, 86, 125, 127, 156
Nicaragua, 7, 120
North Korea, 182
Norway, 137, 171
NPR, 69

Oath Keepers, 53, 82
Orban, Viktor, 3, 69, 83, 87, 127, 224n80
Ortega, Daniel, 183
Ortega y Gasset, José, 36
Orwellian, 3
Osés, Enrique P., 97, 216n10
Oyuela de, Silveyra Eugenia, 35

Pakistan, 38
Palacio, Alfredo, 102
Palacio, Ernesto, 102, 166, 216n10, 237n88
Panunzio, Segio, 150, 151, 155
Pasteur, Louis, 111
Paraguay, 118
Pareto, Vilfredo, 148
Paxton, Robert, 110, 111, 129, 194n16, 197n36
Paz Estenssoro, Victor, 10, 163, 238n98; and National Revolutionary Movement (MNR), 163
Pelosi, Nancy, 48
Perón, Eva Duarte, 11, 41
Perón, Juan Domingo, 10, 40, 74, 83, 89, 123, 131, 163, 167
Peronism, 8, 10, 11, 41, 74, 163, 165, 166

Peronist World, 165
Peru, 13, 55, 171, 173
Philippines, 5, 53, 54, 136
Piccato, Pablo, 192n2
Pinochet, Augusto, 50, 87, 88, 119, 173
Poland, occupied, 29, 72, 179
popular sovereignty, 6, 83, 124, 141, 157, 160, 161, 166, 167
populism, 1, 38, 47, 64, 69, 72, 74, 83, 126, 128, 141, 162, 166, 168, 184; anti-populism, 43, 44, 201n82; authoritarian, 123, 131, 182; Hindu, 53, 136, 204nn102–3; left-wing, 49, 50; macho-populism, 54; racist, 92; right-wing, 1, 3, 7, 9, 24, 82, 90, 91, 92, 173, 228n119
Portuguese Blue Shirts, 25
post-fascism, 9, 14, 44, 47, 87
Primo de Rivera, José Antonio, 35, 36
propaganda, 3, 11, 17, 32, 39, 45, 55, 74, 78, 89, 97, 107, 122, 132, 179
protofascism, 163
Proud Boys, 53
P2, 119
Putin, Vladimir, 183

racism, 4, 9, 20, 27, 39, 68, 78, 81, 86, 92, 97, 113, 130, 137, 166; anti-racism, 101, 184, 185; Aryan race, 47, 56, 88, 101, 108, 111–12, 113, 134, 206n11, 221n56
Rashtriya Swayamsevak Sangh (RSS), 39, 136
Raspail, Jean, 121
Rico, Aldo, 175
Robespierre, Maximilien, 146
Rhodes, Stewart, 82

Rhodesia, 119
Rodrigo, Javier, 127
Romania, 171
romanticism, 215n84
Roosevelt, Franklin Delano, 29, 40, 216n10
Rosenberg, Alfred, 122
Rousseau, Jean-Jacques, 142, 143
Russia, 91, 129, 134, 135, 182
Russian Revolution, 142, 235n69
Rwanda, 183

Salazar, Oliveira, 160, 236n72
Salgado, Plinio, 15, 25, 37, 75, 81, 113
Salvemini, Gaetano, 200n67
Salvini, Matteo, 128, 181
Sangh, Jana, 39
San Martin, José, de, 146
Sartre, Jean-Paul, 41
Saudi Arabia, 182, 183
Sayoc, Cesar, 71–72
Schmitt, Carl, 143, 150, 151, 153, 166, 231n12
Schultze, Walter, 122
Second World War, 10, 11, 31, 41, 46, 71, 91, 145, 162
Silva, Luiz Inacio Lula, da, 175
Sismondi, Jean Charles Leonard, de, 146
socialism, 6, 92, 134, 147, 212n65, 221
Sorel, Georges, 193n15, 221n58
Soros, George, 127
South Africa, 119
Spain, 55, 75, 132, 171, 181, 188
Spanish Civil War, 55, 102, 161, 202n86
Speer, Albert, 180
Stanley, Jason, 59, 97, 205n112, 224n80

Steinweis, Alan, 164, 179
Sternhell, Zeev, 95, 193n15, 196n33
Srisa-nga, Treethep, 204n108, 214n77
Streicher, Julius, 99, 104
Sturzo, Luigi, 147
Sulla, 142
Sweden, 103
Syria, 182

Thailand, 184
totalitarianism: dictatorship, 3, 15, 18, 85, 167, 168; ideology, 9, 11, 22, 64, 89, 98, 149, 150, 185, 197n43, 237n92, 238n98; leaders, 66, 83, 163; order, 147; regime, 168; state, 6, 148; system, 61, 91, 116
Trump, Donald J., 1, 2, 5, 13, 19, 22, 48, 57, 60, 69, 71, 169, 177, 182, 195n23; mini-Trump, 3, 181, 213n73; Trumpism, 4, 9, 14, 16, 18, 21, 74, 78, 85, 132, 176, 180, 190n12, 205n112; Trumpist, 14, 62, 78, 82, 87, 90, 127, 175, 181
tupamaros, 173
Turkey, 182, 183

United Kingdom, 85, 180
United States, 2, 9, 29, 48, 53, 61, 80, 86, 96, 111, 121, 132, 170, 181
Uriburu, General José F., 68, 72, 75, 88, 172–73
Uruguay, 118, 171, 173
Ustaše, 118
Uzbekistan, 184

Vallenilla Lanz, Laureano, 231n18
Valois, Georges, 15

Vargas, Getúlio, 10, 11, 40, 41, 42, 126, 163; Varguismo, 163
Vasconcelos, José, 97
Velasco Ibarra, Jose Maria, 41, 168, 225n93
Venezuela, 10, 11, 12, 50, 163, 165, 168, 171, 173, 182, 183, 238n98
Ventrone, Angelo, 109, 197n43
Videla, Jorge Rafael, 119
Vietnam, 32, 182
Villarroel, Gualberto, 163, 238n98
Volk, 112
von Marées, Jorge González, 37
Vox party, 55, 73

Washington Post, 1
Waterman Wise, James, 226n101
white supremacy, 107, 111, 118, 122; Buffalo attack, 117, 118, 120; Charlottesville attack, 121; Christchurch attack, 120; El Paso attack, 120; Munich attack, 120; Pittsburgh attack, 120; Utoya attack, 120
Whitman, James Q., 101, 217n21
Wise, Stephen, 226n101
World War I, 32, 109, 111
World War II, 10, 11, 31, 41, 46, 71, 91, 145, 162

xenophobia, 3, 12, 17, 19, 22, 39, 49, 87, 94, 97, 101, 106, 116, 126, 185

Zachariah, Benjamin, 195n21, 200n63
Zemmour, Eric, 121
Zimbabwe, 182, 183

Founded in 1893,
UNIVERSITY OF CALIFORNIA PRESS
publishes bold, progressive books and journals
on topics in the arts, humanities, social sciences,
and natural sciences—with a focus on social
justice issues—that inspire thought and action
among readers worldwide.

The UC PRESS FOUNDATION
raises funds to uphold the press's vital role
as an independent, nonprofit publisher, and
receives philanthropic support from a wide
range of individuals and institutions—and from
committed readers like you. To learn more, visit
ucpress.edu/supportus.